JAVA
PANO

A RYOK DANCER.
NOTE THE DELIGHTED EXPRESSION OF THE ONLOOKER ON TIPTOE. YET HE HAS SEEN IT EVERY DAY FOR WEEKS, AND PROBABLY EVERY YEAR SINCE HE CAN REMEMBER!

JAVANESE PANORAMA

More Impressions of the 1930s

H. W. PONDER

SINGAPORE
OXFORD UNIVERSITY PRESS
OXFORD   NEW YORK
1990

Oxford University Press

*Oxford New York Toronto
Delhi Bombay Calcutta Madras Karachi
Petaling Jaya Singapore Hong Kong Tokyo
Nairobi Dar es Salaam Cape Town
Melbourne Auckland
and associated companies in
Berlin Ibadan*

Oxford is a trade mark of Oxford University Press

Originally published as Javanese Panorama *by
Seeley Service & Co. Ltd., London, 1942*

First issued as an Oxford University Press paperback 1990

ISBN 0 19 588940 1

*The Publisher has made every effort to trace the original
copyright of this book, but with no success. Anyone
claiming copyright should write to the Publisher
at the address given below.*

*Printed in Malaysia by Peter Chong Printers Sdn. Bhd.
Published by Oxford University Press Pte. Ltd.,
Unit 221, Ubi Avenue 4, Singapore 1440*

TO MY FRIENDS

MEVROUW AND MIJNHEER J.J.B.V.

IN REMEMBRANCE OF HAPPY DAYS

AT POEDJON

AND GRATEFUL ACKNOWLEDGEMENT

OF THEIR INVALUABLE HELP

PREFACE

I MAKE no apology for returning to the subject of Java. It is inexhaustible; the last word about it is never said. You may live here for years, with eyes and ears open to all around you; you may leave and return over and over again; only to find surprises and fresh discoveries awaiting you round every corner.

Java is one of those rare places with which familiarity never breeds contempt, and added knowledge brings no disillusion. The charm that woos and wins you as a stranger is just as potent when you are a stranger no longer, if not more so. Ripening acquaintance with this magic island might be compared to friendship with a beautiful woman, whose qualities of heart and mind, and even her caprices, attract no less surely than the graces of her person. You fall in love with Java at the beginning for its beauty, and love it better with the passing years as you grow ever more intrigued by its infinite variety. From delight in its charm you pass to friendship with its people, while your interest deepens in their customs and social systems, their village administration, agriculture, and the rest.

But there are pitfalls for the unwary. As little by little you begin to understand the meaning (or think you do) of some of the thousand and one fascinating novelties for ever being presented to your notice, you are apt rashly to take for granted that they are typical of the whole country. You may be right; but you may be wrong; never was there a place where to generalise is so risky. The diversity of ways in Java is endless, and it would need a dozen lifetimes to learn them all. For from time immemorial, countless districts were isolated from each other by impassable natural barriers of rivers and mountain ranges, so that they developed on lines almost as distinct as though there had been the whole width of a continent between them instead of only a few miles, and customs were evolved which became so deeply ingrained that they still remain undisturbed in these days of easy communication. Thus, not only do East, Middle, and West Java differ from each other in a hundred ways, but you may find in some formerly isolated district, covering only a few square miles, customs and ceremonies unknown elsewhere.

It follows therefore that some of the native ways described in the following pages are peculiar to certain districts, and are not common to the whole country, so that visitors to Java must not be disappointed if they do not come across them. On the other hand they are just as likely to come across others as yet unknown to the author, who can only promise a complete picture of the Java scene if the Gods allow it to be revisited in several future incarnations!

May Java soon be returned to her former freedom, happiness, and prosperity!

CONTENTS

CHAPTER		PAGE
I.	The Lazy Native	17
II.	Native Ways, Food, & Fashions	30
III.	Wedding Days	39
IV.	More about Marriage, Birth, & Death	47
V.	The "Dessa"	59
VI.	Life in a "Dessa"	70
VII.	Religious Medley	86
VIII.	"Magic"	100
IX.	For Feminists	122
X.	"Batik," Dyeing, & other Crafts	138
XI.	A Word about Eurasians	151
XII.	Beasts of Burden & "Pets"	158
XIII.	"The Glory of the Garden"	171
XIV.	On Trees	185
XV.	The "Kweekerij"	194
XVI.	The Great Post Road	214
XVII.	Ancient Kingdoms	234
XVIII.	Yesterday, To-day, & To-morrow	243
	Index	261

LIST OF ILLUSTRATIONS

A Ryok dancer . . . . *Frontispiece*

Facing page

A seller of durian 48

Ryok dancers in a bridegroom procession 49

A bridegroom goes in procession to his wedding . . . 49

A "gardoe" house, where a watchman sits & sounds every hour from 7 p.m. to 5 a.m. 64

Rice harvest 65

Doves in cages, run up on tall bamboo poles . . . 80

A sheet of "bilik" 80

Loads of baskets 80

A roadside restaurant 81

Basket carriers 81

Javanese women doing the family washing 81

The Rice Goddess enthroned at a native festival . . . 128

A woman planting rice 129

A native housewife & a firewood seller 176

Drying & storing maize cobs 177

The bridegroom & his steed with their attendants . . 208

European children in sedan chairs or "tandoes" . . . 208

Water supplies being fetched from a stream in petrol tins . 209

A mountain path 209

List of Illustrations

SUNSET ON LAKE SARANGAN	209
REMAINS OF A BRICK TEMPLE AT MADJAPAHIT	240
ONE OF THE ISLAND SHRINES RICHLY CARVED	240
A COUNTRY SCENE IN EAST JAVA	241
SPECIMEN OF THE CARVED STONE PANELS AT BOROBOEDOER	241
A JAVA MOUNTAIN HOTEL & PART OF ITS TERRACED GARDEN	241

INDIA
CEYLON
COCHIN CHINA
MALAY PENIN
SUMATRA
Equator
INDIAN
OCEAN
Cocos or Keeling Is
SUMATRA
Thousand Is.
Sunda Straits
Bantam
Tangerang
Chillinching
Serang
Labuan
Pandeglang
Menes
BATAVIA
Indramayu
Princes I
Java Hd
BANTAM
BUITENZORG
Mt Salak
Mt Gedeh
Mt Cheremai
Cheribon
Mt Tangkuban-Prahu
Bandung
PREANGER
Garut
Telaga-Bodas
Mt Papandayan
Mt Sindoro
Kambangan
INDIAN
OCEAN

JAVA

0 25 50 75 100 125 150 175 200 Miles.

PHILIPPINE ISLANDS
Caroline Islands
EAST INDIES
CELEBES
The Moluccas
NEW GUINEA
NEW BRITAIN ARCHIP
AUSTRALIA
SEA
Straits
MADURA
Demak
Grisee
SURABAYA
Mt Ungaran
Salatiga
Mt MERBABU
Mojokerto
Surakarta
Madura
Pasuruan
Probolinggo
Mt LAWU
Boyolali
Klaten
Brambanan
DJOCJAKARTA
Mt ARJUNA
Kediri
Mt WILIS
Mt KAWI
Mt BROMO
Tengger Mts
Banjuwangi
Mt SEMIRU
Mt BUTAK
Mt KLUT
Straits of Bali
BALI

A Few Javanese and Malay Words in Everyday Use in Java

Atap: roofing material made of palm leaf.

Baboe: maidservant.
Badjoe: jacket.
Baharoe: new.
Batik: cotton material patterned and dyed by hand.
Besar: big, great.
Bilik: split bamboo woven into sheets for building purposes.

Dalang: showman at a puppet show.
Dessa: a district.
Djahat: bad, wicked, naughty.
Djahit: to sew.
Djongos: house-boy.
Doekoen: magic maker.

Gamelan: native orchestra.
Gila: mad.
Golek: doll.

Kain: material (woven).
Kampong: village, hamlet.
Kawin: marriage.
Kepala: head.

Nyonya: lady, madam.

Pandjang: long.
Pasar: market.
Penang: betel or areca nut.
Pikoelan: bamboo shoulder yoke.
Pisang: banana.

Salamat: safe, lucky.
Salamatan: good-luck feast.
Sapoe: duster or cloth.
Sapoe lidi: a switch or brush made of a bunch of palm-leaf midribs.
Sarong: the skirtlike garment worn by most Javanese men and women.
Selendang: a long scarf, usually of *batik*.
Sirih: the leaf in which betel-nut "chew" is wrapped.

Toean: sir, a lord or gentleman. Usual form of respectful address.
Toekang: a craftsman or tradesman. (E.g. *toekang mas* = goldsmith, etc.)
Toko: shop (Chinese).

Wayang: native shadow or puppet show.

Any of the above words containing the letters "*oe*" are spelt in British Malaya with "*u*" instead. Those beginning with "*dj*" are spelt with a "*j*" only.

CHAPTER ONE

The Lazy Native

UNIQUE in this as in all else, Java alone among the East Indian islands is rich in the possession of a large native population. And it is the colourful crowds of these gaily dressed, brown-skinned people, ever moving to and fro across the scene on their lawful occasions, that first arrest the attention of every traveller.

"How picturesque!" "How quaint!" is the typical tourist's comment; and so, perhaps, they are. But there is a great deal more "to" the Javanese natives than that. Though they look as gay and as carefree as butterflies they are also as busy as bees; and the bright flowered *batik* of their national dress camouflages people for the most part as industrious as the Chinese. They are a perfect example of the fallacy of judging by appearances, and many is the casual critic that has fallen into the trap.

Like all Orientals, the Javanese has a secret that we have not: the secret of true repose. Unlike the European, he feels no need to fill up his free time with entertainments (though he greatly enjoys them when they come his way), for he knows as well how to idle as he does how to work. He does neither the one nor the other at high speed as we do, and consequently knows nothing of the "nerves" that drive us feverishly to perpetual motion. He works so hard, so steadily, and so long, that when he does stop, his one desire is to rest, and he asks no more than to be allowed to do nothing. It is this complete relaxation of his that leads European visitors so ludicrously astray in their superficial judgment of the "lazy native."

The Javanese is blessed with a cheery philosophy that enables him to accept, as all in the day's work, labour that the poorest white man would refuse with indignation. You will see coolies plodding up mountain gradients of "one-in-three," carrying porcelain baths and basins, corrugated iron, tiles, bricks, bags of cement, sideboards, teak wardrobes, and even pianos and all the other items that help to make life in the Java highlands so pleasant for the European. The carriers are usually singing and chaffing one another as they go; and their pay is about threepence per journey of several hours' steady climbing, with return down the mountain thrown in. The womenfolk work with equal cheerfulness for even less reward. Loads of tiles are often carried on these same steep roads, on the backs of tiny frail-looking creatures, bowed almost double, who seem to possess the same carrying power, in proportion to their size, as ants. Their wage is about two-thirds of that paid to the men.

It is scarcely surprising that the possessors of such a temperament, tackling the heaviest of donkey work with cheery equanimity, should regard light work as a mere game. Such work as waiting at table the Javanese genuinely enjoys, as you may see if you live in an hotel where the domestic régime is a happy one (an important proviso, for the Javanese is intensely sensitive to the kind of authority under which he works). It is pleasant to sit and watch half a dozen laughing *djongos* (table-boys) vying with each other for the pleasure of serving you. One will bring a fork, another a knife, and another a plate: each polished with gusto under your eyes, as he runs up with it, on the snow-white napkin worn as a sign of office across every table-boy's shoulder, and any request will send one of them off at a swift, short-stepped trot, noiseless on bare feet, to carry out your wishes.

Odd little surprises will be prepared for you now and then. You may come in to dinner, especially when you have guests, to find the napkins elaborately shaped into long-necked birds, with red combs and yellow beaks made of flower petals; while the author of the artistic effort stands shyly by, beaming and eager as a child for your praise and approval.

The Javanese servant (except when he has been over-Europeanised) never considers himself "put upon," but he dearly likes to confide in a sympathetic listener. The hotel *djongos* who brings you your coffee at 6 A.M. (the usual hour in the Dutch East Indies) will tell you that he started work a quarter of an hour or so earlier, after perhaps an hour's walk from his home. He will be on duty till about 2 P.M. and is then free till nearly 4 P.M., at which time tea is taken round. Then he carries on till after dinner, say nine-thirty

The Lazy Native

or so, unless some convivial cocktail party should only go in to dine when everyone else has finished. But even then the philosophic *djongos* shows no sign of resentment, though he seldom gets thanks, and tips never, and often not even ordinary politeness, for his pains.

This is a manifestation of native amiability especially appreciated by visitors from Australia, where the weary traveller who arrives at an hotel later than about seven o'clock in the evening cannot even get a cup of tea, much less dinner, and is forced to starve in impotent rage (in the cause of democracy) till breakfast next morning!

I once had rooms in a Java hotel whence I could look out on the road leading to the back entrance, and thus had some illuminating glimpses of the "off duty" appearance and mannerisms of the varied individualities hidden during working hours beneath the trim uniform of the staff. Punctually at a quarter to six, in the delicious freshness of early morning in this part of the world, all the *djongos* would appear on their way to work, some afoot and some on bicycles, mostly wearing the black or dark-red velvet Malay cap now the fashionable native wear in large towns. Some were in smart Palm-beach jackets, and all wore *sarongs* or *kain* of every imaginable hue from vivid emerald (and silk at that) to glowing orange or deep rich claret, as well as of every variety of *batik* or tartan: these last, unfortunately for Java's local colour, being more and more introduced by the lately established weaving industry. (It should be explained that the term *sarong* has come to be applied indiscriminately by Europeans to any of the skirt-like garments worn by Javanese men and women. Correctly, *sarong* only applies when the two-metre length of *kain*, *i.e.* material, is seamed up into a skirt. This is the working dress. But on more formal occasions men wear an unjoined *kain* elaborately pleated in front and held in place by a clip. To refer to the wearer's "*sarong*" when he is so dressed would be an affront.)

Ten minutes later all these individually attired young Javanese townsmen had been metamorphosed into an impersonal staff of servants in neat starched white drill uniform and *batik* head-dress; in regard to which latter, however, no hotel management would ever dream of insisting upon uniformity. At one time every district had its own style, worn only by the men of that particular region; but nowadays they are worn by all and sundry according to taste. Some choose prim, close-fitting dark-blue and brown *cloches*, V-shaped on the brow, giving the effect of a centre hair parting; others affect brighter colours and jaunty designs with the twisted corners of *batik* sticking out at odd angles.

The Javanese are as cheery people as any in the world, but they take themselves, their affairs and their beliefs, with great seriousness, and their laughter is a sort of froth floating lightly on the surface of their hard working lives. Of the "sense of humour," as we know it, the Javanese has none; or if he has, it is one of the things for ever hidden from the Western mind.

But he has something better. He can make a joke of sudden annoying emergencies and contretemps that would infuriate the average European. He never grumbles or shows the slightest ill-temper on such occasions. For instance, at a particularly well administered hotel of my acquaintance, the house staff were allowed to gather in the late afternoon, when the tables were laid for dinner, for a spell of leisure at one end of what the Dutch call the "voorgalerij," a place almost as spacious as a church and furnished like a club smoking-room with heavy arm-chairs, tables and thick carpets, in reality a giant verandah with its roof supported at front and sides by pillars.

Here, all dressed up, and obviously taking much pride in their smart appearance in freshly starched uniforms, ready to "wait" at table, they would squat in groups on the steps or the floor in their characteristic fashion, smoking and chatting in low voices about their latest love or financial affairs, with no more strenuous work to trouble them till dinner time, except to respond to an occasional call for drinks from the guests.

But every now and then during the West monsoon a terrific storm would break over the town, with drenching downpours of rain driven by wind-gusts of hurricane force, and within a few minutes the great "voorgalerij" was flooded. The happy, idling *djongos* needed no command to spur them to action. With the first low rumble of thunder or heavy spot of rain, off would come the smart white jackets while

The Lazy Native

they raced indoors to hang them safely out of harm's way, and then, laughing and chattering as though the whole affair were an entertainment got up for their benefit, all hands set to with a will, shifting the heavy teak furniture into shelter, rolling up rugs and carpets, racing up and down the tiled floor, fighting back the sudden flood of water with buckets and cloths and the bunches of palm-leaf ribs they call *sapoe lidi*. For a time, it may be anything from ten minutes to half an hour or so, all is excitement; and then, as suddenly as it came, the storm passes. Everything is set in place again with as much cheerfulness as it was removed; and presently you may sit peacefully drinking your after-dinner coffee looking out upon the quiet moonlit river from your favourite corner, where an hour ago all was disorder, waited upon as you were at dinner by a servant as calm and smart and smiling as ever, showing not the slightest trace of the disturbance that so lately broke in upon his little hour of cherished leisure.

A naïf vanity is characteristic of most Javanese, and to take his "portret" (as he calls it) is a sure road to his esteem. But beware of photographing him in groups! I once took some snaps of a friend's native staff, promising a copy of his own "portret" to each if they would come and collect the prints on a certain day. But our cherished idea of fair play for all does not appeal in the least to the Javanese mind, and if you think to please by treating a number all alike you will find yourself greatly mistaken. It was useless to point out to my eager sitters that having duly graced one group of chosen cronies they should not "butt in" to another. Like mischievous children, delighted at their own cleverness, they insinuated themselves into corners of every group they could, the number of their appearances depending upon the strength of their determination.

The fun really began when they came to call for their prints. These simple yet shrewd young Javanese construed my promise of "one man, one portret" on quite a different principle to mine. It had seemed so simple beforehand to make a list of names and cross them off as the prints were delivered; but when I handed each a print of his own legitimate group and waved them away, the delighted faces, eagerly scanning their own counterfeit presentment, would fall at once. "But, *Toean*, there are others," they would say. "The *Toean* took my 'portret' twice" (or three or four times, as the case might be), and their childish dismay at the thought of going away without a copy of every picture in which their ingenuous brown faces appeared made it hard to disappoint them. I weakened, of course; what was a few cents, I thought, compared with the amount of innocent pleasure that it would buy? They should have prints of all as soon as I could get them done.

The complications that followed this rash undertaking lasted for weeks. Almost every day someone would knock at my door, wearing a conspiratorial air, to pour out a tale of the scandalous behaviour of one or other of his colleagues in getting more prints than his share. One had borrowed a print to show to a friend and then denied ever having had it. Another had got two lots from me by impersonating someone else (which was more than likely; by this time I was long past remembering which was which of my fifty odd young friends!); everyone, in fact, except the narrator of the tale appeared to have done something he should not. But every one of my visitors had some perfectly good reason to offer why he himself should be trusted with an extra copy or two, which he assured me he would deliver safely to the rightful owners.

Through all these gravely confided stories of the others' knavish tricks there shone a naughty delight in "going one better" and, at the same time, of convincing me (as they thought) of their own superior virtue. They bore one another not the least ill-will, but each wanted to be singled out for special favour, not to be treated as just one of a crowd. And, added to that, the Javanese have an ingrained love of conspiracy. Like children, they adore a "secret," though they are constitutionally incapable of keeping one, and are for ever coming to you with some confidence or other, often so absurd that it is hard to keep a straight face.

Surprising though it seems in so individualist a type as the Javanese, they are capable at times of real *esprit de corps* as well as personal devotion to a *Toean* of whom they approve. Like the schoolboy, the Javanese appreciates justice as well as kindness, and despises weakness, though he is just as quick as the schoolboy to take advantage of it. In the hotel mentioned earlier in this chapter, whose manager was one of the all too rare kind who take the trouble really to understand their servants, the "boys" identified themselves with the place and took as great a pride in it as if it were their own. Several had been in its service for seventeen or eighteen years, and many more for eight or ten.

They never missed an opportunity of confiding their high opinion of their *Toean Besar* (master), or of singing the praises of the hotel itself. "*Enak di sini*" (it is pleasant here) one would observe quite irrelevantly as he poured out the breakfast coffee, to which of course you would politely agree. "The *Toean Besar* is a very good person," the servitor would continue, as he returned with the toast. "If we *djongos* do anything really wrong it is true that there is that in his eyes of which we are afraid though he speaks softly; but if one should fall and break many plates he is not angry, for he knows it was not done out of evil intent but because an evil spirit tripped our feet, and so he does not cut our wages as other *Toeans* do. And if one of us should be ill in his stomach as sometimes befalls, and asks permission to go home, he is allowed to go and his pay is not cut, for the *Toean* well knows that we serve him gladly and do not wish to be ill." And so on *ad infinitum*.

It should be added, however, that native servants are as easily estranged by unfair and unkind treatment as they are easily won by the reverse, and in such cases lack entirely the spontaneity and pride in their job of those who work in a happy atmosphere, though even so they will give far better service than the average European.

The palm for long service among my acquaintance goes to a native houseboy who has been with a Scottish family for over twenty-five years. During this period he has been supported in his domestic duties by three wives in succession. The first of them went *gila* (out of her mind), and Min had no difficulty in transferring the burden of the poor creature's care from himself to the State (the admirable divorce law in force among the Javanese needing no reform by Mr A. P. Herbert). The second spouse was *djahat* (naughty), and succumbed to the charms of the chauffeur, so once again Min secured his freedom. The third, so far, seems a paragon of all the virtues, and the good old fellow's pock-marked face wears an expression of great content as he serves the excellent meal that he himself has cooked.

The accepted ideas held by Europeans in regard to such a matter as murder are apt to be severely shaken now and then in Java. The young daughters of some planter friends of mine, who were fond of camping in the mountains, were allowed to do so only when accompanied by a valued old native gardener, under whose protection their parents felt them to be perfectly safe, and had not the slightest anxiety about them even if they stayed away for days. The old man had acted as the young girls' devoted watch-dog in this way many a time before it was accidentally discovered that long before entering the family's service he had "done time" for murder, having settled some little argument with a neighbour by stabbing him to death!

The effects of European "higher" education on the Javanese are hard to analyse correctly. Some of the results are unquestionably beneficial: notably the number of native doctors who are doing such valuable work both in Government service and in private practice to improve native public health. Nevertheless the "educated" native is even less fathomable than the simple countryman and apt, in Java as in India and elsewhere, to prove a rod fashioned by a would-be beneficent administration to scourge its own back.

I have met Javanese who have studied in Holland, speak fluent Dutch, and are practising lucrative professions as the result of a generous education system, who yet miss no opportunity to pour out to a foreigner disloyal comments on the very Dutch administration that has made their education available to them. But such cases, I hope and believe, are rare. Many, if not most, European-educated natives are delightful people of whose loyalty to the ruling white race there is no question.

Many Europeans seem quite incapable of grasping the idea of "natives" belonging to any but a low, illiterate coolie class, an error particularly rife among Australians who are apt to describe indiscriminately as "niggers" all persons

The Lazy Native

whose coloured skins debar them from citizenship of "White Australia." They little know how many grades there are in Javanese society, and how rigid is native etiquette; nor how all too easy it is to "drop a brick" by greeting with the usual *"Tabek"* a person whose social rank entitles him to the more formal *"Sembah"*; and that to address as *"Toean"* one whose correct title is *"Radin"* is a far worse insult than to apply plain "Mister" to Sir Jonathan Jones.

How surprised they would be to know that an immense percentage of Javanese are not only literate, but bi-lingual, thanks to the almost universal teaching of Malay in the schools throughout the country as well as the mother-tongue of each region. The ordinary working-class native in the towns sits down to read his daily newspaper in Malay, which is not his own language, as a matter of course. It would be interesting to know how many of the tourists who look down upon him could do as much in, say, French or German! As for *djeroe toelis*, or native clerks, they are usually tri-lingual, speaking perfect Dutch as well, and often type with equal ease in all three languages.

The two leading "native" newspapers, *Mata Hari* and *Sin Po*, both issued in the Malay language, contain the same news cables as those in English, French, Dutch, or other journals, and their editorials would soon disillusion those who think of "natives" as primitive uninformed folk who go about their simple affairs oblivious of the doings of their "betters." One leading article, for instance, commented acidly and quite without reverence upon the pronouncement of a member of the Government regarding the support that might be counted upon from natives in the event of war. "So far from agreeing with the Minister's remarks," comments this native writer, "we find them merely laughable." He goes on to criticise the cool assumption that natives will be content to be used wholesale as baggage-carriers, road-makers, &c.

Another article dealt with air-raid precautions, and remarked upon "the elaborate training being given the populace, not in self-defence, but in running away." Yet another spoke of the number of accidents in the Air Force, "due apparently to faults in construction, thereby wasting not only lives but the costly training of years"; the writer (a mere "native," remember!) proceeded to counsel with all the sententiousness of a *Times* leader, that "at least use should be made of these mishaps to investigate and correct the mechanical defects that caused them"! The suave and polished language in which these articles are always written, too, would enlighten those Europeans who fancy the Malay language is nothing more than the string of half-learned words in which they convey their orders to those who serve them.

In most towns and villages there is a "Volksbibliotek," or People's Library, and these are well patronised. So are the *Balai Poestika*: circulating libraries that tour the country by motor van, and introduce native readers to Shakespeare, Dumas, Swift, Tagore, Kipling, Farnol, "Don Kiset" (Don Quixote), and many other classical and popular works in Malay translations.

On the shelves of many native homes you will find volumes of classical *wayang* plays: far better known to the Javanese of all classes than are Shakespeare's to us. To the average foreigner, the *wayang* is no more than a sort of native Punch and Judy show, but to the Javanese the art of the *wayang* is a matter of as serious importance as was that of the Drama to the Greeks, and though it has suffered many changes under the imported influences of successive conquerors, the Hindus especially, it remains a native Javanese institution, designed originally for the purpose of calling up the spirits of ancestors, but thereafter developed into a unique and elaborate art. Its strange religious origin is probably responsible for the grotesque form of the figures, not quite human, yet one that the imaginative Oriental mind might suppose departed human spirits to assume, and is recalled too in the offerings always made to the spirits before a *wayang* show begins.

Among the volumes of *wayang* plays you may find, too, an interesting text-book called *Uger Pedalangan*: containing the rules for *wayang* showmanship. The vocabulary of this curious art is a rich one, but none the less the *dalang*, or showman, must be able to express by a distinct intonation every mood and emotion, whether love, farce, tragedy, triumph, contempt, and so on; and the slightest departure from the accepted tone would be resented by any native audience. Each of these tones has a name, *prenesan, banolan, &c.*, and the *dalang's* art of expressing them, which is held in high esteem by the Javanese, is called *lakon*.

Natives say that the oldest and true native *wayang* is the shadow-show they call *gedog*, in which krisses are worn by the puppets, and which was in vogue long before the Hindus imported the stories that came in time to dominate the *wayang* repertoire. These, they say, were merely adapted to the original native show. In the *wayang Purwa* the characters had become Hinduised: Arjuno the Indian hero appearing as the leading figure, and his love Subadra as heroine. In this no krisses are worn. The *Purwa* took its name from the *parwas* of the *Mahabharata*, which, with the other great Indian epic *Ramayana*, supplied most of the stories that have now merged with the old Javanese legends in the repertories of all forms of *wayang*. The characters of these are inextricably mixed; ancient Java heroes appear in Hindu stories, and Hindu gods have been turned into clowns!

Another ancient form of *wayang* is the *wayang kelitik*. In this, flat figures like those used in shadow-shows are displayed in front of a screen instead of merely as a means of throwing their shadows upon it. These figures are of thin wood with leather arms, and not, as in the earlier *wayang*, cut entirely out of buffalo-hide. The stories in this *wayang* are all of the the heroes of Madjapahit, the East Java Hindu kingdom, and it is still in vogue in East and Middle Java.

The next development was the *wayang golek*, now general in West Java. In this the figures are wooden dolls cut out of soft *randoe* or *kanari* wood, and elaborately painted and dressed. This gives the puppet-maker much more scope, and the sixty-odd characters are all differently treated, and immediately recognisable by a Javanese. The less observant European, however, seldom succeeds in recognising any but the hero Baladewa, whose magnificent head-dress, called *kuluk*, is unmistakable.

The word *wayang*, it should be explained, originally meant "shadow," but with the introduction of puppet-shows, and later still of plays with living actors, it has come to mean any sort of play or players.

Another, now rare, form of *wayang* is the *wayang beber*. In this there are no puppets, but painted figures and scenes are unrolled and set up while the *dalang* sits behind unseen and speaks the parts. This show is given on special royal occasions in the Sultanates.

Spoken plays by unmasked living actors, called *wayang wong*, were introduced by the Sultans of Djokdja and Solo during the last century, but they remained a royal entertainment and never became popular; perhaps because the Javanese think it unlucky to take the place of puppets. The repertoires are much the same as those of the *wayang purwa*. A few travelling shows give plays by masked actors, called *wayang topeng*; these are farces not unlike the well-known Malay "opera."

At an old-fashioned *wayang*, the *dalang* and the men of the audience sit on one side of the *kelir* or screen, in front of which hangs a brass lamp called a *blentong*, while the women sit on the other side to see the shadow. The unflattering inference suggests itself that at the *wayangs* presented for tourists, at which they see only shadows, they are probably classed in native eyes with the womenfolk as inferior mortals!

Strangers meeting a *wayang* on its way to fulfil an engagement have been known to mistake it (and even to describe it in stories written on their arrival home) for a native funeral. The box, called the *kotak*, in which the puppets are packed much resembles a coffin, so the error in excusable. Another smaller "coffin" contains horses, *krises*, and other stage properties called *ricitan*, and a set of flat metal plates called *keprak* which the *dalang* operates vigorously with his toes to indicate the noise of battle when a fight between two warriors is being staged.

Popular reaction to the first "blackouts" held by way of air-raid precautions in the large towns of Java provided interesting sidelights on native mentality. The leaflets which were distributed, headed "Danger from the Skies!" and dramatically worded in Malay, were received in perfect calm, and the order to show no lights was obeyed almost without exception. It seems probable that to the Javanese, living as they do in a country where sudden and violent storms and floods are everyday affairs, and volcanic eruptions and earthquakes always a possibility, the aeroplanes they are now so well accustomed to hear roaring overhead are simply one more noisy phenomenon added to the rest. And when they are officially warned (just as they are of anticipated volcanic activities) that these latest additions are likely to prove as unpleasant as, say, Mount Merapi, which a few years ago killed hundreds of peaceful country folk as they went about their ordinary affairs in their fields and villages, they accept the new danger as philosophically as they always have the old, as something that it is quite useless to get excited about.

The women, few of whom can read, because they cannot be spared from home in childhood to go to school, were warned of the "blackouts" in another way. They were told by their lords and masters that the kampong head-men had ordered that they must stay indoors in darkness, so that the evil spirits that would be abroad that evening (whom they would hear in the sky) should not be able to find them or do them any harm: which, after all, was not an inapt rendering of air-raid intentions.

CHAPTER TWO

Native Ways, Food, & Fashions

THERE is one generalisation that is quite safe to make about the Javanese, and that is in regard to their personal cleanliness. Running water and these people have a natural affinity for each other; and the running streams that are so lovely a part of every Java landscape would seem incomplete without the brown figures so often to be seen standing ankle deep, pouring water over their shoulders from any and every sort of dipper that comes to hand. The Javanese would no more think of failing to bathe at least once a day than he would of missing his sleep; and even in towns, where the delicious sparkling streams he loves so dearly are not available, he makes shift just as contentedly with the brownish waters of the canals.

At any hour of the day you may see men removing their clothing with becoming modesty before slipping into the warm current, there to stand breast-deep, soaping their hair as assiduously as ever hair was shampooed in a beauty parlour; and when the long, pleasant process is over, ducking and swimming under water, pausing for another soaping, sliding hither and thither with the ease and grace of fishes, while the garments washed before the bath lie spread out on the bank to dry in the sun. Nor do native women allow town life to prevent them from bathing. They do so fully dressed in a *sarong* drawn up and secured round their bodies under the arms, slipping the wet garment off after pulling a dry one over their head.

So long as you live in Java, you take this trait in the Javanese character that sets them for ever washing themselves and their garments, for granted; but you will not spend long in a country where other standards obtain, in France, for instance, before you appreciate it at its proper value. The ingrained greyish grubbiness of many otherwise charming little "white" boys' and girls' skins (to say nothing of that of some of their elders!) is in sorry contrast indeed with the satin-smooth bronze Javanese, bathed several times a day.

Not only the grubbiness, but also the slovenliness, all too

familiar in the countrysides of England and France, is foreign to Javanese ideas. Lovers of "artistic" tumble-down cottages and all that goes with them would find the Java *kampongs* far too neat to be "picturesque," matching as they do the orderly perfection of the fields. Broken fences, gates hanging drunkenly on one hinge, and makeshift fastenings with rusty links of chain or bits of wire, so characteristic of our farms and fields, are unknown in Java. No sooner do repairs become necessary to a fence or bridge, or whatever it may be, than the native makes it as good as new again. The inherent craftsmanship universal among the people is fortunately combined with an inexhaustible supply of bamboo at no more cost than the trouble of planting it from time to time; and thus it is that never a day passes but you will see a native cutting, carrying, or splitting this invaluable material. Europeans too benefit from the general native use of it. A three-foot-high fence put up round a friend's garden recently cost ten cents per three-metre section, about a farthing per foot. The bamboo was cut in the garden, split, and the fence made and erected for this princely sum, the only additional expense being a few cents' worth of nails.

The surfaces of the lanes that serve as main streets to countless thousands of native *kampongs* are kept as smooth as they are neatly fenced; and women and little girls are often to be seen conscientiously sweeping the section outside their family compound. These smooth pathways are in strange contrast to so many lanes in rural England, very often the only means of access, perhaps, to the homes of well-to-do householders; lanes made up of puddles and pot-holes and mud, only to be tackled afoot in over-shoes, or gingerly by car at the risk of broken springs. It is amusing to reflect that if the English gentlefolk who live thereabouts were mere humble Javanese peasants, neither puddle nor pot-hole nor sloppy mud would pollute the surface of that awkward lane! It would be smooth and level, easy alike for shod and unshod feet; and even, if necessary, paved with squared stone, trimmed and laid by hand.

It is unnecessary to say that the Javanese are past-masters in the handling of water. Their irrigation system is admittedly one of the wonders of the world, and there is no detail to which their patience and ingenuity does not extend. A farmer who wants to water a field that cannot be irrigated by a stream above it will rig up a bamboo lever with a tin at one end, and patiently dip up water into furrow after furrow from a stream on a lower level. When he wants to dam a fast-flowing stream, he does not waste time building one with loose stones, having learned by experience that these are no match for the impetuous mountain torrents after rain; instead, he makes baskets of split bamboo, and puts his stones into them, so that his dam hangs together. On somewhat the same principle he binds the earth with which he builds the "bunds" between his water-filled ricefields, with rice-straw, so that they never crumble, narrow as they are. And he well knows how to make running water serve him in other ways besides irrigation. I watched some men one day who were weeding a stone-paved mountain road. It was during the dry monsoon, and the earth between the stones was hard as concrete. But that troubled them not at all. The *mandoer* (foreman) looked round for a handy stream, never far to seek in the Java mountains, dammed it with earth and straw and stones, and deflected its flow over the road till it was soaked and the weeds came up easily; then demolished his little dam, and turned the stream back into its proper course, all as casually as turning a tap on and off.

You will see examples of native ingenuity in everyday matters at every turn. How neatly, for instance, he solves the problem of felling a dead shade-tree in a tea or coffee plantation, without damage to the bushes beneath it. If he cut it at the base it would crash down and smash perhaps a dozen or more in its fall; so he climbs another tree near by, taking a rope with him which he passes over a branch at a good height from the ground; then comes down again and climbs the tree he is about to fell, taking one end of the rope and tying it securely high up among the branches. Then he perches himself a little below and chops into the trunk until he has weakened it enough to break off with a sharp pull on the rope. It looks a risky business, but he knows just when to stop. "*Turun*" (come down) calls his partner below, who has been holding the rope's end on the farther side of the first tree, and down he scrambles, out of harm's way, as the rope tautens. The top of the tree then bends slowly over and breaks off with a splintering crash. Its fall controlled by the rope, it swings harmlessly in mid-air and is carefully lowered to the ground. The process is repeated, once, or perhaps twice, and the thing is done.

The same ingenuity and infinite patience is applied to everything the native does. He will plant a field with *cassava* (tapioca) cuttings with such meticulous exactitude that from whatever angle you view them they stretch away in long, dead straight lines in the distance, forming a perfectly symmetrical network of tiny squares; or set out another field with seedlings, each one of many thousands shaded by a little half hoop of sugarcane waste or screen of banana stem, painstakingly made and stuck in by hand. A municipal road sweeper fits a scraper neatly made of an empty tin at one end of a long bamboo, and a stiff little brush of palm midribs at the other, and is thus equipped with the perfect tool for his purpose.

Everything that we do with machinery the Javanese does by hand. He "mows" the lawn as smoothly as though by a razor, with his small curved knife called an *aret* or the larger *gogok bangan*; and though visitors from more "advanced" countries sometimes smile superiorly when they see rice being harvested a head at a time with a little knife, the native scores heavily if a storm should flatten his crop before it is cut, as happens sometimes in Java as elsewhere. A European farmer, dependent on machinery, would groan that his wheat or oats are ruined, but the Javanese is quite unperturbed; thanks to his "primitive" methods, his crop can be gathered with little trouble and no loss.

The Javanese wooden plough, or *loekoe*, too, is as primitive an implement as you please. But the farmer knows better than to change it for any modern innovation. It is of exactly the same design as that used by his forefathers for countless generations, and is perfectly adapted for its purpose. It can be easily carried on a man's shoulder to and from the fields, and turned with the minimum of trouble when in use.

The native countryman's knowledge of local conditions is of course unrivalled, and the Dutch have the wisdom to make full use of this when occasion arises. When, for instance, a bridge is to be built in a region subject to *bandjir* (floods), local natives are always consulted.

It is difficult for Europeans to realise how humble is the native's financial standard, and how pleased he is with the tiniest coin. It is worth while always to carry a supply of copper cents (of which a roll of fifty, done up in a screw of newspaper, is to be had at any Chinese *toko* (shop) for the equivalent larger coin); for one of these, worth only about a farthing to us, is quite acceptable to a Javanese. It will buy a packet of the tiny cigarettes so dear to his heart, or a portion of most of the eatables sold at the wayside stalls. The possession of this small change will save the European traveller a considerable sum in the course of a few weeks, and achieves just as much in good will as five cent or ten cent pieces.

You have only to watch for awhile, when the tide is low, from one of the bridges over the river at Soerabaya, to realise how much a very little may be worth to the native. You will see men and boys wading waist deep as they dredge in the mud with flat baskets for bits of old iron, bottles, prawns, a possible coin or so, or anything else the gods may send them. The gleaners are so many that the harvest at best must be pitifully small; but the Javanese is an incurable optimist; and at worst he has an excuse for a bathe, which, next to eating, is his favourite occupation.

In the matter of food the Javanese are artists in their way, and no French chef could put more care than they do into the preparation of the queer concoctions they find so delicious. Like the French, too, they have the "restaurant habit," or rather that of "eating out"; the population is too large and too well distributed to be catered for by restaurants, and the demand is met by thousands of itinerant food-sellers who set up little stalls by the roadside or trot along carrying a cooking-stove and pots and pans hanging at one end of their *pikoelan* (bamboo shoulder yoke) and a larderful of dainties at the other: ready to pull up and serve a meal for a few cents to any passing client. A small blue bowl is taken from a pile in the larder, and on to a foundation of rice other portions are ladled to taste, after the inevitable soup made of coconut milk in which float

Native Ways, Food, & Fashions

lumps of *katella* (sweet potato) and other vegetables, and a piece of dried fish. For more prosperous customers there are soft pale-green cookies called *lontong* made of rice steamed in banana leaf, looking, if the truth must be told, rather like Cornish pasties that have gone mouldy! Another popular favourite is the *lemper*, a small rice roll containing minced chicken; it is wrapped in banana leaf and pinned at the ends into a tiny parcel with splinters of bamboo.

The Javanese have a very sweet tooth: so much so in fact that they sometimes even pay for it with their lives. Wild honey abounds in the forests, and to get it they smoke the bees out of their nest in some high tree, and a man will climb up to take the honeycombs. It occasionally happens that the angry swarm returns too soon, and settling on the thief sting him so furiously that he falls out of the branches and is killed.

Among favourite sweetmeats less adventurously acquired are *tjaka ayam*, made of strips of cassava dipped in sugar and fried golden-brown, stuck together in little bunches like chickens' claws, which is the meaning of their name; flat round flour and sugar cakes with a hole in the middle, dyed pink or yellow, which are strung together like Chinese "cash"; and *pisang salé* (sundried bananas). These last are sold not only at native foodstalls, but in packets at railway stations, and are often eaten by European travellers.

Despite the fact that the Javanese eat with their fingers, and so perhaps offend European ideas of propriety, they are extremely finicky about the appearance and colour of their dishes, and dyes therefore play an important part in their menus. Rice, cassava, and coconut cakes are dyed all sorts of brilliant colours, and so are their sauces; native taste inclining for these latter to a particularly garish pink. Some dishes are richly black, an effect for which burnt coconut leaves are used; others are snowy white with grated coconut; for brown ones, caramel or palm sugar is the medium; and for red, hibiscus flowers or the leaves of the red *Colius*; a familiar red-dyed item being a tiny fish like whitebait, called *ikan glagah*, served at a European rice table as well as with native repasts. The sap of almost any non-poisonous leaves may be used to make green dishes, which Europeans often make the mistake of supposing to be mouldy! Blue ones are dyed with the petals of *Clitorea*; yellow, with saffron, Gardenia, or the pith of a huge fruit called *nangka*. Many of the same dyes are used in *batik* making.

Native fritters and fried chicken are excellent, always providing your prejudice against coconut-oil is not insurmountable. And a hungry English motorist who pulls up at a native restaurant may get a meal more to his taste at the cost of a few cents than at an expensive Dutch one. Any passing native in a country town will direct you to one; and there you can help yourself at a laden counter to a portion of fried chicken or a variety of other delicacies for three cents or so, and sit down to eat at a small table adorned with a gay, clean, coloured cloth and a great dish of Ambon bananas as centrepiece. A bowl of steaming rice will cost you one cent; a couple of bananas and a big cup of strong black coffee, three more; and to offer the odd cent change as a tip out of a ten cent piece is neither usual nor polite! The behaviour of the clientèle in these humble eating houses could not be more decorous at the Ritz. I have never known anyone even cock an eye at the intruder, though a European female must be an extremely rare bird in such places (it simply isn't done by the Best People!); and one can only marvel again at the unconscious example in good manners that these simple folk often set to those who regard them as "inferiors."

The motorist who prefers an *al fresco* meal bought from a roadside food vendor will fare almost equally well, except that he will have to take his chicken or *lemper* in his fingers. But so did far greater folk in Merrie England not so many years ago; and in Java there is always a sparkling stream near by to serve as finger-bowl.

Food varies in different parts of Java, and so do fashions, particularly in millinery. In the West Java countryside, when a man wears anything other than the usual *batik* headdress, it is usually a wide straw hat that is the special product of Tanggerang. In East and Middle Java hats are also worn, but they are small, stiff, miniature editions of Chinese coolie hats, rising to a point in the centre, or else a queer basin shape. Either kind is often perched on the top of the *batik* headdress, which the Javanese wears so constantly that he probably forgets it does not grow on his head. Occasionally, however, he will reverse the order, with even more comical effect; and even in the highly sophisticated streets of Batavia, you may see a velvet Malay cap fitted neatly over the crown of a wide brimmed Tanggerang straw. A "dunce's cap," exactly like those used to shade choice chrysanthemums, is sometimes worn in East Java; and in one district a kind of woven helmet is the mode.

It is not only in matters of headgear that Javanese men are greater slaves to fashion than their womenkind. In some places, so perverse is human nature, it is the custom to blacken and polish the white and even teeth, of which most of them are the lucky possessors, with a dentifrice they call *banyon*, made of coconut milk in which iron rust has been steeped. *Djoko* bark is used for polishing, and the processes are repeated until a shine like that on patent leather is attained. Elsewhere the victims of custom tamely submit to the removal of their two upper middle teeth on arrival at adolescence. And in the Preanger, where the people are much lighter-skinned than elsewhere in Java, and the men almost beardless, they pluck out any hairs that may appear on their chins, an occupation at which you may often see them engaged with tweezers and a little looking glass, as they squat on the grass by the roadside.

There are fashions too in umbrellas. In the royal capital of Djokdjakarta, large yellow or black gamps vary the Java wide use of those made of oiled paper, and add a characteristic note to local colour, especially when they are displayed in shop windows against backgrounds of burnt sienna and indigo *batik*.

Tenacious though he is of all these and a thousand other native customs, the Javanese shows himself amusingly susceptible sometimes to European influences, even when these are least appropriate. The native child, for instance, born and bred to tropic heat, thrives in it like a little salamander. Nevertheless house servants in the towns, who have come to regard mountain holidays as the "done thing," will gravely inform you that they have sent their families away to the hills for the hot weather.

The natives of different parts of Java vary as much as do those of our English counties. In the Preanger, people met along the road will greet you of their own accord, a man raising the straw hat perched atop of his *batik* headdress as he does so. In East Java, though they respond at once to your greeting, they seldom take the initiative. But it is easy to get on terms with native children everywhere.

We may smile at native simplicities; yet the Javanese might retort that he has long outgrown some childish things still firmly believed by many people in England. *Old Moore*, for instance! A Javanese equivalent of this immortal work was published about a century and a half ago at the court of the Sultan of Solo; and among many prophecies foretold that "vehicles would move without horses or oxen"; that "lines of metal would carry travellers across the country"; and that "when the *pasars* (markets) lose their echo the women of Java would lose their virtue." An old resident who owned a copy of the book told me sadly that this last prophecy had been fulfilled as well as the others. The *pasars* had lost their once characteristic echo when the old-fashioned high roofs had been replaced by others of modern design; and (so he averred) the modern Javanese "Miss" had travelled far from the modest simplicity of her grandmother!

But however that may be, the fact remains that the Javanese natives are a pleasant people. They differ from ourselves in a thousand ways, great and small; but they possess qualities that give us very seriously to think, before assuming with too much certainty that it is we who are the Superior Race.

CHAPTER THREE

Wedding Days

THE Javanese attitude to marriage and divorce is the exact antithesis of ours. In England marriage is dangerously easy and divorce deplorably difficult. In Java the married state is enviably simple to escape from when occasion demands; there is, for instance, an old custom, still extant in places, which permitted a man whose wife remained childless to return her to her parents and ask for another sister in exchange! But casual register office weddings are not for the Javanese couple, and the long drawn out ceremonial that is their unescapable prelude to matrimony is an infallible preventive of rashness, and would probably scare any European into perpetual celibacy.

As in Europe, there are in Java months that are specially popular for weddings. Many are celebrated just before Ramadan, the Mohammedan month of fasting, and many more when that disturbing period is over. And in Middle and East Java, where the effect of the dry East monsoon is most marked, and rice cannot be planted all the year round as in the West, the favourite marriage months are June and July, after the gathering of the rice harvest.

In Middle Java, above Madioen in the Sultanate of Soerakarta, there is a mountain region between Magetan and Ngerong that celebrates weddings in a way all its own. I lived for some time in this district in a house whose garden overlooked the road through Plaosan, a native and Chinese township possessing no white population except ourselves and the occupants of two or three villas on the outskirts, which therefore was affected but little by modern influences. The more so that it lay almost at the end of the road to the higher ranges, which a mile further on became too steep for ordinary traffic.

Our garden made an ideal "dress circle" from which to look on at the show unconsciously provided for us, day in, day out, by the inhabitants as they passed up and down on their lawful occasions along this road which, with its hedges of roses and hibiscus, and its overarching bamboos and shady trees framing glimpses of the distant mountains, made a perfect setting for the scene.

The revue that passed unceasingly across this natural stage was colourful enough at all times. But in the marriage months it became doubly entertaining. An atmosphere of restless activity pervaded the village during these wedding days, continuing hour after hour, day and night, instead of only before and after the market as at ordinary times. Groups of people in twos and threes would stand about laughing and chattering; and every now and then a native girl, dressed in her best and dainty as a flower, would pass up the road carrying on her head a large tray covered with a white lace cloth. These trays were laden with all kinds of eatables, and might be either contributions from relations to the marriage feasts, or else gifts accompanying invitations to the wedding.

In Java custom demands that the parents of a young couple about to marry shall give presents to the entire circle of their acquaintance. The Javanese have in fact an incorrigible habit of present-giving to all and sundry on the occasion of any sort of *salamatan* (good luck feast) whether personal or public, a habit which it is the accepted thing among Europeans to condemn as extravagance. And yet there is something very likeable about this overwhelming desire of theirs to share any great occasion with their friends. It is, moreover, largely a matter of exchange; for the compliment is always returned either in cash or in kind. Among the Javanese, as with us, it would be unthinkable to go to a wedding without giving a wedding present.

All day the endless cavalcade goes by. Sooner or later the members of the *gamelan* orchestra will pass, laden with their instruments, without whose queer monotonous music no native celebration is complete. The big gong, measuring four feet across, packed in a great bamboo basket like a huge wash-basin; the principal instrument, a kind of giant xylophone ten feet long, and its stand, a gaily painted red and gold contraption like a highly ornate bedstead, are each carried by two young men walking one behind the other, with a stout bamboo resting on their shoulders from which the instrument is slung. Smaller gongs and other instruments are carried in long tubular containers of split bamboo; the whole procession, of a dozen or more, all in appropriately festive mood and laughing and singing as they go.

There is always one discordant note in these otherwise delightful day-long shows. Inevitable as the *gamelan* is the appearance of the limp, dismembered corpse of a *sapi* (steer or bullock), slain like the fatted calf of old to provide meat for the feast. It is usually carried back from the village slaughter-house in a large shallow wooden cradle with barred sides that afford a much too good view of the unsightly contents.

The pretty golden brown head, with horns and soft velvet muzzle all dabbled with blood, will loll grotesquely in a basket borne in the rear: destined most likely to form an offering to ingratiate evil spirits, and turn them from any unkind intentions they might be entertaining towards the bride and bridegroom.

Excitement grows as the day passes, and does not end with the coming of darkness. All through the night, if you happen to wake, you will hear voices and laughter: but always subdued, as is the way with these mannerly people. And a little before dawn, the bang of a shot-gun will announce that the wedding celebrations have officially started. They will go on, first at the bridegroom's home and then at that of the bride, for days; until such time, in fact, as all the provisions, if not the guests, are exhausted.

On this day, about noon, the bridegroom goes in procession to the *Mesigit* (mosque), and it is now that the real show begins. The whole population turns out to see it. Even the *tanis* (farmers) take care to be back from the fields, and see their plough-bufflaloes safely stalled in time to bathe and don their newest *sarong* before either joining the crowds that line the roads or becoming part of the procession itself, which swells and lengthens as it goes. It is as fantastic a sight as ever was devised in pantomime, and as it comes slowly into view in the brilliant tropic sunshine, you are likely, especially when you see it for the first time, to rub your eyes and wonder if you are dreaming.

The wail and squeal of bamboo pipes and a vague thudding of drums, mingled with the murmurous hum of many voices and the soft scuffle of bare feet, comes nearer and nearer.

Then, round a bend in the dappled shade and sunshine of the winding road trot a score or so small boys, all turning fascinated half-frightened glances back over their shoulders at the antics of a huge monster that capers just behind them.

Sometimes leaping high into the air, where it seems to remain uncannily suspended; jumping clear from one side of the road to the other; now facing this way and now that; twirling giddily, or springing suddenly backwards into the midst of its delighted followers, the amazing apparition slowly approaches. It is crowned with an immense fanshaped headdress made of peacocks' feathers, bedizened with streamers and spangles and flowers, towering high above the crimson-scarred hibiscus hedge that borders the road. It has an enormous lion's face with staring eyes, prodigious whiskers and hideously grinning teeth; and the twirling figure itself is decked with every sort of bizarre drapery that Oriental naïveté could devise. Yards of muslin and scraps of *batik* of every hue hang about it indiscriminately, touched up here and there with bows and tassels. And finally, a pair of magnificently muscular calves emerge from three-quarter-length loose breeches trimmed with ludicrously feminine frills. A ten-foot-long tail of extremely grubby calico whirls with the agile giant's leaps and bounds, its end held by another masked dancer who plays up faultlessly to his leader's complicated performance, while missing no opportunity to capture the applause with a solo on his own account whenever opportunity offers.

Behind these come two lads dressed as female characters, their brown cheeks rouged, wearing bejewelled headdresses and dangling earrings, and their thin braceleted bare arms hanging from modish quasi-European *décolletages*. They are followed by the "band," whose instruments consist of three or four small oblong drums hung from the players' necks, and tapped with the fingers at each end; some tambourines; and a mixture of bamboo pipes and whistles, producing between them a rhythmical and not unpleasing accompaniment.

But all this is merely accessory to the procession proper. The real hero of the occasion, the bridegroom, is now seen approaching, riding on a pony and shaded by a large umbrella

Wedding Days

carried by an attendant walking beside him. The benedict-to-be is an even odder figure in his way than the capering dancers that preceded him. He sits absolutely rigid, impassive and expressionless as a doll, his face whitened like that of a circus clown, his hands in loose white cotton gloves, the left arm stiffly a-kimbo, and the right hand with gold rings (worn outside the glove) gleaming on the first and fourth fingers, as he stiffly holds the reins.

He wears a heavily braided black cloth military cap and long coat, with loose black breeches ending below the knees to reveal the suspenders that hold up barred red-and-white stockings; and black laced shoes of generous size to accommodate feet better accustomed to go bare. A *kris* is stuck in his belt at the back, and from its hilt dangles a string of glass beads, in contrast to a chain of real gold and silver coins, hung round his neck and falling to his waist. The bewildering ensemble is completed by a pink muslin sash tied round his waist in a big bow.

The bridegroom's mount is draped with red netting trimmed with tassels; and the saddle is a sort of winged boat with a Garuda head, suggesting the probability that these ceremonies must date back to Hindu times, five centuries or more ago; for Garuda was the god Shiva's favourite mount. Bracelets of bells jingle on the pony's fetlocks and on its tinsel crown, and round its neck is a pink sash to match its rider's. Trained specially for these occasions (and hired out at a not inconsiderable fee by its owner, a well-to-do local Javanese) the animal dances along with mincing steps, in time, more or less, to the band.

It is the duty of the attendant umbrella-bearer to keep the umbrella twirling over the bridegroom's head without pause from beginning to end of his progress to the *Mesigit*, for it is by this means that an abundant offspring is assured to the coming marriage; and this is a consideration of the first importance in Java, where children begin to earn their contribution to the family exchequer almost as soon as they can toddle. The umbrella man does his duty conscientiously; with only a slight lapse now and then when some superlatively funny antic by the dancers distracts him, and he pauses to join in the delighted chorus of "*Wah!*" with which the

Javanese express applause; but he always resumes his fertilising exertions the next moment with redoubled vigour.

The bridegroom's procession consists only of men: all dressed in their smartest batik *sarongs* and headdress, and starched white jackets. And as every available man in the village turns out to support each bridegroom in turn, and the latter's costume, the pony, and its trappings are all hired for each successive marriage, is it any wonder that it is hard to distinguish between the wedding parties of Paiman, Sapari, Osman, or Matradji, even though you may be on the friendliest of terms with them in everyday life?

The dancers are known as "*Ryoks*"; they are local men whose skill has been acquired in a lifetime of practice, and genuine skill it is, suggestive at times of the methods of the Russian Ballet. Their art is often a family one, handed down from father to son. Their services are considered indispensable at any *comme-il-faut* wedding in their district, so that during the marriage months they make a substantial addition to their income. In ordinary life they are farmers and cultivators like the rest of the community. Their elaborate masks are communal property, for which an association called *atoeran sinoman* make themselves responsible. In our village they are kept at the school, in full view both of scholars and passers-by, but familiarity does not seem to detract in the least from the thrill they produce when the *Ryoks* appear in them.

The procession winds slowly along, with many halts to allow the dancers to entertain the populace, until at last it comes to the *Mesigit*, where the *Modin* (whose function it is, among many others, to look after local religious affairs and to marry and divorce any who desire his services) is sitting on the steps, smoking the odd little tapering cigarettes beloved of all Javanese natives, while he awaits the arrival of the party.

The bridegroom is helped from his pony by two of his friends (his unaccustomed clothes apparently making him incapable of independent action) and then walks stiffly across the compound with an attendant on each side of him, to the foot of the steps, from which the *Modin* has now disappeared behind a curtain. One attendant here takes off the groom's cap while the other stoops down to unlace and remove the clumsy shoes, and then for a few minutes they leave him standing there alone, a quaint unreal-looking figure, expressionless as ever, while they go off to wash their feet in a little room at the side, before entering the *Mesigit*.

Then, all together, the three young men ascend the steps, lift the curtain, and disappear. Further we cannot follow them; but I am assured that in the very few minutes they remain out of sight, inside, the bridal knot is securely tied (in exchange for two and a half guilders) despite the absence of a bride. That is until such time, of course, if the marriage should not be a success, as the husband may see fit to spend the same modest sum in having it untied again!

Meanwhile, outside in the road, the *Ryok* dancers have seized the opportunity to relax: to raise their masks and exchange pleasantries with their friends in the crowd, until the bridegroom returns and stiffly mounts his pony again, to sit there motionless as a Horse Guard, the umbrella still faithfully twirling above his head, while the *Ryoks* proceed to give a whirlwind performance of mock fights and wild caperings to which all their previous efforts have been a mere curtain-raiser. This show outside the *Mesigit* is the most important item of their performance, and its omission would not only deeply offend the village public, but reflect most adversely on the prestige and reputation for generosity of the bridegroom's parents. So he doubtless accepts it with the rest of the tiresome preliminaries to connubial bliss, as he sits on his pony, his immobility in odd contrast to the general hilarity, visibly the only person present who is not enjoying the entertainment: though it is probable that, even if he were, custom would forbid him to show any sort of expression.

The crowd has grown by this time until it has completely filled the street between the low-browed Chinese shops, but remains a most mannerly audience in spite of its enthusiasm. Sometimes, from one end of it or the other, there will come a cry of "Mo-tor-r-r-r—" the final "r" trilling from mouth to mouth, like the purr of a giant cat. And with the sound the crowd splits in two as though a wedge had been driven into it, and dancers, band, bridegroom, wedding-guests and onlookers all press back helter-skelter to the sides of the narrow road, overflowing into shops and front gardens and tumbling into the deep ditches, as a car (usually driven at high speed, for there is no "30-mile limit" here) with blaring horn tears through the human avenue thus formed, yielding glimpses of massive figures and pasty faces, and perhaps the echo of a contemptuous laugh at these silly native pranks.

But it has no sooner passed than the crowd, quite without resentment, flows out over the road again, even giving the white man's car a cheer to speed it on its way, while the *Ryoks* start their gymnastics again as though they had never been interrupted.

The bride's progress to the mosque is a very different story. So unobtrusive is it that you must keep a keen look out if you are to see it at all. No drums or dancers give warning of its coming as it makes its way humbly along the same road that the bridegroom travelled so triumphantly a few hours earlier. And if ever proof were wanted of woman's insignificant place in the Oriental scheme of things, this almost furtive little party would supply it.

With whitened face, wearing a crown of paper and tinsel flowers, and a new, but quite ordinary, *sarong* and little muslin coat, the bride-to-be rides past in a primitive *tandoe* (sedan-chair) surrounded by a score or so of her women friends, all, of course, wearing their best. They are dressed, in fact, exactly like the bride herself, except that no crown adorns the sleekly brushed dark hair coiled so neatly on the nape of each slim neck, and their brown cheeks are innocent of her disguising white make-up. They steal sedately down the road, scarcely receiving even the tribute of a glance from the passers-by, and presently the bride in her turn disappears behind the curtain of the *Mesigit*. Soon she creeps shyly out again, climbs back into her chair, and the little party melts away into the distance once more as inconspicuously as it had come.

The whole programme is repeated day after day, without any variation that an outsider can see, so long as the marriage boom continues. But interest never flags, and both *Ryok* performers and audiences seem as full of enthusiasm at the end of a month or so of weddings as they were at the beginning.

CHAPTER FOUR

More about Marriage, Birth, & Death

THE queer eatables that accompany invitations to a Javanese wedding are a source of much embarrassment to a European guest. It would be a bold stomach indeed that would tackle them, and it is most difficult to dispose of them otherwise, without being caught in the act by your native servants, whose feelings would be outraged. To refuse the gifts would be unthinkable; for not only would it be an unpardonable affront to the donors, but it would bring bad luck to your own home as well as theirs for a whole year if you did so, or failed to put in an appearance at the marriage.

While I was living in the village described in the previous chapter, the son of the *Kamitoewoe*, an important native local official, was married; and though the bridegroom's procession appeared to be identical in every detail with the others that were taking place almost daily, the other ceremonies were on a rather more elaborate scale. The festivities began the night before the wedding with a *tanakan*, a formal wedding dance with prescribed movements, led on this occasion by the highest local official, the assistant *wedono*, in honour of the happy event in his colleague's family.

The bamboo gateway at the end of the path leading to the *Kamitoewoe's* house was gaily decorated with palm fronds and hibiscus when we arrived in the early afternoon of the great day, and we were received in a big room where rows of chairs and two long tables awaited the guests, the tables however being bare, while a lavish supply of food was displayed on the mat-covered floor.

Lace curtains veiled doorways leading into rooms on either side, in one of which a *gamelan* orchestra was softly playing. It was only when we were startled by the shrill neigh of a pony from what we had supposed to be a bedroom, behind one of the lacey draperies, and the unmistakable "moo" of a *sapi* from another, that we realised we were not in the house proper at all, but in an addition built on for the occasion in the compound in front of the one large, windowless, living and sleeping room of which many Javanese houses consist. So that actually we were encroaching on the lawful domain of the worthy *Kamitoewoe's* domestic animals.

The house into which this fine new addition led was a bewildering hotch-potch of East and West. The whole floor was covered with beautiful new woven grass mats, across whose expanse we looked to an alcove in the centre of the farther wall. This was curtained with heavy red plush, looped back in a style ludicrously reminiscent of small old-fashioned Parisian hotels, and gave a secretive sort of effect to the bridal couch, a large, brand-new double kapok mattress which almost covered the floor of the little inner room. On it we could just catch a glimpse between the curtains of two "Dutch wives" (a sort of bolster) in frilly covers, and of a spotless mosquito net looped up with tinsel and flowers.

In front of this alcove, on a velvet pile mat of startling design, two upright chairs with red velvet seats covered by white lace antimacassars stood primly side by side awaiting the bride and bridegroom. At intervals round the walls were seven large cupboards and wardrobes, and in one corner a double bed, enclosed in a mosquito net, was half hidden by a screen.

The walls were hung with oleographs, among which was a highly coloured portrait of Queen Wilhelmina of Holland, with enlarged photographs of the *Kamitoewoe's* family, and some highly glazed pottery ware, lobsters and fish. Light (to say nothing of heat) was supplied by a paraffin lamp hanging from the roof, and two "fat-lamps" on the floor. The two stout posts supporting the roof were banded with red and white paper, and at the top of both of them, and at each corner of the room, there hung a big bunch of bananas, always much in evidence at native weddings. For among Javanese and Malays the banana (*pisang*) and betel-nut (*penang*) are the chief marriage tokens. To offer either to a young girl is equivalent to a proposal, and her acceptance implies a favourable answer. The Malay word meaning "to ask in marriage" is *menimang*, derived from *penang*.

Little groups of friends sat on the floor chatting softly together, while they were served with cups of tea and coffee by the ladies of the house and by wives and daughters of the

A SELLER OF DURIAN.

EACH DURIAN IS TIED UP IN PALM-LEAF TWISTED INTO A HANDLE TO ENABLE PURCHASERS TO CARRY THE PRICKLY, VERY HEAVY FRUIT AWAY WITHOUT DIFFICULTY. NOTE THE BEARER'S PALM-LEAF HAT. HE WILL PUT IT ON OVER HIS VELVET *Songkok* IF IT RAINS. HIS *Sarong* IS TWISTED UP AND CARRIED OVER HIS SHOULDER.

RYOK DANCERS IN A BRIDEGROOM'S PROCESSION.

A BRIDEGROOM GOES IN PROCESSION TO HIS WEDDING.

THE UMBRELLA HELD OVER HIS HEAD MUST BE KEPT TWIRLING IN ORDER TO ENSURE PLENTIFUL OFFSPRING OF THE MARRIAGE!

atoeran sinoman, this being among their official duties. They moved noiselessly to and fro, inviting the guests to help themselves from a long double row of dishes set out on the floor, laden with all sorts of odd looking dainties.

All this we had plenty of time to observe at our first visit, paid before the arrival of the young couple from the bride's home in a *kampong* a few miles away, whither the bridegroom had gone in state, complete with his whole entourage, to take delivery of his bride.

The oftener guests come and go at these days-long receptions, the better the luck for both hosts and guests. So it was quite in order that after awhile we should take our leave, promising to return later. Meanwhile we took the opportunity to put in an appearance at another wedding which was taking place on the same day. Returned home from that also, we presently heard from our garden the distant sound of drums and shouting, and set out once more for the *Kamitoewoe's* so as to be in time for the reception ceremony.

We took our places at the invitation of our host, who was looking very stately in his stiffly starched white jacket and new golden-brown *sarong* and headdress, standing close behind a new grass mat spread just inside the entrance. Upon this mat, which custom demands must be virgin new and undefiled by any foot before that of the bride is set upon it, we were very earnestly warned not to tread.

We had not long to wait before the head of the procession appeared in the narrow bamboo fenced lane leading to the house, in much the same order as usual. The small boys were in the lead, yelling with joy at the antics of the *Ryoks* who, far from appearing tired, seemed to be reaching with this final scene the very apex of their inspiration. This time it was the second dancer, slender and powdered under his tinsel crown, who came whirling with fluttering hands towards us, before his leader, the *parongan*, with one last tremendous bound, fell into a dramatic pose just outside the door. Then came the musicians, who drew apart to make way for the bride in her floral carrying-chair (called the "*Kronok*"), to be set down in front of the new mat, beside which her father-in-law stood gravely waiting.

The little bride sat stiff as a doll in her chair, her face

utterly blank under its thick coat of white paste, crowned by a top heavy headdress of imitation pearls and wired metal flowers, while the *Kamitoewoe* stepped solemnly forward. Stooping down, he gathered up his son's wife in his arms and carried her, according to custom, over the threshold into the house, moving slowly so as to allow time for her to be plentifully bestrewn with rice. Then he set her down on her feet on the mat; for thus, and in no other way, must a Javanese bride be received on her marriage day into her husband's home.

Looking more like a doll than ever, she stood there on the mat for a minute or two while the bridegroom, who was close behind, dismounted awkwardly from the grey wedding pony in its Garuda trappings, and came to stand beside her. Then the queer little figure sank to her knees and clasped her husband's left ankle, bowing her head and touching his knee with her face. Rising to her feet again, they stood stiffly side by side, and an egg was placed in the hand of each of them. This they held while attendants transferred a flower from the bride's headdress to that of her husband and *vice versa*, and then dropped over the shoulders of both a loop of strong white cord. Thus united, hand in hand, the other hand of each still grasping the egg, they walked through to the inner room and sat down on the two chairs in front of the marriage bed. A small table was placed before them and they were served with two plates of rice, elaborately decorated; but before they helped themselves a big brass bowl of water was brought, in which they washed their hands together and then clasped hands on the table for all to see. During this part of the ceremony the eggs were handed to attendants to hold, as an English bride hands her gloves to a bridesmaid. The eggs having been returned to them, each then took a little rice in the hand not occupied with the egg, and offered it to the other, both eating a few mouthfuls.

While this was going on, plates of rice and dishes of every imaginable sort of *etcetera* had been handed round by the attendant womenfolk to the company who by now were crowding the floor, but, strange to say, nobody seemed to be eating anything. This was explained when after a while squares of banana leaf were distributed. On to these the plates were emptied, and the food, safely wrapped up in neat packages, disappeared into the folds of the guests' garments to be carried home and enjoyed at leisure.

All this went leisurely on for about an hour, during which the bride and groom sat silent and unmoving on their chairs. Outside the *gamelan* played its odd monotonous music, broken now and then by a muffled bang from a drum, lying at the entrance, which is beaten to announce the arrival of each guest.

At last the newly married pair stood up, and the bridegroom walked through the assembled guests to the outer room, while his bride, supported from behind by her mother with a hand under each arm, followed humbly in his wake. A brass *sirih* box containing the ingredients for betel-nut chewing, and some tobacco, were placed in her left hand, and an earthenware drinking vessel in her right. These she handed to her new lord and master in token that in future it would be her care to serve him with the daily necessities of life. This done, she was free at last to slip away and sit at ease among her own friends, while the bridegroom vanished into the darkness outside the house.

The formal proceedings were now over; and having pressed our small wedding contribution into the host's expectant hand (there is no false modesty about the Javanese!) we took leave once more, receiving a pressing invitation to attend the celebrations which would go on all night at the home of the bride, to which the whole party was to set out shortly.

A heavy thunderstorm came on soon after we reached home, and it was not until some hours later, when we were beginning to think about bedtime, that we saw the flickering light of a number of torches wavering along the road, and the procession with the bride's chair in its midst passed our gate in the warm scented darkness on its way to the next stage of the festivities, which, we had been told with pride by one of the party, would alternate between the two houses for five or six days.

These post-nuptial celebrations we did not this time attend. They are all very much the same and, to a European, after the first few experiences, extremely wearisome, for, once in the party, it is difficult to escape before daylight. There is almost always a *wayang* show; the queer monotonous *gamelan* music goes on and on, rising and falling like the sound of wind or water; native guests drift in and out and eat and drink, which latter you too must try to do if you would not hurt your host's feelings; the bride sits on view in her finery looking like a doll; and the master of the house accepts without the least embarrassment the coins slipped into his hand by departing guests as wedding gifts.[1]

There are few *kampongs* in this part of Java in which you will not see preparations for marriages going forward during these "marriage months." As at the *Kamitoewoe's*, the usual plan is to wall and roof in part of the compound in front of the house, an area perhaps thirty or forty feet square. The walls are of split and woven bamboo and the roof of palm-leaf *atap*. To see the care and labour with which the sections are planned and measured out on the ground, you would never think that the building in course of construction was only a temporary one, destined to be demolished after only a few days' ceremonies.

All standards of labour are different from ours among these slow-moving, slow-thinking, eternally toiling people. Nothing to them is too much trouble. They do not look at things that way. If, for whatever reason, they decide to do a thing, whether it be building a house, tilling a field, or carrying some enormous load all day and all night for an infinitesimal profit, they simply go ahead and do it, without haste or delay, comment or complaint. The same spirit that sets these humble country folk building what are in effect whole houses for a daughter's wedding feast, inspires the natives of the big towns to erect the elaborate *Pasar Gambar* and *Pasar Malem* pavilions, involving months of labour, only to be torn down again after the twelve days' annual fair.

The life of a Javanese bride-to-be during the weeks preceding her wedding must be anything but a happy one. Every day for two months, unless she breaks away from prescribed custom, which is probably rare among so conservative a people, she submits to massage, or *dilalar*, from head to heels by the village matrons, with a coarse powder called *lalar*,

[1] See *Java Pageant*, chapter iv.

made of *temoe-giring*, *pandan*, *ketan*, and *kemoening* leaves,[1] ground up together. Then, after having bathed, she is rubbed down again with a finer powder called *bedak wida*, made of *temoe-giring*, *sarinaga*, *dempo*, and *penang*.[1] These recipes are strictly adhered to and the ingredients regarded as indispensable. Daily, for the last ten days before the event, she is rubbed with a sort of cold cream, a mixture of fat with the *bedak wida*, to make her skin soft and supple, and the hairs are plucked out of her body. Two days before the wedding the thick long rope of black hair that is every Javanese woman's crowning glory is washed and smoked over a fire of sweet-scented wood to give it a pleasant odour, and she herself is rubbed with a sweet-smelling mixture called *tapel*. On the last night before the marriage an emblem called the *sadjen* is often placed beside the bride-elect's sleeping place. It consists of some bananas, betel-nut, and two yellow coconuts called *klapagading*, on one of which is a drawing of Ardjoeno and on the other of Soembadja, his wife. In some villages the bride sits up all night dressed in her wedding finery, surrounded by brass pots full of flowers.

On the great day itself she is dressed, after bathing and massage, by a local *doekoen* or magic-maker who, before setting the heavy bridal headdress in place, cuts off a lock of the bride's hair, to be snipped up and divided among the relations, each of whom should put a few hairs in the shell of a young coconut and throw it into a river or the sea.

The bridegroom on his wedding morning, before being dressed in his Gilbertian costume, sits in the front room of his father's house surrounded by his male friends, while the *Modin* reads aloud instructive passages from the Koran. He then hands round for inspection the *Sri-kawin*, a gold ornament that he will present to his bride at their meeting.

The wedding day is called "day of meeting"—*ketoemoe*—from the fact that the bride and groom meet officially for the first time outside the bride's door when the groom goes to fetch her. This is the first formal part of the ceremony shared by both, and each is given a rolled *sirih* leaf, which they throw at each other before their joint procession sets out to the home of the bridegroom's father.

[1] All cultivated in native gardens or easily obtainable.

Tiresome formalities do not end for the Javanese wife with her marriage. In the seventh month of her first pregnancy she must prepare a good-luck feast called *Tingkeban* for all her friends. And native methods of midwifery can scarcely add to the joys of childbirth, though they do not seem to have the adverse effect upon the population that might be expected. These methods and beliefs differ in all parts of Java. One that is widespread is that difficult childbirth is rendered as easy as Twilight Sleep if a dried gut from a panther or, better still, a tigress, killed when in whelp, is bound round the woman's abdomen.

When the baby is born, another feast, the *Sepasaran*, is held and kept up for six days, and another, the *Selapanan*, thirty-five days after the birth. When the child is seven months old a ceremony not unlike Christian baptism takes place, an example of which I saw recently at the home of one of our native neighbours, a well-to-do gentleman aptly described locally as *orang tjoekoep*, meaning, literally, "a man who has enough" or, as we might say, "a warm man."

Early one morning we noticed several servants emerging from this worthy's door, carrying a large brass bowl of water which they set on the ground in the middle of the compound in front of the house. The *Modin* then arrived and, after bowing gravely to the little group of people standing around, squatted beside the bowl, muttering long strings of unintelligible words as he scattered flower petals, looking suspiciously like those of the pink roses in our hedge, on the surface of the water. The proud father then threw in a handful of small coins, to ensure wealth for the child in the future, and the baby was carried out from the house, dressed in bright silks and swathed in a handsome *selendang* or scarf of *batik*. It was undressed and plunged into the water without raising the slightest objection, and with its tiny face smeared with white paste looked even more like a doll than had the bride and bridegroom. When it had been wrapped in its *batik* again and carried off indoors, the *Modin* and his assistants frugally gathered up the infant's symbolic future wealth from the bottom of the bowl, no doubt to prevent it from falling into evil hands and thus bringing bad luck, and the water

Birth, & Death

with its rose petals completed its beneficent work on the roots of a bougainvillea growing by the house door.

Death too, of course, has its ceremonial in Java, though the dignified simplicity of a native burial is in most marked contrast to the noisy demonstrations of the Chinese. When a Javanese dies, the body is carried out of the house and washed from head to foot, after which wads of fibre or kapok are placed over the eyes, and in the ears, mouth, and nostrils, to prevent the entry of evil spirits into the body, and the corpse is tightly wrapped in a length of new white cotton material.

An old native called on me one day to ask if he might borrow sixty cents to buy a piece of this white *kain* in which to wrap his aunt after her death. When I condoled with him on his bereavement and gave him the money, he explained that the old lady was still well and hearty (she lived in fact for another year or more), but that she herself had expressed a wish to have everything all ready. He had some time previously asked for, and been given, two nice pieces of teak to mark the head and foot of the grave, and now, he said, nothing more was needed except the bamboo for the bier! He added ingenuously that as he was sole heir to his aunt's house and a field of *djagong* (maize) he felt it his duty to carry out her wishes.

Javanese employees, like Europeans, are fond of using a relative's funeral as a pretext for a day or half day off. In their case the funeral is always perfectly genuine, but their relationship with the deceased is sometimes hard to establish. The simplicity of divorce leads to a multiplicity of step-relations, all of whom regard one another with complete amity, and the conveniently elastic word *saudara* (family) includes them all. When, for instance, my maid Moerti asked leave to attend a family funeral recently, she was assisting, as far as I was able to discover, at the obsequies of a sister by her father's last wife but two, for whom she had a warm affection and shed many tears.

A native funeral on its way to the burial place is a very simple sight, and perhaps for that reason a very touching one. The body is carried on a bamboo bier called a *bandoesa*, under a sort of cradle something like those used in hospitals to keep the weight of bedclothes off a broken limb. Over this are laid the batik *kains* of the departed, and across them chains of *Kembodja*[1] blossoms. Ahead walks the *Modin*, scattering yellow rice (very frugally) out of a small china bowl. Somewhere in the procession that follows the bier you will see two young men, each carrying one of the roughly carved teak head and foot posts that will be set up when the burial is over, a sight that never fails to suggest to me the sensation that would be caused at an English funeral if the tombstone were carried behind the hearse.

At the funerals of better-off persons, especially in towns, the bier is often covered by a mosquito net set up on cornerposts as on a bedstead, so that the dead appear to be carried to the grave on a bed, hung with garlands of *Kembodja* flowers. The effect of one of these, with an umbrella carried ahead of it, indicating that the dead person was of good position, threading its way across tramlines and among modern motor traffic, is extremely incongruous to European eyes, but the mourners are quite unaware of it, and go on their way with all due dignity.

There is no other burial place in the world that conveys so completely the fitting atmosphere of Death as some of those long established among the Java mountains. Nor are there any that, in their own eerie way, can compete with them in beauty. You will often see one on a low hillock, or tucked away in a sheltered corner in a fold of the hills, a dark patch touched with scarlet amid the green and silver of the surrounding ricefields. Around the edge, poinsettias flare like living flame against the sombre darkness inside, under the gnarled, grotesquely twisted trunks and branches of ancient *Kembodja* trees, planted long, long ago, as cuttings, at the heads and feet of the forgotten dead. They crowd close together as though to prevent all intrusion upon those they still guard so jealously; and their branches, interlacing a bare four or five feet above the ground, make with their thick glossy leaves an impenetrable roof that shuts out entirely the light of the sky. So that, peering in

---

[1] Kembodja (*Plumeria Acutifolia*), known in Australia and elsewhere as Frangipani, is called *Boenga Koebor*—the "grave flower"—by Javanese and Malays.

Birth, & Death

from the bright sunshine outside, it seems like an enchanted forest, whose mysterious gloom must inevitably be peopled with ghosts and all manner of strange, terrifying spirits.

As your eyes grow accustomed to the darkness, you may perhaps distinguish one or two graves enclosed with stone or cement, but this is rare. For the most part nothing marks the last resting place of the Javanese dead but stout teak posts whose carved heads stand a foot or so out of the ground. These bear no inscription and are seldom or never replaced. For the Javanese, wiser perhaps than we are, does not attempt to perpetuate the memory of his dead for a posterity for whom they can have no concern. He plants a *Kembodja* beside them, which will add its shade to the place when he too, and his children and his children's children, have come to rest there. The teak posts will last as long as the memory of the dead in the hearts and minds of those left behind; and after that, who will be left to know or care who it is that is lying here? The posts will rot and fall; all trace of the grave is lost, as that of hundreds before it. But the dust of those who were buried here is safe, mingled with that of their fathers and forefathers, in the shade and keeping of the "grave trees."

Sometimes, on the outskirts of a village, you will see one of these trees, huge, gnarled, and immensely ancient, on a little artificial mound surrounded with a neat bamboo fence or perhaps a hedge of poinsettias. This marks the grave of some specially revered person of long ago, perhaps a "wise man" or religious teacher. Even he is now long forgotten; probably not even his name survives, but the people of a village always treat such a place with reverence and keep the fence in repair, and it is seldom that you will not see little offerings of rice, cakes, or flowers among the roots of the tree. Some of these graves are said to be so old that the *Kembodja* tree, old as it is, may have been replaced by a new one several times.

The Javanese observe many feasts after the death of someone belonging to them. One takes place immediately after death, one three days later, and another after seven days. The first anniversary is honoured with a celebration called *mendak sepisan* and the second with *mendak pindo*. A thousand days after death one called the *njewoe* is held. Thereafter the dead are remembered all together at a feast held in one of the "holy" months, in somewhat the same way as the French celebrate the "Jour des Morts."

CHAPTER FIVE

The Dessa

THE foundation of the native social system in Java is the *dessa*. And *dessa* administration, though it appears strange to the European, works with a smoothness that any of our systems, from parliaments to parish or county councils, well might envy.

The *dessa* is an agricultural area, usually a large one, surrounding and including a village or town ("township," as Americans or Australians would call it) which serves as its heart and commercial centre; and also a number of *kampongs* or subsidiary hamlets scattered far and wide among the rice-fields, where live the peasant farmers and their families.

The system of *dessa* government is entirely native, a survival of earlier times left almost intact by the modern Dutch rulers who wisely recognise its efficiency in the special conditions for which it was devised. It varies somewhat in different parts of the island, as do also the titles of the officials and their duties: these divergencies having doubtless been evolved under individual local conditions in the days when districts were entirely cut off from one another for lack of means to cross mountains and rivers. But fundamentally the system is the same in every *dessa*. In the Javanese scheme of things the town exists as an adjunct to the land, not *vice versa*, as has come to be the accepted rule in our Western world. And the whole structure of local government is based on that idea, so to administer the affairs of the community as to assure its well-being through the land by which it lives.

Dessa land law is extremely complicated and many weighty tomes have been devoted by Dutch writers to the subject. It is of interest to English readers that the system described in these treatises on native land tenure is that inaugurated during the five years of British rule in Java, by Sir Stamford Raffles, and that Dutch administrators who followed him paid him the compliment of adopting it. One authoritative article on the subject begins: "When the English took over control of Java they found a system based on monopoly, forced labour, and forced delivery of produce ... which Raffles regarded as oppressive for the people and bad for the Treasury." [1]

Briefly, it may be stated that the land composing each *dessa* is divided among a number of families in which it is handed on from generation to generation, but with one curious proviso. If one of the landholders breaks the law, for instance by theft, or by an affair with his neighbour's wife, and especially if he should lay himself open to a sentence of imprisonment, then he forfeits the right to his land for himself and his heirs, and the *dessa* council decides to which of the hitherto landless families the culprit's portion shall be given. By which it can be seen that a fall from grace on the part of one of its members is not a matter of unmixed regret in the community, for in no *dessa* is there ever quite enough land to provide a piece for everybody.

All the *dessa* officials are natives, and all except one are local residents, elected by local native vote. The exception is the head of them all, a sort of Mayor, called *Wedono* in East and Middle Java and *Wedana* in the West. In small *dessas* this official is called "assistant" *Wedono* or *Wedana*, as the case may be. This head man is a well-educated native from elsewhere, appointed by the government, and usually transferred to fresh fields every few years. He enjoys a special prestige due to his ability to speak Dutch, and his quasi-European standing, and he acts as a sort of liaison officer between Dutch and native, a delicate position calling for considerable tact, which is seldom found wanting.

Next to him comes the chief of the really local officials, the *Loera* or *Bekel*, who may also be called *kepala dessa* (*kepala*=head) or *Petinggi* (meaning literally the tall or high one). Through this important person and his next in command, the *Kamitoewoe* or *Kami-toea*, the *Wedono's* orders are transmitted to those lower in authority. Then comes the *bayan* or *kebayan*, a sort of Public Works controller, who apportions and directs the communal work of the *dessa*, such as cutting or planting trees, trimming banks, repairing flood damage, and the like. He also acts as go-between in

[1] *Encyclopædia van N. Indie*, M. Nijhoff, 's Gravenshage, E. J. Brill, Leiden (J. F. Snelman; van der Lith).

the matter of orders from the authorities to the humble ordinary countryman. The *Djogobojo* is an official whose duties are many, and vary in different places. One I know in Middle Java was known as the Keeper of Buffaloes, being responsible for the safety and welfare of these important animals and of all other cattle, without which the fields could not be ploughed. It is his special duty in most *dessas* to catch thieves, whether of live stock or smaller fry.

The *Sambong* is another indispensable official, who, in the *dessa* mentioned above, was the arbiter of the water-supply. This is the most delicate and difficult of all administrative posts, for irrigation water is literally the life of the community in a rice growing country. Quarrels are frequent; the temptation to tap a neighbour's channel at night proves irresistible at times. All such disputes must be dealt with by the water-chief, and it is whispered that in Java, as elsewhere, bribery is by no means unknown, and that it is the farmer who can offer the best arbitration fee who is always found to be in the right in such an argument!

In country *dessas* where the *mesigit* is a combination of mosque, *hôtel-de-ville*, and town-clerk's office, the *Modin* is an important functionary, taking the place of the *Penghoeloe* who presides over the mosque in large towns. He plays an even greater diversity of parts than his *mesigit*. He acts as priest, so far as priests can be said to exist in the Mohammedan church, collects religious dues and taxes, makes and breaks marriages, presides at *salamatans*, indicates lucky days for weddings and other important events; takes measures against evil spirits when required, this being considered a more dignified method among persons of standing than recourse to the *doekoen* or magic maker; he gives instruction in the Koran, and hunts up children for vaccination! He is, in short, a very useful member of the community, though he is not always regarded with as much respect as he could wish. In West Java the Soendanese have a saying: "The *Lebé* is a goat!"—meaning that he will eat anything; or in other words, that he will take on any old job that is offered to him. (*Lebé*, or *Amil*, are this industrious functionary's titles in West Java. In East and Middle Java he is *Modin* or *Kaoem*.)

All these officials, and any others there may be, are easily located by a painted board, the equivalent of our professional men's brass plate, bearing their style and title, such as PONDJOSARI ... MODIN, usually set up on the ornate bamboo archway giving access to their homes.

In addition to all those officials who live in the central town of the *dessa*, every one of the surrounding *kampongs* has its own head man, called *Kepala Kampong* or *Petinggi*. These gather with the rest on appointed days, once or twice a week, at the *Koempoelan* or council meeting at the *Wedono's* house. Usually they ride up on ponies, which are noticeably well fed and groomed. The well-to-do Javanese countryman is a keen horseman and takes great pride in his mount, especially if it be a *koré*, a pony trained to a smart "amble" pace. These are rare, and command very high prices. A prettier sight in its way than these native councillors cantering or "ambling" down the village street under the great overarching trees, with the dappled sunshine striking now and then on a pony's glossy flank or on the polished hilt of a *kris*, it would be hard to find. One by one they dismount and the ponies are tied up in shady corners here and there, and the *dessa* parliament gathers solemnly on the "voorgalerij" of the *Wedono's* house. The "voorgalerij" is a verandah on a very large scale: in reality an open-air room with the roof supported on three sides by pillars. Here they sit all the morning cross-legged on the tiled floor, discussing, and very effectively legislating, local affairs, fortified from time to time by cups of black coffee.

The councillors wear a distinctive dress for the meeting. Their *sarong*, more properly called a *kain*, is always a handsome one, and a *kris* is stuck into an embroidered belt. A short black jacket, often piped with red, is worn over a white shirt. And a broad ribbon—red when the meeting concerns exclusively local affairs, and orange when it is "Queen's business," such as roads or bridges, that has to be dealt with —crosses the breast from shoulder to waist. The usual jaunty *batik* headdress completes the costume, and sandals are worn as a sign of social superiority.

Elections are held from time to time. Balloting is done with small pieces of bamboo, dyed a different colour for each candidate, adding much to the picturesqueness of the occasion.

Survivals of ancient troublous times, when Java was as

warlike in its small way as modern Europe, are the *dessa's gardoe* or watch-houses, in each of which hangs a hollow tree trunk called a *kentongan* or *tong-tong*, on which the hours are struck during the darkness, from 7 P.M. to 5 A.M. One of these little buildings, which may be built of concrete, split bamboo, or stone, according to local fancy, must always stand at the entrance of every path leading to a kampong, and at any other points deemed desirable by the *dessa* authorities. The watchmen are appointed weekly, and every man in the *dessa* takes his turn sooner or later at this honourable duty. The hours thus sounded are a sort of "all's well" signal like a ship's bells, for the *kentongan* are the recognised means of giving an alarm. In the days when inter *dessa* skirmishes were as much a national sport in Java as football to-day in England, they served to call the men of the *kampongs* to defend their homes or help their neighbours in case of an attack. When the warning sounded, all the *kampongs* within earshot of the one first sounding the alarm and, snowball-wise, all those in turn surrounding each of the others so summoned, rushed to the assistance of the one attacked: the perfect anti-aggression pact in practice. More settled conditions under Dutch rule—and above all the Field Police—have rendered this system of mutual defence, which was known as *kawan-gangsal* or *montjapet*, no longer necessary. But the *kentongans* remain, and are still used as fire alarms or when a theft has been discovered. Some ultra modern *Wedonos*, eager to show their thorough conversion to European ways, have abolished the striking of the hours during the night. But native opinion is conservative, and this rather charming custom is still fairly general outside the large towns, especially in East Java.

It is oddly companionable, if you happen to be awake in the night, to hear the muffled musical "klonk" of wood on hollow wood in the distance, picked up and repeated, or overlapping like striking clocks, from half a dozen or more different points. You lie drowsily seeing in imagination the tiny fire, whose ashes are to be found in each *gardoe* house next morning, glowing and flickering softly in the starry darkness, and the watchman, having faithfully discharged his duty, settling down to sleep again for another hour after rewarding himself with a puff or two of one of his queer little cigarettes. Admirably devoted to duty these native watchmen seem to be. But I am bound to record that their ardour is rather apt to wane with the night. You will be able to pick out a much greater number of separate notes from different watch-houses at 10 or 11 p.m. than at four o'clock next morning. And by 5 a.m. the falling off in the volume of the *kentongan* orchestra suggests that most of the performers have decided to "cut" the last hour of all and have a good sleep before going off to their everyday work.

The *kentongan* also serve as a sort of curfew. At 9 p.m. the nine strokes are followed by a further series of taps which indicate to all and sundry that now shops must be shut; the roadside food-stalls, round each of which with its tiny gleaming oil lamp a few gossips are always gathered, must be packed up and carried off, and all good people go quietly home to bed.

Old residents say that in some *dessas* there were formerly also night watchmen who marched round in threes, beating a tattoo on pieces of bamboo to rouse Chinese merchants who were heavy sleepers and were afraid of thieves. The custom was, not unnaturally, anything but popular with other sections of the community, and appears to have quite died out. Many *dessas* however still employ a night patrol.

In the daytime the little *gardoe* houses are used as shelters by wayfarers, and very often a food-vendor will set up a stall under their friendly roof.

Just as the *Wedono's* council is the brain of the *dessa*, so the *pasar* (market) is its heart. It is the business centre, the exchange and mart, the agricultural show, fun-fair, social club, and a hundred and one other things combined. And that on no mean scale, for the *pasar* of many an unpretentious township serves a wide and densely populated area, and on market days will be packed with a mass of humanity numbering thousands, through which it is scarcely possible to push your way.

Despite the great numbers of buyers and sellers, there is none of the casualness of a French or English market about a Java *pasar*. It is fenced in, and there is only one entrance, where a native clerk from the *Wedono's* office sits issuing tickets at one cent apiece to every vendor. A market is held

A *Gardoe* HOUSE, WHERE A WATCHMAN SITS AND SOUNDS EVERY HOUR FROM 7 P.M. TO 5 A.M. ON THE HOLLOW TREE-TRUNK OR *Kentongan* HANGING FROM THE BAMBOO STAND OUTSIDE. THESE LITTLE SHELTERS ARE FAVOURITE RESTING AND MEETING-PLACES BY DAY WITH PEDLARS AND OTHERS. A TRAVELLING HABERDASHER IS HERE RE-ARRANGING HIS STOCK.

RICE HARVEST.
CARRYING HOME A LOAD OF GRAIN FROM HIS *Sawah*.

in very large *dessas* every day; in others, twice in the seven day week; and in Middle Java once or twice in the old five day week, now called "*pasar* week," as it survives only in this custom.[1]

On those days, long before it is light enough to see them, you will hear the low clank of the big bells worn by the oxen drawing the heavily laden, creaking *grobaks* or *tjikars* (heavy wagons built of teak), and the laughter and chatter of the men and women who think nothing of walking all through the night carrying enormous loads to market from their fields and gardens. As the light increases you will be able to watch the endless procession passing down the road to market, the perfect pageant of country life. You may see it a thousand times, but it never loses its novelty or its fascination, or the illusion it creates that it is a scene staged for your entertainment rather than an ordinary episode in a workaday world.

It is full of variety and yet bewilderingly the same. As you see the ever moving stream pouring down the lovely sun flecked road under the sheltering trees, it seems almost as though all these busy chattering people must be marching round and round, reappearing over and over again, as in Drury Lane dramas of the good old days, so alike they look with their brown faces and colourful garments. But this is a stage on which there is no lack of "supers." The people come from all the countless *kampongs* scattered among the surrounding miles of cultivated fields: tiny hamlets which, when you see them from the mountain slopes above them, are only visible as darker patches made by the shade of trees and bamboos amid the brighter green of the rice crops. And all these passing eager folk have the same goal and the same object: to sell their produce and to exchange gossip with their friends at the *pasar*.

Women are much in the majority, and they provide their own transport. Every one of them carries a big round basket slung in her *selendang* (a length of stout cotton material a yard wide and three yards long: usually of *batik*), which she wears across one shoulder with the ends tied together, and this is filled with all sorts of produce according to the district and the season of the year. It may be piled high with coconuts,

[1] See Chapter Eight, p. 119.

with maize or cassava, bunches of carrots or tiny pink onions, with enormous *nangka*, twice as big as a man's head, with papayas, peas, beans, sapodilla, oranges, potatoes, mangoes or durian; or the heads of half a dozen or so luckless fowls, unmindful of their destiny and apparently quite contented, though their legs are tied together, poke out above the top of the load, looking absurdly like a bunch of grotesque flowers.

Most of the women wear a tight-fitting long-sleeved cotton or coloured muslin jacket called a *badjoe*; but many, especially in mountain villages in the poorer parts of Middle Java, wear instead a long piece of *batik* or blue-dyed calico wound tightly round the upper part of the body under the armpits, leaving uncovered smooth shapely arms and shoulders that any society woman well might envy.

Beside many of the women trot miniature replicas of themselves: little girls, scarcely more than babies, with unnaturally solemn faces and hair screwed into a bun, dressed in tiny *sarong* and *badjoe*, and carrying tiny well filled baskets in tiny *selendang* to match, with nothing childish about them except an occasional frightened clutch at mother's hand or dress. Often a baby is sharing the big basket, the *selendang* slung across its mother's back, its little behind fitting snugly to the tight-stretched cloth, and a small fat leg protruding on either side. Usually the tiny face is smeared with white paste, and sometimes it is ridiculously crowned with a man's grey felt hat or a cloth cap, lamentable evidence of European influences and Japanese trade, but obviously, in the proud mother's eyes, the last word in smartness.

When the women stop, as many of them do, at the roadside food-stalls to buy their breakfast, a baby hand is pretty sure to be stretched out and dipped into the sticky mess for a share. The people eat as they walk along, usually a handful of steamed rice over which is poured a spoonful of henna coloured sauce; pinches of various vegetables are added, all these being kept cooking in their several iron pots at the roadside. The mixture is served on a square of banana leaf, of which the restaurateur has a pile on the little stall beside him.

For the men of the *dessa*, the *pasar*, when they attend it, is a respite from their hard work in the fields, and for the most

The Dessa

part you will see them walking proudly along, alone, or in twos and threes, very rarely indeed with their womenfolk, smoking their small tapering cigarettes. All wear the *batik* headdress of universal Java custom, and some a conical or basin shaped rice straw hat, painted a vivid red, blue, or green, perched on the top of it. Many are unencumbered by any sort of burden; others carry a stout bamboo and a coil of rope, ready for the goods they plan to carry home, bought at the *pasar* with the price of the produce their wives are bringing to it. Others are carrying a *patjoel* (the native farmer's favourite tool) for repair or re-tempering at the blacksmith's forge, whence there sounds, almost unnoticed, an intermittent musical accompaniment to the scene. A few are well loaded with great bunches of bananas, or bundles of firewood as tall as themselves, fixed at each end of their *pikoelan* (bamboo yoke); or with twin baskets of manure or piles of palm-leaf roofing.

Few of the endless stream of passers-by seem to have any concern other than the all-engrossing *pasar*. But now and then a man may emerge from the bamboo grove near by, balancing a great smooth green freshly cut bamboo across his shoulder with one hand, while in the other he carries the sharp curved *parang* with which he has just chopped it down. For him the *pasar* does not exist; he is only concerned with some needful repair to his house or stable.

Dozens of little boys run free, laughing and chasing each other round their elders, on their way to school; though some of them will probably be pressed into service on their way home again to help carry their parents' purchases back to their *kampongs*.

Sometimes on *pasar* days a better class native lady will stroll down the road, in the crowd but very manifestly not of it. Her costume is invariably that known as *sarong* and *kebaya*: the latter a long cutaway jacket, usually white, trimmed with embroidery. This style, believed to have been introduced by the Chinese, was formerly worn in Java by European women, but is now only the fashion for upper-class Javanese and Chinese. She is pretty sure to be wearing high-heeled mules or sandals, which alone would mark her out as belonging to a different world from the rest who, without exception, go barefoot, but she too may conform to universal custom and carry a baby in her pretty *selendang*. She will be greeted very respectfully by the lesser folk, and by the *Wedono's* staff of clerks, who appear in due course, immaculate in starched white jackets, golden-brown *batik kain* and headdress, and sandals, carrying important-looking document-cases under their arms.

As the sun rises higher, the stream moving down the road towards the market gradually thins, and for an hour or two, while activity at the *pasar* is at its highest, the road will be almost empty. Then, by degrees, the stream of humanity starts to flow again, but this time in the opposite direction. The people are still laden, but differently. The women's baskets are filled now with their household purchases, and crowned, nine times out of ten, with a *koekoesan*. This is the conical split bamboo basket in which the family rice is daily steamed, and which, from such constant use, wears out quickly. It should be noted that in Java rice is never boiled, as by European "barbarians"; and the difference in its flavour when thus cooked as it ought to be is extraordinary. Another very general purchase is a bunch of the indispensable *lidi*, midribs of palm leaf, out of which every sort of broom, brush and mosquito switch is made. And some women are now laden with local products for sale in some distant *dessa*, which their labour in transporting it will enable them to turn into a microscopic profit.

For the most part the men return as they went, less heavily laden than the women, and are carrying nothing more than new tools or *patjoel* handles, or perhaps the baby, so as to enable mother to deal with the heavier load! But there are some exceptions. Some carry weighty hardwood planks, half as long again as they are themselves, ingeniously lashed in pairs on to the shoulder-yoke in the form of a giant inverted V, for convenience in transport. Others will be entirely hidden behind sheets of split, woven bamboo called *bilik*; literally as big as the side of a house, that being exactly what they are destined to become. These are lashed to a stout bamboo and balanced so that they can be carried upright with nothing visible of the bearer from one side except his feet.

Many of the men will be resplendent in fine new hats, perched of course on the top of their ordinary *batik* headdress. The purchaser of a new hat is always unmistakable, because he is unable to resist the temptation to take it off and admire it as he strolls back along the road.

CHAPTER SIX

Life in a Dessa

JAVANESE country folk are poor, but seldom too poor to spend a cent or two on their children, or rather on their little boys. There will be few of the little lads who do not carry toys of some sort as they pass on the homeward journey with their parents. Some run along with bright eyes fixed on paper windmills whirling on slender bamboo sticks, or on jolly little *wayang* figures made of paper. Others swing ingeniously made rattles of various kinds, or suck the coloured ices on sticks which are brought up from the town below in big vacuum flasks by the Java equivalent of our "Stop Me," and find a ready sale in all country places.

The housewife's own purchases are not all strictly utilitarian, either. Few go home without a supply of pink and white cassava-flour cakes impaled on a stick or strung on a grass cord; or a bunch of the popular sugar "chickens' claws." And a bouquet of paper flowers to brighten the dark windowless living-room of her home often nods from the top of a woman's basket in place of the fowls that peered from it on her outward journey, which fowls by now, poor wretches, are probably sizzling in the pan for someone's dinner!

The *pasar* itself is a perfect index to the life of the *dessa* in which it is held, and is a fascinating study to the foreign visitor, providing that its pungent blend of smells, and the inevitable close contact with humanity in a hot and humid mass, are not too great a deterrent. If you join the procession you will find on reaching the *pasar* that, for lack of *lebensraum*, it has overflowed its boundaries and that vendors of all sorts of goods as well as of food line both sides of the road outside. The vendor of rice straw hats plies a busy trade on the grass verge by the roadside, where the purchasers, all men, make their choice with as much care as a lady of fashion in Bond Street, but at somewhat lower cost. The ordinary conical shape, with coloured straws cunningly woven in to make a pattern, is sold for ten to fifteen cents. Painted over with enamel in some gay shade the price is five cents or so higher.

Life in a Dessa

There are sellers of toys, cakes, haberdashery, and unclassifiable oddments which include soap cut into one inch cubes, and salt in slightly larger ones, wrapped in banana leaf; sewing cotton wound off in short lengths on paper balls, full reels being too expensive for these humble purchasers; palm-sugar done up in small round wheels of dried palm leaf; tiny tapering packets of native cigarettes wrapped in maize leaf; the woven grass cigarette cases which every Mid-Javanese carries; matches, big coarse hairpins, sold singly, buttons, also sold singly, peppermints, spoons, pencils, and so on *ad infinitum*: a sort of very humble Woolworth's where nothing costs more than one or two cents, say a halfpenny or farthing.

Having nothing to sell, you are admitted free with a genial grin, by the *Wedono's* clerk in the ticket office, to find yourself at once part of the ever moving, closely packed, good natured crowd whose chatter blends into a murmur as vague as that of the sea; a crowd that, congested as it is, never jostles roughly or shows the least sign of irritation or impatience. So dense is the mass of people that it is almost as impossible to see the merchandise, much of which is laid out on the ground, as it would be to see the sea bed when you are swimming. You can only get glimpses here and there of cabbages and coconuts and carrots, beans, lettuce, tarong, tomatoes, sawoes, papayas, soursop, artichokes, chillies, potatoes, cucumbers, melons and the rest, with here and there a picturesque little group of women stripping maize from the cobs into great golden heaps. The crowds surge round all this without doing it any damage, for the Javanese as a rule are careful to do as they would be done by in the matter of respect for their neighbours' property.

Threading your way carefully through the throng, you come to the raised floors of the roofed-in market proper, where the produce is exposed in a more conventional way, on benches, and here the variety is infinite indeed. Tobacco is heaped in dark piles on green banana leaves, looking as attractive as it smells. Near by are huge quantities of the popular *tempé* cake made of partly fermented soya beans and cassava flour; it is sold in great slabs a foot or more long, is about six inches wide and looks rather like oil-cake. The yeast used by natives, called *raggie*, is there in small white balls that look like moth-balls; so are little brown cubes of *gambir*, side by side with its partners, betel nuts and chalk, for use in the universal *sirih* chew.

All sorts and sizes of ugly-looking roots and nuts and scrapings are displayed, every one of which, if you ask, you will be told are the ingredients of various medicines guaranteed to cure every ill that flesh is heir to. The names of these remedies differ in every district, and even if they did not, would convey little to European ears. But it is evident that they are all as well known to the native marketers as though they were labelled in bottles or packets in a chemist's shop, and there is always a thriving trade in them, for the native has a blind faith in the efficacy of a dose of medicine. Sometimes there is a stall where a primitive apothecary, usually a woman, dispenses strange concoctions after whispered conversations with the patients: consultations that have an air of mystery that suggests dealings with some medieval sorceress. And you wonder whether it is a love potion that is afterwards handed over, or perhaps the means to get rid of an unwanted mother-in-law.

There are fragrant many coloured heaps of scented flower petals, of which you can buy a handful to scatter on a grave, or adorn your hair, or make chains for the children's necks. And you can buy too a tiny phial filled with any scent you choose for no more than one *gobeng* ($2\frac{1}{2}$ cents: about a halfpenny). A popular stall this with young girls, especially at *Lebaran* time, the so called Native New Year.

At another stall you may find a woman making up small packets containing a pinch of several of the medicinal roots, an orange petal or two, a slice of carrot, and a few pepper seeds, which she wraps in the ubiquitous banana leaf, and sells like the proverbial hot cakes. What this odd mixture is designed to do for the purchaser I have never been able to find out. Whenever I have asked I have always received a shy smile and a shake of the head; and information, usually so eagerly given, is not forthcoming. So whether it is a form of magic of more than ordinarily confidential kind, or merely a Javanese version of the French housewife's *bouquet garni*, I am unable to say.

The sight of the banana section of a *pasar* is unforgettable. The green and golden bunches, called *sisir*, many of them as

Life in a Dessa

tall as a man, hanging close together as though growing in a fairy tale forest, give the narrow dark passage between them something of the character of a jungle path, filling it by their colour with a weird and false illumination. Here too, in some corner, there will be a pile of the strange torpedo shaped purple banana flowers: a much prized delicacy among the Javanese, who cook them with chillies and coconut milk, and serve them on special occasions with their rice.

To pass on from the banana jungle to the fish section is a transition from the sublime to the ridiculous; but there was never a Java *pasar* yet that lacked this department, a very important one in the life of the people. The *bareng*, a small herring which is common round the coast, and also bred extensively in artificial ponds under Government supervision, is dried and salted to become a staple article of diet known as *trassi*. It announces its importance in the national scheme of things by permeating an unduly wide area of the *pasar* with its unpleasant aroma.

A familiar sight are masses of the tiny sprouting beans the Dutch aptly call "little commas," a popular adjunct to both Dutch and native rice tables. Less attractive are big, bloated, jellylike cakes, quivering and flabby, made of banana and palm sugar, sold by the slice. There is hardware of all sorts, from the tiny *ani-ani* or *etam* for cutting the heads of rice from the stalk, sharp as a razor and sold for one cent, to *patjoel*-blades and ploughshares, *parangs* and *arets* (large and small knives for outdoor work): to say nothing of all the imported delights now so beloved of these once unsophisticated people, such as safety razors, cigarette lighters, and electric torches. There are "departments" for everything: firewood, tiles, pottery, hats, baskets of every shape and size from three inches to three or four feet deep; enormous piles of *koekoesan*, mats made of grass or coconut fibre; palm-leaf roofing called *atap*, house walls of *bilik*, maize-fibre brooms, stacks of *lidi*, and of wooden *patjoel* handles.

There is a drapery section with piles upon piles of cotton goods, beside which squat the sewing men with their machines, ready to make up garments to measure while the customer waits. Business always appears to be thriving, and you will seldom see one of the dozen or more sewing machines that is not hard at work. More often than not, several are crowded out, and tailor, sewing machine, shirt or jacket in the making, and anxiously waiting customer, are all out in the open, among the maize and melons and the rest. *Batik* sellers are legion, for this is the national dress material of the people; and in Middle Java there are also great quantities of cotton goods dyed blue with locally grown indigo. Belts embroidered with silk in many colours, very popular with Javanese men on dress occasions, hang in dozens from a bamboo in a dark corner, illuminating it with gay colours.

Inside, outside, in round, flat, covered baskets, or in bunches of two or three or half a dozen, in every corner, lying on the ground with their feet tied together, are the luckless fowls that are the mainstay of every menu in the tropic East. Unluckily the climate demands that they be marketed alive, and the sight of them is distressing to the compassionate onlooker; yet the victims are themselves so little concerned at their situation that they peck greedily at the grain scattered round them until they are picked up, pinched or poked appraisingly by prospective purchasers, and either carried away or else dumped down again to snatch another grain or two before their inevitable doom overtakes them.

There is food and drink of all kinds to tempt the marketers. There are fruit syrups in intimidating shades of verdigris green and petunia pink, and cakes and biscuits no less highly coloured; and though few Europeans would care to tackle any of these, the appetising smell of grilled meat that sometimes tickles your nostrils is quite another matter. It comes from a row of small charcoal fires over which small pieces of meat, liver, or chicken, impaled on skewers, are being grilled. These are called *saté*, and are as popular at European tables as they are with the Javanese.

When a market day coincides with a killing day at the *dessa* slaughter house, as for popular convenience it very often does, there is sure to be in the *pasar* a gruesome meat exhibit calculated to convert any European visitor to a strict vegetarian diet. And among the horrid shapeless bloody relics, which look as though the animal had been torn to pieces rather than cut up, you will always see the hooves, still muddy from the poor beast's last journey, as likely as not from the compound where it had been the children's companion and pet from babyhood.

You may go to any *pasar* of all the thousands throughout Java, and yet be sure to come across something that is new to you, or some small incident worth adding to your memories of them. I once saw an old man, gnarled, smiling and deeply wrinkled like a Balinese carving, selling smokes and sundry small *etceteras*, among them the flint-and-steel cigarette lighters that have become popular in Java of late years. He was singing, softly and ceaselessly, a jolly little song, obviously improvised, about the wares he had to sell, and I caught something about "pretty flowers of fire that would light up the hands of those who used his fire stones." Catching my eye, and what I hoped would be accepted as an appreciative murmur, he immediately introduced a personal and embarrassingly complimentary note into his improvisation: after which, having no use for a "fire stone," who could do less than stop and buy two boxes of matches for three cents?

At another *pasar*, a stout Chinese had arranged a table and four heavy teak armchairs by the roadside near the entrance. Here he graciously played the host, inviting passers-by to sit down and drink tea to the strains of a gramophone, while he displayed samples of shaving cream.

On *pasar* days, an official is always on duty at the *Loembong*, or *dessa* bank, another most important item in *dessa* administration. Much gold is deposited here in the form of smooth shining bunches of ripe golden heads of rice. It is at the *Loembong* that a certain proportion of his crop must, by *dessa* law, be deposited by each farmer to ensure enough seed for the next sowing; a most necessary precaution, without which the light-hearted Javanese would quite likely sell or consume the whole lot, leaving the future to take care of itself. Outside this curious "bank," at any time that it is open, you will always see some of the golden grain being unloaded from the *grobaks* while the big creamy coloured oxen lie peacefully chewing the cud on the grass at the roadside.

The amount of rice thus deposited for seed is regulated by the *dessa* authorities. This and all other matters of bookkeeping are in the hands of the *Tjarik*, the local writer or accountant, who, like the other officials, enjoys the distinction of a board bearing his title at his gate.

Extra entertainment for the crowds that gather on *pasar* days is provided from time to time in many *dessas* by the advertising methods of various European manufacturers. The directors of these enterprises are well aware that however small the purchases of the individual native, they represent in the aggregate an immense trade that it would be folly to neglect. Motor vans, equipped with loud speakers and gramophones, tour the country, penetrating into the most remote corners, taking care that their visits shall coincide with market days, when the scattered populations of the *dessas* are drawn as though by a magnet to their exchange and mart, and villages that are quiet and sleepy at other times are thronged with thousands of people.

The van pulls up near the *pasar*; the salesman turns on the gramophone, and proceeds to broadcast a lively dialogue between two natives, man and woman, in which the charms and cheapness of, say, Palmolive soap, which has a factory in Java, are extolled, interspersed with some extremely highly spiced jokes, which delight the crowd that immediately collects. The entertainment is given in Malay, and also in Javanese or Soendanese, according to the locality visited.

When the audience has been entertained and got into a thoroughly good humour, the salesman turns off the gramophone and gets down among the crowd, giving away hundreds of small samples, cajoling delighted girls to use this soap that will make them irresistible, and persuading married women that it will beautify their babies: in short, writing "Palmolive" on the local consciousness in such a way that it will never be forgotten. The local storekeepers, well knowing the mentality of their customers, lay in a supply and arrange for more; attractive posters in gay colours, announcing the soap as "*Saboen oeangi boeat moeka, boeat badan, boeat sehat*" (fragrant soap for your face, your body, and your health), are posted up; and off goes the car to repeat the programme at the next *dessa* on its list.

The designing of posters to attract the native eye is an art as yet only in its infancy, but one or two firms have learned it to a nicety. The palm in this respect should certainly go, up to the present, to Mr Wood of "Wood's Great Peppermint Cure," who is a familiar figure on the walls of every native or Chinese *kampong*, even the smallest, and the "cure" a much trusted *obat* in countless native homes. For despite his own enormous pharmacopœia of herbal remedies, the Javanese is always ready to pin his faith to any new one recommended to him by the white man. Mr Wood is represented as a benevolent Eastern potentate in flowing robes with a long white beard, dispensing to a worshipful populace his miraculous mixture, whose innumerable virtues are set forth in flowery Malay as guaranteed to cure *penjakit roepa-roepa* (illnesses of all sorts). Chinese storekeepers, from whose shelves the "cure" is seldom absent, have told me that it is in immense demand, and is firmly believed to be a panacea for a variety of quite unmentionable ills.

Even the important Dutch tea-growing industry does not find it beneath its dignity to establish direct contact with Chinese and native buyers. The motor vans of the *Nederlandsch Indische The Propaganda* tour the country as thoroughly as do those of manufacturing firms. So far as my experience of them goes, they do not employ quite such entertaining methods; but they distribute attractive posters showing natives dispensing the "cup that cheers" to groups of friends, making eloquent speeches about it the while; and in every village, storekeepers are appointed their official agents. It would be rare indeed to find even the smallest *dessa* town in which a board bearing the words *Waroeng Teh* (*lit*. "tea-shop"), and the agent's number, does not appear on at least one small Chinese or native shop—or more likely on several. Competition for the honour is keen, as indicated by the numbers, which run into five figures.

Tea has become a popular drink among the Javanese, though it has not, and probably never will, replaced coffee. But even so, just as twopenny cups of tea are said to have laid the foundations of Lyons' great business, so the tiny purchases of Java's forty odd millions of people may well have an effect by no means to be despised upon the fortunes of the Dutch tea-growers.

Even on days when there is no *pasar* there is never any lack of entertainment in a country *dessa* if you care to watch the passing show. There are the farmers going off to their fields in the early morning, their *sarongs* pulled up and worn shawlwise to keep out the cold, carrying a heavy primitive wooden plough across one shoulder, and driving in front of them the great water buffalo or golden brown oxen that will draw it. There are women of all ages, some young and charming, and others ancient crones that must be great-grandmothers at least, going down to the stream for water, with earthenware jars, as big as themselves and far heavier, carried either on their heads or held in place on their backs with the ever useful *selendang*. There are men carrying loads of every sort and kind at the ends of their *pikoelans* which they shift adroitly from one shoulder to the other in one lithe movement, without even stopping in their stride. There are huge clumsy creaking *grobaks* (for some reason no one ever seems to oil them!) of the same pattern as those used by countless generations in these same regions, drawn by two oxen with a tall slender tapering upright rod fixed between their yokes, painted in bright colours and often tipped with a bunch of flowers. There are strings of pack ponies, almost hidden under their cruelly heavy loads; and sometimes in mountain districts you may see a Chinese or well-to-do native being carried along in a heavy teak and bamboo sedan chair.

On most days the travelling native barber will pass, carrying his apparatus in a wooden box labelled BARBIER, and a camp-stool for his clients. He will take up his stand under a shady tree, hanging a little mirror on a nail he drives into the trunk; and there the men of the *dessa*, swathed in a sheet, will have as neat a hair-cut as any man could desire. These barbers ply their trade also, with equal lack of embarrassment, under the great trees beside road or river in the heart of the big European towns.

In places off the main highways, where there is not much motor traffic, the native has not yet abandoned his age old custom of squatting down for a rest and a gossip, whenever he happens to meet a friend, right in the middle of the road. The small boys too will gather there at all hours of the day except when they are at school, using the open road as a convenient board on which to play the popular "stone game," a sort of "noughts and crosses" played with twenty-one small pebbles of which you will find traces scratched on the ground in every *kampong*. Should they hear an approaching car or *grobak*, they simply withdraw quietly to the side of the road until the intruder has passed, and then resume gossip or game without the slightest agitation.

After dark the road becomes even more of a social centre. And when the food vendors have set down their portable stalls and kitchens at their regular nightly pitches at the corners of all the bamboo fenced paths leading from the surrounding *kampongs* to the road, the faint smoky yellow light from each of their tiny paraffin lamps illuminates dimly a ring of gossipers who, having bought their right to a place by the purchase of a cent's worth or so of some queer eatable or other, sit straggling half across the road. These stalls are the ordinary *dessa* man's club, and he would be regarded as a *djewa soenji* indeed (a hermit: lonely soul) who did not join the group around one of them. There is no sight in all *dessa* life that is more characteristic and familiar; and there is no memory that comes more vividly to mind in after years than that of these faintly seen glimpses of village night life.

The *batik* headdress (called *iket kepala* or *oeding*) which custom demands must be worn by every Javanese man, except those who have succumbed to imported fashion and wear instead the velvet Malay cap, is as necessary a part of his equipment as his nose and ears. The conversion of the squares of *batik* dyed specially for this purpose is a difficult art, and the principal village of most *dessas* has its native *modiste*, who squats on the floor of his tiny shop and showroom, surrounded by dummy heads stuck all over with pins, on foot-high wooden stands. On these dummies, on stiff muslin foundations, he makes up the intricately folded little turbans to his customers' orders, in any style they may desire. As a rule only half the square is used, cut across diagonally, as modern fashion, and perhaps economy, dictates a smaller, closer fitting headdress than formerly, when it was the custom for the wearer to twist up his own headgear for himself.

In large towns and *pasars* the finished headdresses are sold ready made; but in country places the milliner's business is all "bespoke." No finished models are on view, but all round the walls of the shop, which may be a bare six or eight feet square, hang squares of *batik* of various designs from which the client may select. An *iket kepala* thus made to order costs from one to two guilders.

Apart from such specialists, the storekeepers are almost all Chinese who do a steady business quite unaffected by the *pasars*. An important institution in most *dessas*, too, is the *tjandoe* or *chandu* (opium) depot. This is opened at fixed hours, and is of service to all classes of the community as well as to opium smokers, as it is the recognised place at which small change is certain to be found! Thus proving how small are the quantities in which this so-called curse of the East is consumed. The Javanese is far from being so affluent that he can afford to buy enough to do him any harm, and the Chinese too are very moderate in its use. I know many a Chinese storekeeper whose one evening pipeful is passed round all the adult members of his family, providing one short puff for each; surely a very modest indulgence compared with that of the ordinary European cigarette smoker whom it never occurs to anyone to accuse of being an addict to vice.

This much prized luxury has been the subject of endless Government commissions and of a ponderous mass of literature; but there is one point about it that admits of no argument, and that is the handsome profit it yields to those controlling its supply in both Dutch and British colonies. The Dutch East India Company made over two million guilders out of it in 1794, and a century later it brought the Government more than eighteen million. The unlicensed planting of the opium poppy is forbidden, and even this is being diminished; but it is hard to believe that so valuable a source of income will ever be seriously discouraged, except on paper.

The schools, of which there are now well over 15,000 in Java, play an important part in *dessa* life. The teachers are all natives, themselves the products of the same admirable Dutch-instituted education system that they are engaged in passing on to the next generation. Most of those I have met are polished and delightful people who take their responsibilities very seriously. They are extremely successful in their handling of the pupils, by virtue of an instinctive understanding and love of children that is characteristic of the Javanese people.

NO JAVANESE COUNTRYMAN FEELS HIS HOME IS COMPLETE WITHOUT A DOVE IN A CAGE, RUN UP A TALL BAMBOO POLE LIKE A FLAG. THIS IS HOW THEY LOOK AGAINST A STORMY SKY.

A SHEET OF *BILIK*.
THIS HAS JUST BEEN BOUGHT AT THE *Pasar* AND IS BEING CARRIED HOME BY THE PURCHASER TO FORM A WALL IN THE NEW HOUSE HE IS BUILDING.

LOADS OF BASKETS BEING CARRIED OVER A MOUNTAIN-PASS TO A MARKET TWENTY MILES AWAY.

A ROADSIDE RESTAURANT.
THE PROPRIETOR IS GRILLING *Sate* (SMALL PIECES OF MEAT ON SKEWERS) OVER A CHARCOAL FIRE. A PILE OF BANANA-LEAF "PLATES" IS ON THE TOP OF THE LARDER BESIDE HIM.

BASKET-CARRIERS CROSSING THE MOUNTAINS TO MARKET.

JAVANESE WOMEN DOING THE FAMILY "WASHING" IN A MOUNTAIN STREAM.

Life in a Dessa

School buildings are more or less uniform throughout the Java country *dessas*. They are long, low, and whitewashed, built of *bilik*, stone, or cement, and roofed with brown tiles. The spotlessly clean and airy classrooms are plentifully hung with pictures designed to add entertainment to geography and other lessons. Australia's charms, for instance, are illustrated for the youthful Javanese in giant kangaroos that leap right across the map of the Commonwealth from Perth to Brisbane. And in Africa the chief product would appear to be the elephant. This pictorial method is turned also to practical purposes by charts showing the tools used in agricultural work, building devices, and so on.

The children are taught their lessons in the local mother-tongue of their district: Javanese, Soendanese, or whatever it may be, and are also taught Malay, which it is desired to make a *lingua franca* throughout Java. The "readers" published for the purpose by the Education Department are exceptionally good, and are as useful to Europeans desirous of acquiring a sound knowledge of the language as they are to the children for whom they were compiled. They contain, moreover, numbers of delightful pen and ink sketches illustrating native everyday life, and are well worth buying for those alone.[1] The increase of Malay-speaking natives all over Java, as well as in the outer islands, is very noticeable to anyone who has known the Indies long enough to see a generation of school children come out into the world. The illustrated "readers" published for the use of natives who wish to study Dutch are invaluable also to English students.

All the schools have gardens, and in many of them, if the headmaster is, as most country-bred Javanese are, a keen agriculturist, the boys are taught to cultivate small plots of various crops under his skilled direction, so that they return to the paternal fields less inclined to join in the "drift to the towns" that is one of the drawbacks to school education, even in such an agricultural paradise as Java.

The teachers say that as a rule the children are very quick and keen at all their studies. For some reason, they almost

[1] The two volumes of *Mata Hari Terbit* are specially recommended to students of Malay, as used in Java.

invariably take a special pride in neat handwriting, and consequently many Javanese write a faultless copperplate script that no European could ever hope to emulate: a far cry indeed from the days when the point of a *lontar* palm leaf was the only pen of the few natives who could write at all. The proportion of boys to girls is typical of the East; there are rarely more than half a dozen or so girls to a hundred boys in any country school, the parents considering it mere foolishness that their little girls should waste time at school that can be so usefully employed at home.

Native parents are expected to pay a small fee, if they can afford it, for the education of their children. The amounts vary with the district, from five cents per month in the lowest class and ten to fifteen cents in the second and third classes, upwards.

The *kampongs* have a life of their own; and in them, as in the central town or village of the *dessa*, all duties for the common weal are shared by the members of the community. The *Kepala* of the *kampong* is a mere subordinate member of the central *dessa* council, but in his own *kampong* he rules supreme; usually without much difficulty, for local pride in each *kampong* is strong, and they vie with each other in the perfection of their close trimmed banks, their bridges and fences, and their paths, swept as meticulously as your drawing-room floor.

For the most part these *kampongs* are charming, especially in cool mountain regions, where in each little garden there is a proud display of flowers and vegetables, and orange or *pommelo* trees fill the air with the lovely scent of their blossom, or stand laden with golden fruit. There are always waving palms and bananas and clumps of bamboo, none the less ornamental because it is grown for strictly practical purposes; and often palisades of burnished green *sirih* or other climbing plants. The houses will be of split bamboo *bilik*; and nowadays almost if not quite all are roofed with the pretty red-brown tiles which are one of a thousand and one other minor native industries. A wise Dutch regulation has ordained of late years that the formerly much used palm leaf *atap* roofing, which gave dangerously hospitable harbourage to rats, must be abolished, as a precaution against plague.

Life in a Dessa

Other simple and admirable hygienic regulations ordered by the Dutch, and transmitted through the *dessa* council to the heads of the *kampongs*, are rigorously enforced by each of them among their little groups of subjects. In every small compound you will see all rubbish neatly gathered and burned, bedding being aired in the sunshine, and walls freshly whitewashed at regular intervals. The people of the *kampongs* usually pay their head man's salary, or part of it, in kind. And in maize growing districts the long rows of tall bamboo drying-racks laden with the cobs thus paid in are a sight well worth seeing.

Every *kampong* has a more or less elaborate entrance gate and porch built of bamboo. Often these are most decorative, for this is a matter in which the community take special pride. Usually the large double gates, often eight feet or more high, made of *bilik*, are closed at night; and many of the entrances are provided with a covered platform and a *kentongan* where the hours of darkness are struck by a watchman. This same platform is also used to accommodate a *gamelan* orchestra on public festive occasions. In a particularly prosperous *kampong* there may be a fine avenue leading to the gate, and the approach may be beautified with hedges of alamanda or acalypha, or by walls covered with a veil of maidenhair fern. There is no need to teach these simple people the "community spirit." It is part of their natural make up; and despite their long hours of labour in the fields, nothing is too much trouble that will enhance the beauty of their "home town," and incidentally give them an opportunity to crow over the inferior attractions of their neighbours' *kampong*.

No *kampong* is complete without its communal laundry and bathing place, made in the bed of some convenient stream, and fenced round with the indispensable bamboo. These are the women's clubs. Here, all and every morning, happy groups of women and children are busy, washing themselves, their babies, and the many coloured garments of their families, beating soapy *sarongs* on flat stones as they stand ankle or knee deep in the warm, soft, gently flowing stream, in a glorious mix up of splashing water, mud, ducks, soapsuds, laughter, and gossip. While higher up the stream, other women are washing rice for dinner, in bamboo baskets under the bamboo pipe that brings them their unfailing supply of running water.

Among the many communal customs of the *kampongs*, one which concerns theft might be recommended to other communities, for it is remarkably productive of honesty. If the property of any stranger visiting the *kampong* should be stolen, the whole community is held to share the responsibility, and every member of the population must contribute to the cost of replacing it. Hospitality to travellers is one of the accepted rules of Javanese native life, and no one is ever refused shelter for the night. That he should be robbed while the guest of the *kampong*, therefore, brings shame to everyone living in it.

Consideration for weary travellers is also shown in the custom, in many *dessas*, of keeping an earthenware jar filled daily with fresh water in a bamboo basket fixed on a post by the roadside. One of these is often to be seen at the point where the path to a *kampong* joins the road. The jar in its deftly woven split bamboo cover looks at first glance temptingly like a giant bottle of Chianti!

The *kampong* dweller, simple fellow though he may be, is not so unsophisticated that wireless is unknown to him, and in the most remote hamlets you will probably see several aerials made of slender, immensely tall bamboos, rearing their heads high above the thick foliage that hides the small houses. Their erection presents no difficulty, thanks to the genuine community feeling that prevails.

No sooner does Si Soswosipotro or Ah Woeng or some other village worthy announce his purchase of this latest kind of white man's magic, and his desire to appease the spirits that serve it with a tall pole, as advised by the Chinese who sold it to him, than all the male youth of the *kampong* not otherwise occupied at the moment will turn out to give a hand, well knowing that they will share as a matter of course in all the fun it may provide in the future.

Native houses in country *kampongs* are of extremely simple design. They rarely have any windows; and the one large room is carpeted with grass mats and crowded with furniture. Conservative though he is in the matter of house design, the Javanese, when he can afford it, is a convert to European furnishings at their very worst. Wardrobes and "whatnots," china cabinets, occasional tables, and Nottingham lace curtains are his delight. He does not feel his home complete without an immense iron double bed for the heads of the family, the rest being quite content to sleep on the floor, for the Javanese have the happy knack of being able to sleep anyhow and anywhere. Even the hospitable instinct that is one of his most ancient traditions is given a European flavour when a card on which the words SALAMAT DATANG (Welcome) are printed, in large letters, is framed and glazed in the latest Dutch style and hung just inside the door.

Javanese taste in music, however, remains unchanged; and the vague indeterminate rhythms of the *gamelan* to be heard as you pass by any *kampong*, through all the countless *dessas* of Java, have probably changed little, if at all, through many hundreds of years. They are almost as indispensable to native life as light and air and food. These village *gamelans* usually consist only of the giant xylophone already mentioned: made of two long converging bamboos supporting the "notes" of metal, wood, or split bamboo, called *saron* in the former case, and *gambang* in the latter, and of various drums and gongs. The full *gamelan*, which is an orchestra of about twenty-four players, is rare in Java outside the two royal palaces, though it is common in Bali.

In the old days, when every village was an independent fortress, Java shared with many other parts of tropical Asia the admirably practical custom of planting a dense grove of bamboo round each *kampong*, as the best of all defences against surprise attack, and a supply of all-purposes building material. The peaceful modern Javanese has happily no longer need of it to protect him from treacherous neighbours, but he still finds it as necessary as ever for a thousand peaceful purposes. To the casual passer-by the appearance of any *kampong* in a country *dessa* to-day, half hidden among its feathery bamboos, probably differs but little from what he would have seen if he had passed that way a thousand years ago.

CHAPTER SEVEN

Religious Medley

THE religious and quasi religious customs of the Javanese are inextricably mixed. His devotion to the orthodox observances of Islam is as intense, or almost, as that of a good Catholic to Mother Church. But that does not make him any less faithful to the ancient beliefs of his remote ancestors, as well as to some of those introduced by the Hindus who ruled his forefathers for a thousand years. He celebrates innumerable *salamatans* on religious occasions; but as to which department of his voluminous theology any of them really belong it would be hard to say. He himself would be the last person who could tell you, for even those held on the orthodox Mohammedan feast days have borrowed so much from old-time Java customs that the Faithful from other Mohammedan lands might well be hard put to it to recognise them.

Salamatan is an elastic and untranslatable term, applied equally to religious festivals and to feasts and ceremonies designed to bring good luck and, still more, to avert bad luck and appease evil spirits. Every sort of event in public or private life is held to be a suitable occasion for one of these celebrations. It celebrates, quite impartially, the Birth of the Prophet, the pregnancy, birth, marriage, or death of any humble native, the building of a house or a bridge, the crushing season at a sugarmill, the end of the month of fasting, or the departure of an employer on leave to Europe!

To European eyes, all these *salamatans* are very much alike, and leave a general impression of picturesque native crowds, dressed in their best and most colourful garments, and of unlimited quantities of queer and, to us, most unappetising eatables, most of them smelling pungently of coconut oil. But to the Javanese, a *salamatan* is a very different matter. Each and every one of these occasions have their own special conventions, especially in the way of food; and a native housewife would no sooner dream of departing from them than we should from our Christmas turkey, roast beef, and plum pudding.

It might be expected that the most important of all the feasts of a devoutly Mohammedan population like the Javanese should be the *Garebeg Moeloed*, the equivalent of our Christmas, which celebrates the Prophet Mahomet's birthday on the twelfth day of Moeloed, the third month of the Mohammedan year. But important though this may be in a religious sense, it cuts no ice in Javanese native life in comparison with the *Garebeg Poesa*, *Hari Raya*, or, as it is more often called, *Lebaran*, which marks the end of Ramadan, the month of fasting, called in Java *Boelan Poesa*. This is the day of days in the Javanese calendar. It falls at the beginning of Sawal, the tenth month of the Mohammedan calendar, but in Java and for the Javanese it is the New Year.

It must be mentioned in passing that every year, as *Lebaran* comes round, it happens as regularly as clockwork that some erudite individual or other will sit down and indite a letter to the Press to correct those ignorant persons who *will* insist on falling into the error of describing this feast as "Native New Year"! It may be that the misinformed Europeans who do so will mend their ways, though I doubt it. But what is to be done about the forty odd million natives who fall into the selfsame error, and greet one another wherever they happen to meet on the great day with "*Salamat Tahoen Bahroe!*" (Happy New Year!)?

However, New Year or not, the *Lebaran* feast is the most delightful of all occasions to see in Java, for every native goes avisiting, dressed in new clothes. And the scene on the roads, especially in a prosperous country district, is like an endless colour film, only a thousand times more charming and entertaining.

The colours that the people wear are as gay as those of the flower fields that in many mountain regions border the roads. The women wear *sarongs* in varied patterns, of henna-brown, red, and orange, with tight little *badjoe* jackets, some of plain red, green, blue, yellow, or petunia silk or muslin, and others of dainty floral patterns. Some young girls wear a *kodoengan*, a yard or so of bright hued chiffon, scalloped and embroidered, thrown lightly over the head as our grandmothers used to wear what they called a "cloud" when they went to an evening party. These are in every conceivable combination of colour with the wearers' *badjoes*: bright pink with mauve; blue with green; yellow with claret colour; and all or any of them with golden brown *batik sarongs*; yet they all harmonise as naturally as wild flowers with charming effect.

Others are bareheaded, to show their immaculately smooth hair coiled in a great knob at the nape of the neck, adorned with flowers and gold pins and ornaments; and a few, especially smart, have whitened their faces with "liquid" powder, ending at a well defined highwater mark across the forehead. Some walk in pairs, hand in hand; some lead tiny tots like pocket editions of themselves, just as smart as their elders in their brand-new miniature garments, with an absurd baby bun of hair adorned with an hibiscus blossom; and some carry a smaller edition still, pick-a-back, with wee hands sticking out on each side of big sister's neck.

The men are all in stiff new *sarong* or *kain*, mostly worn hitched up at one side to show their equally new shorts. They wear freshly starched white or khaki drill jackets and open shirts, and almost all sport the Malay velvet cap, rather than the ordinary Javanese *batik* headdress, the cap being considered smarter for these festive occasions. Some wear sandals, but more often they carry them in their hands, as do also the women. A dainty little lady walking with obvious discomfort in a smart pair of high-heeled mules will suddenly give up in disgust, and slipping them off will stride away with them swinging in her hand, to be resumed, no doubt, when she reaches her destination, if she has one that is, for the important thing on *Lebaran* day is simply to be on the road to see and to be seen.

For this reason the crowds going in one direction are as great as those going in the other. Taxis, "mosquito" buses, and pony *sadoes* all do good business, packed to doors and roof, racing to and fro, going apparently nowhere in particular, charging their passengers only a cent or two per head. A few rather arrogant looking young native "bloods" ride smart ponies up and down, the admired of all beholders. Now and then a flower farm employee, smartly dressed as the rest, will pass carrying a glorious bouquet of multicoloured

Religious Medley

flowers: most likely a "St Nikolas" gift, for it happens sometimes that the native and Dutch festivals fall on the same day, the fifth of December. Sometimes, but happily, as a rule, not often, there may be a discordant note in the bright colour harmony of the scene, when some misguided native mother has seen fit to score over her neighbours by dressing her children in European fashion. I once saw two little brothers in native dress leading a younger one in shirt and navy-blue knickers, a solar topee much too big for him, and brown lace shoes, in which the poor little lad clattered awkwardly along, stumbling now and then, between his luckier barefooted brothers. Just behind them were two small girls in shoes and socks and pink silk frocks, and a third, aged about four, in a white shirt-blouse on to which a dark serge skirt was buttoned: she too, poor mite, stumbling painfully in unaccustomed shoes. Then there was a toddler scarcely able to stand alone, in a knitted red and white cap, white shirt, horrid little red knickers, and long loose stockings that kept tumbling down his legs and flapping round his toes, as two little girls tried to lead him along. They stopped on the grass by the side of the road, and while one held him, the other pulled the stockings up above his skinny little bow-legged knees, and fixed them with strings of grass. Then, apparently deciding that these improvised suspenders would not stand the strain of any more pedestrian exploits, the bigger girl picked him up and sat him astride her hip; and the little group tripped away obviously as proud as Punch to be the bearers of such an up to date baby brother.

There are other sartorial effects somewhat startling to European eyes: as for instance a muscular pony driver in a transparent white sprigged muslin jacket worn over a violent red and white striped football jersey, with the usual *batik* head-dress and *sarong*; and a lad racing past on the carrier of a friend's bicycle, wearing a Malay cap, a shiny new white satin jacket, a mauve "zip" shirt, tartan *sarong*, and *batik kepala*. Javanese young men and little boys, as well as Chinese, are much addicted to striped cotton suits exactly like European pyjamas; but this is a fashion that has something to recommend it, for it is cool, clean, gay, and comfortable.

Now and then two or three young Chinese will stroll past,

in the same holiday mood as the rest, with arms round each other's shoulders, very slim and trim in their well starched white suits. But, sad to say, when Europeans appear on the scene it is seldom that they contribute to its charm. Robust ladies in revealingly tight shirts and trousers, for instance, set one wondering why, in a period when feminine fashion is kinder to women, when they please, than ever before, they should be at such pains to appear at their worst by contrast with the festive attire of the crowds on a native holiday!

Even on this general holiday not everyone is idle; and you will see mingling with the throng here and there a coolie, bare to the waist, swinging cheerily along with piled-up loads of carrots, cauliflower, or cabbages, all adding their touch of colour to the pageant.

It is noticeable that in all such crowds you will always see groups of little boys walking together, and others of little girls. They never mix, except when a family party of father, mother, and children take the road together. The little girls walk sedately, their muslin *badjoes* fastened with gold brooches, wearing chains of fresh flower blossoms, and each grasping a tiny *payong* (umbrella). The boys swagger along, and there is scarcely one of them, even tiny lads of three or four years old, who will not be smoking a little tapering cigarette, often in a holder, which adds the finishing touch to their absurdly grown up air. Each little boy is as perfect a replica of his father or elder brother as his little sister is of her feminine elders.

This great occasion is celebrated, like those of the Chinese, with crackers, the use of which has been shrewdly introduced to the Javanese by Chinese storekeepers. So another touch of colour is added in every town and village by the piles of these fireworks in crude pink and green wrappers, displayed on tables in front of all the Chinese shops.

The *Lebaran* is no more forgotten by the Javanese when they are absent from their country than is Christmas by Britons abroad. Native nursemaids, taken home to Holland by Dutch families on leave, always do their best to celebrate the feast even in the dismal chilliness of European winter.

The great day of *Lebaran* is followed by the *Salamatan*

Religious Medley

Maleman (the word *malem* means "night"), which is kept up for the next seven nights, those on uneven dates calling for the chief celebrations. It ends with *Salamatan Bada Sawat* —also called *Salamatan Ketoepat*, the latter being the name of the rice cakes proper to the day. These, though unpalatable to European taste (at least they are to mine), are most pleasing to the eye. They consist of steamed rice pressed solid, done up in little packets about four inches square, beautifully covered with plaited green palm leaf, with a sort of handle at one end. During the seven days preceding the feast, the women in every *kampong* are hard at work making them, for custom demands that they should be given as presents to every acquaintance. All along the roads on the *pasar* day before the proper day of presentation, you will see women carrying baskets piled high with the pretty things; and you will be lucky indeed if you are not presented with a dozen or more. They are most difficult to dispose of under the watchful eyes of your devoted native servants, whose feelings you would not hurt for the world; but, in modern parlance, they are "too, too, sick-making"!

The month of fasting is faithfully observed in country districts, and the native population take no food between sun-up and sundown; but they certainly do all that is humanly possible to supply the deficiency at night. They have a meal just after sunset, and then settle down to sleep, which the fortunate native seems always able to do at any time at a moment's notice. But one remains awake and on watch, a duty that, of course, is taken in turn, and at midnight he goes round the *kampong* banging on a short piece of bamboo to waken the people for the midnight meal, or *saoer*, calling out a long-drawn cry of "*Sa-a-oe-rr*" as he goes. At the same time, the *bedoek* (a great hanging drum with ends of buffalo hide) booms out from the *mesigit* (mosque), and its dull, muffled sound is heard for an hour: rather intermittently as a rule, for it is banged in turn by the young *santri*, or mosque apprentices, who are apt to fight for the *taboeh* with which the drum is beaten. When this duty, of which the *santris* are very proud, is done, they go home to a heavy meal, leaving the *Modin* to watch over the *mesigit* till dawn.

Strict observance of the month of fasting is to a great

extent dying out among the younger generation in the large towns. They often keep it strictly only on the first day of the month, and for the rest of the period get a dispensation from their *Penghoeloe* (head of their church) just as Catholics do in Lent from the priest. They argue, not unreasonably, that the long complete fast interferes too much with their jobs, and that jobs are all too easily lost in the keen competition of the modern Java town world.

Especially is this noticeable in the so called "factory district" of Soerabaya, which is like no other in the world, and must surely be the pleasantest. It is strung out along the bank of the river just outside the town, where the big, cool looking, spotlessly whitewashed buildings stand back from the road, screened by huge shady Flamboyant trees which spread their branches out across the roadway to join those of others on the opposite side. There, on the wide grass verge of the river bank, under their shade, come the vendors of food and coffee and syrups, to cater for the factory workers, no less during the month of fasting than at any other time.

It is a charming sight to see the workers in their multi-coloured garb come tumbling out, laughing and chattering, at midday, or when work is over in the afternoon, to gather in groups round the food-sellers' little kitchens with their extraordinary variety of the weird edibles dear to the native heart. Many of the men and boys (the girls are far too modest for anything like mixed bathing!) go into the river for a swim, slipping easily out of their scanty garments, and soon the shining water is alive with smooth brown bodies among the bright green and blue of the water hyacinth that comes slowly drifting down with the stream. A jolly crowd of youngsters, some carefully soaping themselves, hair and all; others laughing and splashing and fooling, in the way of all young people. Watching them, it is hard to believe that they are a part of the same ruthless industrial system that produces the weary unsmiling workers of other lands.

In the big towns the end of the twelve hours' fast is announced daily by the firing of a cannon at 6 P.M., for the benefit of those who are not within earshot of the *bedoek* at the mosque, which is always sounded at this hour. But nowadays it is not, I fancy, such an eagerly awaited sound as it was a generation ago.

The easy absorption of the Mohammedan religion by the Javanese by grafting it, as it were, upon their previous beliefs is better understood when it is realised in what manner the teaching of the Prophet came to them. It reached Java by way of Malaya, where it had taken a firm hold centuries earlier, probably soon after Mahomet's death in A.D. 632. Malay and Arab traders made the Java ports of Grissee and Toeban ports of call on their way to the Moluccas for spices; and, finding Java a land flowing, if not with milk and honey, with many other equally delectable things, began to settle there. The rich Mohammedan Malay merchants, people of a race having much in common with the Javanese, were regarded as desirable matrimonial catches for the daughters of Javanese of good family; and as Malay settlement increased, no doubt the humbler classes followed the example of the "best people" and intermarriage became general. In this way there was a peaceful penetration of the new religion with the minimum of friction; a strange chapter in the fiery history of Islam's triumphal sweep across the world.

The first known Mohammedan missionary to Java was Malik Ibraham, who died at Grissee in 1419. His tomb, on a hill just outside the town, is still a place of pious pilgrimage.

The Mohammedans, in fact, seem to have "Islamised" Java and other East Indian islands in much the same way as we "Christianised" various parts of the world. Then, as so often occurred in the case of Christianity, traders and missionaries paved the way for conquest. As the new faith spread, the power of the old Hindu-Javanese kingdoms, even that of the great Madjapahit, dwindled by degrees till they became an easy prey for the Malays; and by 1579 all but one of the Hindu states had disappeared and were replaced by Mohammedan powers. The exception was Balambangan, in the extreme south-eastern corner of the island, which, like the adjoining island of Bali, the invaders seem to have ignored.

And now there comes a third great religion, Christianity, to "try its luck." Not for the first time, for Portuguese Catholic missionaries visited Java early in the fourteenth century, but they do not appear to have found the Javanese responsive. They tried again late in the sixteenth century, and established a mission which existed for a few years until it was expelled by the conquering Mohammedans.

Then came the Dutch; not, like the French in Indo-China, preceded by their missionaries. They conquered and overthrew the Mohammedan kingdoms one by one, but whatever may have been the severity of their conquest in other respects, they certainly did not attempt to impose Christianity upon the vanquished by the sword. The Dutch East India Company was far more concerned with exploiting the Javanese than with converting them; and any attempts by the expelled Catholics to renew their missionary work among the natives were frustrated by the Company's edict that no religion might be practised except that of the Dutch Reformed Protestant Church.

It was not until the great Company had died an unlamented death as a bankrupt that religious freedom was permitted by its successor, the Batavian Republic, and missionaries of various denominations began by degrees to make their appearance, though at first they do not seem to have been very popular with the Government, and only gained a strong footing when the nineteenth century was well advanced.

So far as actual religious "conversion" is concerned, none of them has made an appreciable mark on the Javanese population. A Catholic missionary early in the last century is said to have remarked plaintively that the Javanese were too firmly attached to Islam to give the new faith a chance; though, he added, "they don't really know anything about Mohammedanism"—a remark which would have been equally true of Christianity or any other creed they might have been persuaded to adopt.

It is in more practical ways that the Christian missions, Protestant, Catholic, and Salvation Army, have benefited the people of Java. The missions of each of these bodies provide hospitals, home nursing, dispensaries, and "poliklinieks" for the natives, and the work they have achieved in this way in the improvement of public health, supplementing the fine Government Health Services, is inestimable. All are deserving of the highest praise; but specially notable are the two leper colonies maintained by the Salvation Army, one at

Soerabaya and one at Samarang, and "superior" persons who are inclined to jeer at "Salvation lasses" would do well to visit one of them, to see for themselves the amazing, genuine happiness that they have brought to these poor outcasts.

In a varied life I have seen many memorable sights; but one stands out as unique: that of the leper orchestra in their quasi military uniforms, some playing their instruments with the remnants of hands from which the fingers had all but disappeared; some minus ears or nose or feet, or in process of losing by slow corruption those and other portions of their anatomy; but all of them playing with as much gusto, and as much noise, as any normal "army" band unhampered by such tragic disabilities; and the choir they accompanied sang the familiar cheery, not-too-musical hymns with an enthusiasm equal to that of the orchestra.

The actual means by which leprosy is communicated from an infected person to another is still uncertain, but it is considered unlikely that it is simply by touch. Doctors and nurses handle the poor maimed limbs and bodies of their patients every day as a matter of course. So that when the casual visitor is told that there is no surer way of giving pleasure to these unfortunate people than by shaking hands with them, if the pitiful contact with an often shapeless stump can be so called, is it not surely up to him to make that very small contribution? It is the custom to wash your hands in strong disinfectant on leaving the buildings of the colony, and as in this part of the world a constant change of clean clothing once or twice a day is the rule in any case, no other precaution against infection is necessary.

The "poliklinieks" provided for the natives both by the Government and the various religious bodies are, if anything, more invaluable to the population than the hospitals. In all the large towns there are several at which a native doctor and dispenser give free advice, treatment, and medicine daily. The Salvation Army maintain three in Soerabaya alone; and in most country places a "kliniek" is open two or three times a week. They are used and appreciated by an ever increasing number of the population as education becomes more and more widespread.

In conjunction with an organisation called the "Algemeene

Steun Inlands Behoeftingen" (General Support for Native Necessities), popularly known as the "A.S.I.B.," the Salvation Army provide some 1500 to 1600 very poor natives of Soerabaya with a good meal every day.

The "A.S.I.B." was started by Mevrouw de Jonge, wife of a former Governor-General, well remembered and beloved for her benevolence. It is generously supported and carried on by Chinese and European residents, and the Salvation Army has shouldered the practical side of the work.

The poorest and most densely populated districts of the city are served by five depots, at one of which is the kitchen where the food for all five is cooked. To each of these centres every morning the poor people come, each with his or her card, showing to how many portions they are entitled. The system has been worked out with the co-operation of the people's *kampong* head men, who investigate the needs of the poorest inhabitants of their districts, and report them to the committee. Rice, of course, is the staple of the meals provided, and three whole sacks of it per day are steamed (not even for Java's poorest is it boiled in the wasteful western way) in a huge drum over an open fire. Dried fish and many kinds of vegetables and other native dishes are all cooked according to native methods by native helpers in the same building, a *bilik* shed erected for the purpose. The poor people form a queue, each carrying some pathetically humble receptacle in which to take away the food: old earthenware pots, rusty enamel basins, pieces of ancient calico, *batik*, or even newspaper, and file slowly past a table where each card is taken and the number of portions called out. These are ladled out one after the other by a row of voluntary native assistants. First, out of an enormous bowl, constantly replenished by the cook, comes the steaming unbleached rice, which, by the way, is delicious; and then the other foods, which, as far as possible, are varied every day. They are bought at the *pasar* each morning by a Javanese woman superintendent who lives in a little room adjoining the kitchen.

One point about these poor folks who are thus assured of one meal per day is remarkable, and should be recorded. Desperately poor they undoubtedly are; their *sarongs* and jackets are faded and patched, and the headdress of some of the men, which, however destitute, not one of these conscientious Mohammedans would ever dream of going without, is no more than a twist of threadbare rag. But none of them, not even the raggedest, is dirty. And here, in a shed, under the blazing tropic sun, only a few degrees from the Equator, there is no vestige of that horrible pervading smell of unwashed bodies and garments that is characteristic of European or Australian soup kitchens.

It is the same at all the depots, to which the food is taken in turn by the "army" car, and gives the foreign visitor an added respect for these humblest of Java's people, whose instinct for personal cleanliness survives even the direst poverty.

The buildings at all the depots are of the simplest and cheapest kind, mere shelters of *bilik* and tile, as is so fortunately possible in Java, and the necessary space has been provided in every case at very low cost. The fine influence of the "army," combined with natural Javanese kindliness, has resulted in most of the labour connected with the scheme being voluntary and unpaid; consequently the expenses are very small, and almost every guilder contributed can be spent on actual food. The average cost of the meals thus provided is only about two cents ($\frac{1}{2}d$.) per person. The average amount spent per month is 800 guilders.

Modern Christian missionaries in Java, mindful perhaps of their medieval predecessors' failures, approach their desired converts in a very tolerant spirit, and some have been known even to press the national Hindu-Javanese *wayang* into Christian service, by presenting Bible stories with *wayang* puppets! In the missionary hospitals, native prejudices, such as an objection to a day for which an operation has been fixed as unlucky, are treated with sympathy, and no direct attempt is made to convert the patients, whose friends may come and go freely, and who may observe the Mohammedan forms of prayer in a Christian hospital without let or hindrance.

As a result of these tolerant methods there are said to be some 50,000 Protestant and 25,000 Catholic natives in Java, and, in places, there are whole *kampongs* whose populations have embraced the Christian faith.

Happily most of these Javanese converts, unlike the

Christian natives of other parts of the Dutch East Indies, have retained their charming national costume, and with it their natural grace of manner. They continue to celebrate the traditional *salamatans* with their indefinite relation to this or that religion, attend the same *wayang* performances of stories from the Hindu *Ramayana*, and listen to the *gamelan* with as much zest as ever. In fact, to the passing stranger, most of them are quite indistinguishable from their Mohammedan brethren, and except that they attend a Christian church service, and sing hymns instead of gabbling the Koran, one is rather tempted to wonder just what the change may be that their conversion has wrought in them. For the average Javanese, whether he professes and calls himself Mohammedan or Christian, remains still the same mannerly, industrious, kindly, hospitable individual, possessed indeed of more of the Christian virtues than most of us, but he also remains at heart the same convinced animist, with a few added trimmings garnered from each superimposed religion in turn, without dropping any of the previous ones. That is why, as a Mohammedan, he is unique, as he doubtless was also as a Hindu or a Buddhist: and as he is when he is persuaded to turn Christian.

The very mild form of Christianity that is accepted by Javanese converts, at all events those of the humbler class, is the only one that would ever really suit them. They have a genius for adapting a religion to themselves rather than themselves to the religion, in which they differ widely from most other Orientals. It is a melancholy fact that although the Christian religion had its birth in the East, it is a misfit in its modern fulldress form to the average Oriental. Introduced to Eastern peoples as it is by European missionaries, after nearly 2000 years of modification to European standards, Christianity is inevitably associated in Eastern minds with the aping of the white man's clothes and manners. Probably they imagine that the first disciples of Jesus wore trousers and collars and ties! And indeed, so completely have we "westernised" His teachings, that we have all but succeeded in convincing ourselves, to say nothing of the "heathen," that Christianity is our own exclusive property and a product of western civilisation.

There are, of course, some well and truly "westernised" natives in Java, mostly of the upper social class. But it is more likely that the generous Dutch education system, with the facilities it offers for study in Holland and to qualify in one or other of the learned professions, is responsible for their metamorphosis, rather than that they owe it to missionary effort. They appear usually to have "adopted" Christianity; but the dispassionate observer is tempted to surmise that they have done so more with a view to putting the finishing touch to the near European figure to which they have attained, rather than as the result of any religious conviction.

An example of the all embracing tolerance of the ordinary Javanese native's attitude to religion may serve to illustrate the rich blend of which his faith is composed. The native postmaster of a small country *dessa*, a simple fellow, whom I had long known as a Mohammedan, appeared one day to my surprise in his little office not only in a European suit, but bareheaded, which, to the followers of Mahomet, is unthinkable.

I asked him if he had been converted to Christianity: there could be, I thought, no other explanation. "No, *Toean*," he said; "but it seems to me that it is well to belong a little to all religions!" And he proceeded to embroider the theme, while he drew a diagram on his post office counter to show that all roads may lead to *Toean Allah*!

Whether or not Christianity will ever replace Islam in Java, as Islam replaced Hinduism, no one can tell. But it may already have had effects that will add to the problems of future archæologists. Centuries hence perhaps, when civilisation is struggling painfully to life again, and students come to search in Java, as elsewhere, for traces of an earlier, lost civilisation blotted out by barbarians of the twentieth century, they may find among the ruins, with the Buddhas and the Hindu giants, some of the Madonnas and Christian angels in Oriental poses that now adorn native Catholic churches; and they will speculate upon the confusion of influences revealed in the art of a vanished race, as we do to-day upon that of the Greeks in India.

CHAPTER EIGHT

"Magic"

REFERENCE to the ingrained animism of the Javanese, despite their conversion and apparent devotion to Islam, has already been made. But the extent to which that animism is expressed in almost every action of native daily life is an endless revelation.

Your Javanese may have made the pilgrimage to Mecca: thousands of them do so every year; he may be a doctor or a lawyer as the result of Dutch higher education, or a skilled mechanic or electrician; in any case he will certainly have adapted himself more than willingly to all the innovations that Western progress has brought him in the way of electricity, transport, and so on. But he can never quite shake himself free of the ancient belief of his ancestors in the spirits that inhabit every nook and corner of the country. A faith that permeates the whole atmosphere of the archipelago, and that of Java, for all its civilisation, as much as the rest. So much so, that even hard-headed Europeans can only shrug their shoulders and murmur the overworked tag about "more things in heaven and earth," etc. Certainly not one of them who has won the confidence of his native friends will ever doubt their unshakable belief in the strange tales they tell, or will be so foolish or so unkind as to laugh at their fears and fancies.

As a typical example: a native electrician, skilful as any European at his trade, was sent for to repair a connection running through our garden. He arrived just at sundown, ready and eager to put all in order for us, having come on foot the five miles up the steep mountain road from the town. But when he learned that the trouble was outside, and that he would have to brave the darkness of the garden, even though illuminated by our torches, he sorrowfully shook his head and departed down the road again, saying he would return next morning, for, if he touched their haunts at night, the spirits of the garden would be angry and punish him severely!

But after all, there is not so very much to choose between the Javanese native's methods of propitiating any spirits that may happen to be about, and those of the conventional Christian. At planting and harvesting seasons all the farmers of a *dessa* will gather at a sort of service under some ancient holy tree, bringing offerings with them which they deposit among its enormous roots. And near the fields that they wish to place under spiritual protection they place little offerings of food on small altars; or light tapers and set them up beside any tree or rock that they have been taught to regard as holy. Whereas we bring apples and vegetable marrows to the harvest festival, or burn candles and tapers to the saints, according to taste.

It is impossible to live long in Java without noticing these expressions of the natives' respect for the spirits. The offerings are to be seen here, there, and everywhere, and you may pass a dozen of them on any country walk. The little altars look rather like big toadstools, the top formed of a round tray made of woven split bamboo, with a bamboo section serving as stem. On these, tiny cakes, sweetmeats, and handfuls of rice are arranged on pieces of banana leaf, and adorned with a flower or two. You will find them on the earth banks surrounding the ricefields; in quiet shady corners under a *waringen* tree; or beside lonely paths where protection from lurking dangers might be especially welcome.

I once asked an elderly Javanese, a village head man and devout Mohammedan who had made the pilgrimage to Mecca, and was very proud of the prestige as a *Hadji* that it gave him, why, if his people really believed in the One True God, they should think it necessary to "keep in" with the field spirits in this way. He gravely explained that *Toean Allah* was a very great God, and had great affairs on his hands to attend to: such things as pilgrimages to Mecca, for instance. How then could he be expected at the same time to keep his eye on Ahmat's and Soedji's rice crops, and those of all the other millions of cultivators in Java, to see that the rats did not get at them, or other mishap befall? It was not reasonable. He could not do it. It was a matter for Sri Dewa, the Rice Goddess, and, under her, the Field Spirits to look after; and the old man, squatting on his heels, puffing away at his tiny cigarette, gazed at me sadly, as though I ought to have known better.

The Javanese farmer, having duly fulfilled his obligations to the spirits, gets steadily on with his job, conscious that he has done all that is possible to secure the co-operation of the unseen powers, and that the rest depends on his own efforts. It has always seemed to me that his is a much more reasonable blending of spiritual matters with agriculture than that of the British farmer who, having, as is his way, bemoaned the weather and the rain that endangers the wheat or oats he has cut, will let a fine sunny Sunday go by entirely wasted rather than cart and stack the crop on the sacred Day of Rest, to awaken, as he deserves, on Monday to another wild, wet morning, and curse anew the vagaries of the English climate.

Offerings to the gods and spirits of volcanoes are constantly made, for the Javanese have only too good cause to know what these are capable of doing to them if they are angry. So, in times of epidemic, failure of crops, or other adversities, or indeed at any time, they will climb the mountains and place their gifts there in the hope of appeasing the unseen powers. Near the summit of Goenong Kloet (one of the most sinister volcanoes in Java, with an even blacker record to its discredit than Goenong Merapi, having erupted every eight or nine years since 1811) there is a knife-edge above a precipice some 1500 feet high which, according to native legend, has been from time immemorial a place of human sacrifice. It is whispered that whenever the wise men predict another outburst there are always to be found those whose faith and courage are sublime enough to offer themselves as a sacrifice to the mountain gods, by leaping into the crater.

Not long before the last eruption a party of Europeans who were climbing the mountain found the traces of a camp. There was a blanket, the ashes of a fire, some cakes, brass pots, and other small offerings; but no sign whatever of who it was who had brought them there, nor any trace of returning footprints in the soft ground that showed clearly those going upwards. The coolies with the European party told them that the vanished camper had certainly thrown himself over the precipice in the hope of turning away the wrath of the gods: a vain hope as it proved, for the eruption duly followed not long after. But in the face of such things who shall dare to say that the humble Javanese have no faith, or that they are not truly "religious"? Which of us would dare do the same, even to avert a world war?

Europeans who wish to climb any of the active volcanoes in Java will find that it may not be done without the concurrence of the spirits. Your coolies will carry offerings with them, and will stop to place them at some holy spot, in return for which it is understood that permission is granted to climb further, or to camp for the night, as the case may be. A party whose coolies had thus secured permission for them to camp for one night were overtaken by heavy rain, which made the climb to the summit impossible. They decided to stay where they were for a second night and continue the expedition on the following day. This, however, their coolies very gravely explained, was impossible, as only one night was covered by the permit they had received; but they would soon put it right. So down they scrambled, an hour's journey or more over the rough path they had just ascended, back to the Holy Place to offer a second gift to the gods. Then, having arranged the matter to their satisfaction, back they came to the camp, saying that now all was well, and the party could safely climb to the crater next morning!

In some curious limestone mountain formations visible from the winding road that crosses the ranges near Bandoeng, not even the materialistic presence of several chalk-works, sources of some of the loads of lime so often to be met, carried on the backs of trains of pack ponies, has been able to frighten away evil spirits. One of them especially, Goenong Pawan, is inhabited by particularly fearsome *hantoes*, and on leaving my car by the roadside one day, and walking towards some caves in the gleaming white precipice, I was gravely cautioned by a native not to enter them. I took his advice; otherwise, I gathered, I should not be alive to tell the tale.

Every volcano in Java has its own legends, firmly believed by every native. Of the terrible Goenong Kloet, mentioned above, for instance, they say that there sleeps beneath the triple craters a giant prince with the head of a buffalo, and that whenever he stirs or turns over in his sleep there is an eruption, serious or slight, according to the degree of his restlessness. But if ever it should happen that he wakes up completely and rises from his hard couch, then the whole of Java and its people will be overwhelmed in a disaster a thousand times more terrible even than the eruption of Krakatoe.

The legend about the Ardjoeno mountains is of another kind. Arjuno or Ardjoeno, the great Indian warrior who is also one of the heroes of the Javanese *wayang*, gave his name to the whole range, the two principal peaks being called Ardjoeno and Wedadarin (Arjuno and the Angels), to commemorate the fact that the hero spent many days and nights here in meditation without once succumbing to the charms of the angels in exquisite female form who took it in turns to tempt him. His pious retreat to the mountains had been undertaken in order to consult the gods about a "brothers' war" he had dreamed was to break out, and according to which "men should fly over on wings from other lands and kill them"—a curious prediction in a story some 2000 years old!

Javanese legends are of course not confined to the mountains, and most of them, like all respectable fairy tales, have a "moral," taking care to avenge the sufferings of the hero and bring down a terrible vengeance on the villain of the piece. The story of Lake Sitoe Bagendit, near Garoet, is a typical one. Where the lake now is, there was once a prosperous village among whose residents was a very wealthy widow called Nji Endit, who was hated for her miserly ways. She had a fine house and many servants, but never gave anything away. Once a year, however, she gave a great feast after the harvest by way of showing off before her poorer neighbours. While this feast was going on, there appeared a poor beggar, terribly emaciated and almost naked, asking for a little rice for pity's sake, as he had not eaten for three days. But the widow laughed at him and said: "Do you think I grow rice to waste it on beggars? Get out, or I'll set my servants on you!" She hunted the old man away, and he crept out of sight, sitting down to rest beside a *bagbagan* (a bathing place in a running stream) behind the house, with the tears running down his cheeks in his weakness and hunger. Suddenly he heard a voice, and looked up to see a dignified old man who asked him so kindly what ailed him that he told the story of Nji Endit's cruelty. The old man was the Spirit of the Stream and said to him: "Fear not, I shall avenge you. Go away from here as far and as fast as you can." The beggar hobbled off as fast as his feeble legs would carry him, and presently, as he looked back from a hillside where he had sat down again to rest, he saw the water rising. The stream, commanded by its Spirit, had overflowed until the whole village was under water, and thus the present lake came into existence. The greedy widow was changed into a big leech, which lives on the shores of the lake to this day.

The ancient custom of currying favour with the gods by an animal sacrifice will sometimes crop up among the natives of Java. A sugar planter friend of mine, making his rounds in the mill one day, came upon the scene just in time to rescue from a grisly fate a wretched kitten which was about to be thrown into the crusher tied to a bunch of sugarcane "to bring good luck to the crushing," as the millworkers earnestly informed their master when, much to their puzzlement and distress, they were told to stop the machine, untie the little creature, and take it to the planter's house. That particular kitten lives to this day, a sleek and pampered household pet; but the custom may be more general in the mills than any of us guess. Cats are cheap enough, heaven knows, but it is not a pleasing reflection as you drop a lump of sugar into your afternoon tea!

The heads of cattle slaughtered for feasts of any ceremonial kind are usually offered as sacrifices to the spirits. This is especially the case at the inauguration of a new building; and during the great Java sugar boom, now, alas, only a matter of history, when many huge new mills were erected, these sacrificial offerings of rows of wide horned buffalo heads were a sight not easily forgotten.

How all the "holy" trees and stones and rocks and springs acquired their holiness, no native can ever say. But holy they are, and the Javanese will run no risks of offending the spirits that inhabit them. All *waringen* trees are holy, more or less, when they have attained any age, which is most fortunate, for if it were not so, many of the magnificent old trees that preside over the *pasars* and the big open grass covered space, called *aloon-aloon*, in the centre of most native towns, sheltering an immense area with their wide-flung branches, might well have been swept away by the tide of progress. But happily their holiness protects them. No native would dare to strike an axe at the sacred trunk, and it would be a brave white man indeed that would order him to cut one down.

The *waringen* is one of the most characteristic of Java trees. It is a member of the *ficus* (fig) family, to which *Ficus elastica*, from which rubber was tapped before the cultivation of *Hevea*, also belongs. They closely resemble one another, and the *elastica* is often mistaken for its "holy" relation.

A fine old *waringen* that stands on a piece of land leased from the native owner some years ago by a European, as a site for a country house and garden, created a curious situation. Native prejudice would not permit the holy tree to be included in the very beautiful garden that the new tenant soon caused to be made around it, and certainly no white man might ever sit and drink tea or gossip in its shade! The difficulty was overcome by putting up a fence all round the tree, with a pathway, also fenced, leading to it through the garden from the outside boundary, so that natives might bring their offerings to it without let or hindrance as before.

You may sometimes see, under the deep shade of one of these old *waringen*, such relics as a carved stone Hindu god, or Nandi, the sacred bull, tucked in the natural shrines formed by the huge sprawling roots. They were probably brought there, perhaps generations ago, by natives who found them in the neighbourhood, who would think the holy tree a suitable place. There is such a tree at Simpang, Soerabaya, and another at Poedjon, in the eastern mountains. These, and all others similarly distinguished, have an added holiness, and it is rarely that there are not small votive offerings among the great roots, and always the ashes and remnants of countless tapers.

A stone or rock of any unusual shape is quite sure to be regarded as the habitation of a spirit, and often a *bilik* house is built over it, in which offerings are placed. If by the wayside on a mountain path you see what looks like a neat bamboo dog kennel, it is long odds that inside you will find a queer shaped stone with faded flowers and some rice or cakes beside it.

So long as native superstition is confined to such things as rocks and trees, it does not cause the European resident of

Java much inconvenience. But when it is a stream or a spring whose water he needs that is found to possess the embarrassing quality of holiness it is quite another matter. He may be very seriously inconvenienced and be put to heavy expense; but his material interests will carry no weight in competition with the Javanese spirits, and in the end he is almost sure to have to admit himself beaten.

As a case in point: an hotel was built recently on a high pass across one of the lovely mountain ranges, the site being chosen, as is the custom, in convenient proximity to a sparkling stream which runs splashing and gurgling past it from the heights above. From this it was proposed to connect a running water supply according to the delightfully simple method in vogue in these parts. A bamboo pipe, often with its end covered with a small round tin, perforated to form a filter, is fixed under a fall from over some high rock, or in the bank of the stream at a point where the water flows swiftly; the bamboo pipeline is carried on along the hillside to a concrete tank outside the house. Thus a constant water supply is yours at the cost of a few shillings and without payment of a water rate!

This is done in country places, especially in the mountains, all over Java; and the hotel in question, in common with all others in the Dutch East Indies, was luxuriously fitted with baths and wash-basins and all the latest sanitary appliances which had to be carried by coolies up the steep mountain track in readiness for the bountiful supply of clear spring water provided by nature: which incidentally was an item given prominence in the advertised attractions of the establishment.

At last all was ready; the plumbing done, and every fitting in its place; but when it came to the last and simplest item, the tapping of the stream and laying the pipeline, there came a hitch. The coolies, who till now had worked at the job as cheerily as is their wont, shook their heads and looked frightened. The hotel proprietor, thinking they were waiting for his promise of the usual *salamatan*, hastened to promise that one should be held the moment the water was connected; but still they hung back, and at last their head man spoke for them. "It may not be, *Toean*," he said very solemnly. "The water of that stream is holy. The spirits will be angry and some great evil befall, if we steal the water from their stream!"

No orders or promises or persuasions would induce those or any other coolies to place in position the bamboo piping across the short distance that would have led the sacred water to the house. There stood the new hotel spick-and-span and ready for its guests. All around it was the music of running water; but to conjure that melodious sound within doors, to flow from the shining chromium taps into the much advertised modern baths and basins, was beyond the white man's power.

At last, after many consultations with the wise men of the village near by, the coolies' head man announced that, provided the proper offerings of rice were regularly made to the spirits of the stream, water might be dipped from it in sufficient quantity to fill the hotel tank, but that on no account might it be run off in a pipe. So the hotelier, grateful for small mercies in a situation that had looked for a time like being even worse that it was, had to be content with a tank filled by buckets; and the inadequacy of the supply in proportion to his costly fittings is a constant mocking reminder of how impotent the blessings of civilisation may be, at times, to compete with an ancient primitive faith.

Holy objects such as *krises*, shields, and other things, which are said to fit none but men of royal blood, and which make their wearers both invincible and invulnerable, are still preserved in the palaces of the sultans at Soerakarta and Djokdjakarta, jealously guarded in an inner room by women especially chosen for the task. These *poesakas*, as they are called, are much revered by the people, who bring offerings to them in the hope of help in curing sickness, and of procuring fruitfulness in women.

Every village has its *doekoen*: a wise man or magic maker who is consulted upon every sort of medical, domestic, social, or other problem. And the natives' blind and utter faith in all things supernatural makes the *doekoen's* job a profitable and easy one. The average Javanese, however poor, would far rather pay the wise man as much money as a coolie can earn in a month, to make magic over his sick child, than allow a white doctor to treat it free. There is in some villages also

"*Magic*"

a wise woman, called *nini towok*, whose speciality it is to discover thieves and other evildoers.

Odd stories of these *doekoens*' powers are told even by Europeans: as witness the following, vouched for by a well-known Dutch business man. Some years ago, a friend of his who had a native wife decided it was time to turn "respectable" and marry a white girl. But he was genuinely attached to his native partner, and shrank from breaking the news to her and still more from the thought of sending her away. So torn was the young man between his two loves that several of his bachelor friends put their heads together and decided to tackle the affair in the native way by consulting a *doekoen*, found for them by a native servant. The ancient man listened gravely to the tale they told him and, after deep thought, said that all would be well if they carried out his instructions. Then, taking a sodawater bottle, still adorned with its label, and putting a small piece of bamboo inside it while muttering a charm, he corked it and handed it to the young men, telling them to throw it into the water from the first bridge they should cross on their way home. This they did, throwing the ridiculous bottle into the river from a bridge in the heart of the town; a place swarming with traffic and a most unlikely *milieu*, one would have thought, for magic. Nevertheless it worked. Their friend, who knew nothing of their efforts on his behalf, announced next day that, to his astonishment and relief, his native wife had packed her baggage while he was out, and had disappeared, never to be seen by any of them again.

Many people will remember a recent African travel film in which a native was seen "calling the crocodiles." The same extraordinary power is claimed by many East Indian *doekoens*, and undoubtedly possessed by some. I have not come across any authenticated case in Java itself, but at Banjowangi, Dutch Borneo, just over the water, a *doekoen* performed the feat in the presence of hundreds of onlookers, including many Europeans. A native had been taken by a crocodile, and his friends wished to avenge him and punish his murderer. But a promiscuous crocodile hunt would not do. Crocodiles are regarded with great respect in all the islands of the East Indian Archipelago, and in Borneo they are inhabited by the spirits of the Dyaks' ancestors, so that they must never be killed wantonly or without good reason. But it is understood that if one of the creatures so far forgets its manners and the canons of good taste as to devour a descendant of the spirit that uses its body as a habitation, then it must pay the death penalty.

The local *doekoen* was accordingly consulted, and he assured the bereaved relatives that he would certainly bring the guilty reptile to justice. Down to the muddy river bank, right in the middle of the town, he went, followed by the entire native population, and there, squatting in the usual native fashion on his heels, he started to croon a queer monotonous chant. On and on it went, rising and falling weirdly, while the crowd, deeply awed, watched in dead silence. "*Baiya!*" (crocodile) "*Baiya!*" he called, over and over again. "Come, *Baiya*, come! One of you has broken the law. You have killed a man, and eaten him. Come! Come! You too must die! You must die. Come!" ... And presently, while the chant went on unbroken, dark shapes were seen approaching swiftly and silently, leaving the surface of the sluggish stream unruffled save for the wake that widened in two silver lines behind each of them, as though they were small boats. They were the heads of a score or more of crocodiles; and as they came nearer one separated itself from the rest. The *doekoen* now changed his chant a little, and addressed himself to the nearest approaching head only, while the others one by one turned round and disappeared.

The hideous brute reached the point just opposite the *doekoen*, climbed the bank and, waddling clumsily forward, stopped close in front of him. Fearlessly, still singing his uncanny chant, he approached it, and bound first its great jaws and then its fore and hind claws with rope that he had brought with him, to which it made not the least resistance. The *doekoen* then stopped chanting and, turning round, said to the awestruck crowd: "Here is the one who devoured your brother! Kill him! It is the law!" Nothing loth, the executioners hastened to do their grisly part. The helpless crocodile was cut open; and there in its stomach were recognisable traces of the unfortunate man whose death was thus lawfully avenged!

The Javanese greatly revere white hair; and, provided of course that they have reason to like and respect its possessor on other counts, they are very ready to accredit him with supernatural powers. An old planter friend of mine who was born in the country, and speaks Javanese, Malay, Madoerese, and several dialects as fluently as the natives among whom he has spent his long life, is regarded far and wide as a wise and holy man from whom no secrets are hidden. From all over the district they come to consult the *Toean Toea* (the Old Lord) as they call him; and there is seldom a day when you will not find him dispensing wisdom and counsel from a seat in his garden to some figure squatted before him on the ground.

It may be a man suspected of theft or some other misdemeanour. On such occasions my old friend is in his element. Gazing benevolently upon the delinquent crouched humbly at his feet, he slowly shakes his head with its thick white thatch as he raises his right hand and points heavenward. "*Awas!*" (Beware!) says he, with awful solemnity. "Up there in the sky sits the Lord Allah, Who looks into your heart and sees all things! He knows whether you lie or speak truth. And now, mark well what I say. *If you are lying* . . . in two full days from now—that is on Friday at this hour—He will make your stomach swell till it is so big you cannot walk! *Awas! Awas!*"

The man stares, fascinated, at the pointing finger and the gently wagging white-crowned head. And so convinced is he that the *Toean Toea* is on terms of the utmost intimacy with the gods, that he will certainly confess if he is guilty. But that is no guarantee that upon occasion even such a confession of guilt may not be turned to the sinner's advantage in dealing with a white-haired seer whose kindness of heart is as famed as his omniscience. One wily rascal, his bluff of innocence wholly broken down by the awesome thought of Divine intervention in his stomach, replied, grovelling: "Why should I lie when the *Toean* knows all? It is true that I was guilty of the theft, for Ardjo was a fool and it was easy. Such men as he are a temptation to those wiser than themselves. But no matter. I will go now to the *poliss* and confess, and they will put me in prison. And because I speak the truth the *Toean* who is great and good, knowing all the secrets of the gods, will see that while I am in prison my wife and my children, of whom I have many, do not starve!" And it was so! The *Toean* not only provided for the thief's large family while he went to jail, but gave him a job when he was discharged: he was pointed out to me, where he worked among the flower beds, while I listened to the story.

Belief in my old friend's supernatural powers, already strong, received irrefutable and terrifying proof in native eyes through the fulfilment, needless to say wholly unforeseen by the prophet, of one of his prophecies. He had rented a piece of land from an adjoining native landowner, paying him three years' rent in advance in cash, the man, as commonly happens, needing money to meet the expenses of a daughter's wedding. At the end of the first year, however, on going with his coolies to direct a fresh planting, Mr X. to his astonishment found the native owner hard at work on the land in question, and on asking for an explanation the man calmly asserted that the arrangement, which had been made merely by word of mouth, as is usual in such transactions, had been for one year only.

The native farmer, who was elderly and of some importance among his neighbours, stuck stubbornly to his version even when the *Toean*, adopting his usual tactics, solemnly wagged a finger at him and told him that unless he admitted he was lying he would certainly be dead within three days. To my old friend's horror, on the third day the man's wife appeared weeping and wringing her hands, to say that her husband had died in the night, from what cause no one was ever able to discover. Grovelling on the ground in front of the Old Lord, placing her forehead against his boot, she sobbed out: "*Wah! Wah!* Alas that Soemo should have lied to the *Toean* who knows all things and has the power of life and death! I stood unseen behind the door when the *Toean* paid the three years' rent, but I dared not tell Soemo for he would have been very angry. But now he is dead, and I pray to the *Toean* to take the land and plant it, for it is lawfully his!"

Is it any wonder that after such tragic proof the "Old Lord's" fame spread far and wide, and that he is regarded as having powers far greater than any *doekoen*? So much so, indeed, that when plans to murder all the Europeans in the district (during a native plot organised in 1927 with the avowed object of wiping out the Europeans throughout Java) were discovered, it was found that Mr and Mrs X. had been specifically excepted—surely a unique honour!

This plot was "given away" in the district in which my white haired old friend and his family are residents, by an anonymous letter from a friendly native to the *Wedono* of the *dessa*, who promptly handed it on to the European authority in the nearest large town. The letter contained the startling announcement that on a certain day all the local Europeans, except Mr and Mrs X., were to be killed, and that weapons and other proofs would be found in certain native houses.

Soldiers and police were sent up; a search revealed the promised proofs; and a hundred or so of the conspirators were rounded up. They were roped together and made to trot behind a police motor bicycle to the *Wedono's* office at a very slow pace, as an example to their neighbours. Later on they and their fellow-conspirators from elsewhere in Java were deported to a convict settlement deep in the wilds of Dutch New Guinea, several days' difficult journey from Merauké, which is itself surely one of the loneliest places in the world.

Of course there are "haunted houses" in Java. It could not be otherwise in so spirit haunted a community. The strangest example I have come across is a large hotel on the outskirts of a populous village in one of the most famous mountain beauty spots in Java. It is a solid stone building standing back from a main road at the end of an avenue of stately palms, on the slope of a magnificent natural amphitheatre looking out over a panorama of rare loveliness. There is a spacious terrace from which to view the scenery, a fine tennis court, a garden full of flowers and shrubs, and long rows of bedrooms, each with its own bathroom and verandah. The last word, in fact, in attraction and comfort. The whole place is fully furnished; but it was abandoned years ago, just as it stands, to the dust and ants and spiders—and to the spirits.

You can walk through a broken shutter, held in place by a chair pushed against it, into the once pleasant lounge, full of armchairs and small tables, on which there are still ashtrays, and shelves and cabinets still adorned with books and ornaments. On the walls hang blue china plates, framed pictures, and a calendar from some insurance company dated seven years ago!

Through the dirt-grimed windows of the dining-room, where yellowish, rotting lace curtains droop forlornly, you can see the long table on which stands a dead palm in a blackened brass pot. Drawn up to it are two long rows of chairs; and along the walls are buffets and sideboard laden with piles of plates and rows of jugs and cups and glasses; even a stone filter is not lacking.

So it has stood, needing apparently little more than a thorough spring cleaning to make it fit for human habitation, for more than seven years; and so it will in all probability go on standing until it falls down.

A wrinkled old native came hobbling across the garden from an outhouse when he caught sight of me on the day when, my curiosity aroused by the stories I had heard, I made my way in to see for myself. I asked him if he knew why the place had been deserted; and he shuddered and looked nervously over his shoulder as he replied in a low voice: "The place is accursed, *Toean*. It is built over an old burial-place, and the spirits of the dead who were laid to rest there were angry. And as though that were not enough, there is more. It was a *Toean Tjina* (Chinese) who had it built: a very rich man and vain, and he would not listen when the old men of the *dessa* went to him and told him that he must not raise a house here because the place was unholy. He laughed at them and insulted them, saying they were only ignorant men, and that many *Toean Belanda* (Dutchmen) would come to his fine hotel, and that they were not afraid of spirits.

"So the house was built. And when it was finished we went to him again, and said that at least a great *salamatan* should be given, for, as all men know, unless a *salamatan* is held when a house is built it cannot prosper, and how much more when it stands on such a place as this. But he would not listen, and sent us away, and though he was so rich there was no feast. Then he himself came to stay in the hotel though he was more than fifty years old (and if a man go to live in a new house at that age he will die) and because we men of the *dessa* did not wish evil to come to him, and because evil would come to us if we did not warn him, we went to him once more and told him that if he stayed he would surely die. And this time he was frightened, for he did not want to die, and he went away. And so he went on: at first many *Toean Belanda* came to the hotel. But soon there came also evil insects and swarmed like a plague. And then one *Toean* died there and then another and another, and yet two more, as well as two children. And so men knew at last that the place was accursed and they must not live here; and they shut the doors and went away and no one has been inside since."

Such a silly childish story it seems. Just native nonsense that no one could take seriously. And when I went and had another look through the windows at the smug conventionality of the rooms inside, it all seemed more ridiculous still. And yet—it was all true. Four persons actually had died in the hotel, though one at least was an invalid sent to the mountains as a last hope. As for the "evil insects," they might have been no more and no less than bugs. Scarcely a spiritual visitation! Another native reason sometimes given for the hotel's abandonment is that the Sultan of Solo once spent a night there, and that no ordinary person dare sleep in the place where so august a prince had condescended to rest, lest their presumption be punished with death by the spirits in the High One's service.

But whatever the explanation, there the odd fact is. There stands the haunted hotel *Girimojo*, as a proof of the power of the spiritual over the material in modern Java. It is still so attractive in appearance from the road at the end of its fine avenue that, even to-day, passing motorists who do not know its story will sometimes pull up in the hope of being able to stay there. With its furnishings it is worth many thousands of guilders, and many thousands more in profits, if only its builders had listened to the native wise men and chosen its site fifty yards or so away. But as it is, it is doomed to stand for ever empty for no other reason than that "the spirits have willed it so."

There is a belief handed down from very ancient times which proved quite recently to be still not extinct among Java country folk. In the bad old days, according to Javanese legend, it was the custom to placate evil spirits by mixing children's eyes with the mortar in the foundations of important new buildings, and particularly of new bridges, in the hope of saving them from being swept away in the sudden heavy floods that are so common in mountainous regions. To get eyes for the purpose a magician called the *doelitan* or *tjoelikan* was employed. He had only to point his enchanted finger at them and the children would follow him as willingly as those of Hamelin followed the Pied Piper. The rest was easy. He lured them out of sight of the village, then caught them and tore their eyes out and let them go. As soon as he had enough for the amount of mortar required he took his "bag" of eyes to the builders, the mixture was made, and the bridge was as safe as magic could make it. It is scarcely surprising that, when the foundations of any such building were about to be laid, all the parents in the surrounding districts lived in daily terror, and every child was warned to run away as fast as he could whenever a stranger appeared, and never on any account to let such a one come near them, lest it be the dreaded *doelitan*.

The *doelitan* is used as a bogey man by Javanese mothers to frighten disobedient children who will not come in when they are called. "Hurry, hurry!" you will sometimes hear a woman call from her gate to a group of happy little boys busy with their "stone game" in the dust of the mountain pathway. "Come back! Don't play so far away. The *doelitan* is out and he will catch you!"

But the great difference between this Javanese bogey and ours is that many Javanese mothers believe that the *doelitan* does actually exist. Occasionally it happens that a cry of "*doelitan!*" will rouse a whole *kampong*, and all the people will stream out to save their children, the women armed with *aloes* (the heavy clubs with which they stamp rice) and the men with their *pikoelans*, and then woe betide any passing stranger who may unwittingly have aroused their suspicions.

A case of this kind occurred recently when two Dutch sailors spending a day's leave in the country tried to make friends with some native children so that they could take photographs of them. Suddenly they heard shouts, and the whole population of the *kampong* came tearing down the path, brandishing their clubs and throwing stones, evidently in a very ugly mood indeed. The two gallant mariners had never heard of the *doelitan*, but they could see that the natives meant business, so they took to their heels and gained the main road just in time to board an opportunely passing motor bus, leaving the baffled *kampong* folk wildly gesticulating in the roadway behind them. An official inquiry into the affair was held, and it came out in evidence, quite seriously given, that the two strangers had been mistaken for *doelitan*.

Belief in *were*-tigers or, as the Javanese call them, *matjan gadoengan*, still persists in out of the way parts of Java, and much more, of course, in the outer islands. There were in Java quite recently, and there probably still are, *kampongs* where the people, both men and women, were firmly believed to possess the power of transforming themselves at will into tigers. In such places, natives have told me, no travelling Javanese would ever think of asking shelter for the night for fear of what might befall him. If, however, some stranger were to do so in ignorance of the *kampong's* sinister reputation, he would be refused, as it would not be consistent with Javanese ideas of hospitality to expose a guest to such a danger as the possibility of being killed and eaten. One village still bears the name of "Gadoengan," which serves, no doubt, as a warning to all whom it may concern.

Natives will tell you that the *gadoengan* goes about his affairs by day as an ordinary person though, if you look carefully, you can recognise him (or her) because there will be no cleft in the upper lip. At night he goes ahunting in tiger form, but is more to be feared than any real tiger, for he has none of their fear of man, and possesses all man's craft as well as his own. There is just one thing to be done if you should meet the *gadoengan*; if you know who he or she is in human form, and address the tiger by name, it will be forced to resume its real shape and will be powerless to do you harm. It seems, however, that few have had the presence of mind to attempt this experiment; it would be so easy, they say, to make a mistake!

In the islands beyond Java the belief varies. In parts of Lombok the *gadoengan* becomes not a tiger, but a crocodile;

and in Timor, a dog or cat. In Middle Celebes the natives believe that such persons can change themselves at will at night into all sorts of animal forms, even that of a rat, so that they can go spying on their neighbours' affairs.

Among many queer beliefs the Javanese hold in connection with animals is that anyone who eats the flesh of a white water buffalo will become an albino. So that while the black buffalo is killed in Java but rarely, being too valuable as a draught animal to be sacrificed lightly, his white brother is in even less danger of the butcher's knife. Anyone who has ever seen an East Indian albino will easily understand the natives' horror of falling under a similar curse. I only came across one once, and a truly terrible sight he was: a heavy, powerful man with a shock of almost tow coloured hair, pinkish mottled skin, great hairy red hands, weak, watering eyes, and flat nose: hideously conspicuous among a crowd of cheery brown men, and quite evidently conscious of it; silent and morose though all the rest were laughing, and as alien to them as a pariah dog.

A queer game, with a strong flavour of Maskelyne and Devant about it, is said by old residents of West Java to have been played in some Soendanese villages. A dozen or so children would form a ring and march round and round another child who was wrapped up and entirely hidden in a *sarong*. After they had been round twenty times, singing a monotonous sort of chant all the while, they would stop, the *sarong* was unwrapped, and the child had vanished. Then the ring would be formed again and the children march round twenty times in the other direction, singing a different song: after which the vanished child would be found in the *sarong* again, very dazed and saying he had been asleep. No explanation of the trick, if trick it was, was ever discovered; but as it was not considered a healthy form of juvenile entertainment it was eventually banned officially by the authorities. It is more than likely, however, that it is still played in places remote enough to feel themselves safe from interference with their little pleasures.

The old Javanese five-day week, though it was abolished, as was obviously inevitable in a colony developed by Europeans, long ago by the Dutch, still survives in the Sultanates of Solo

"*Magic*"

and Djokdja in what is known as the *Minggoe Pasar* or Market Week. For here the markets are held, as of old, once or more times in the five-day week, the "week" consisting of the five days, Kliwon, Legi, Pahing, Pon, and Wagé. In most *dessas* a *pasaran besar* (big market) is held once a "week" —that is to say, at intervals of five days—and thus falls, according to our week, on different days: Monday, Saturday, Thursday, Tuesday, Sunday, Friday, and so on. The various combinations of days of the five and seven day weeks are regarded by natives as of great importance, for the reason that some are approved by the spirits and some are not.

Some indeed are so distasteful to the powers of the unseen world that when the market day falls on such a combination all sorts of precautions have to be taken. Tapers are lighted, gifts of rice and cakes offered, and even, at times, fowls sacrificed, in order to appease the evil spirits. The days regarded as undesirable differ in various *dessas*; but it is curious to note that, even here, Friday is a bad day, and any combination with it is regarded as a bad one, though some are worse than others. The markets are held on different days in different places; just as with us, one town's market day may be Wednesday and another Thursday. So in Middle Java one *dessa* will choose Pon, another Wagé, another Kliwon, and so on. Those places whose *pasar* is held on Kliwon have to be most careful of all: for the combination of Djoemat (Friday) with Kliwon is that most particularly resented by the spirits.

The following table will explain the combinations of days:

(1) Sunday (Minggoe) (1) Kliwon
(2) Monday (Selasa) (2) Legi
(3) Tuesday (Senen) (3) Pahing
(4) Wednesday (Rebo) (4) Pon
(5) Thursday (Kermis) (5) Wagé
(6) Friday (Djoemat) (1) &c.
(7) Saturday (Saptoe) (2) &c.
&c.

The Javanese of the Sultanates always call the days by their double name, putting that of the seven-day week first. They will say they went to the *pasar* at Plaosan on Rebo-Pon, or Minggoe-Legi, or whatever it may be.

In small country places where the market is held only once in the five-day week the difficulties of European housekeeping are considerable when the unlucky Djoemat-Kliwon combination comes round. For then, when the cook goes to the *pasar* to lay in the next five days' provisions, she will not dream of doing so until she has taken whatever she may have been brought up to believe are the proper precautions, perhaps the sacrifice of a white cockerel, which may be hard to come by, the demand for these luckless birds for sacrificial purposes making the mortality among them very high.

Natives of Soerabaya firmly believe that at least one shower, usually the first of the West Monsoon, is bound to fall during the *Pasar Malem*, their annual fair. The Dutch, for once equally superstitious, believe as firmly that this first shower, being the gift of St Nikolas, will fall on or about this saint's day, the 5th of December. Strange to say, both predictions are almost invariably fulfilled!

The heat of the East Monsoon, much more severe in East Java than in the West, reaches its climax in November, and the relief that comes with the first rain is eagerly awaited. Day after day hopes are raised by masses of grey clouds; by an occasional peal of thunder, or by sudden, shortlived windstorms, scattering a few raindrops here and there. And then, usually at night, it comes at last. It may be a short, sharp rattle like machine gun fire on the roof, tropically heavy but lasting a bare sixty seconds or so. Or it may gather volume like a flood, falling more and more heavily and steadily, with increasing, unbroken roar for an hour or more, drawing from the parched and grateful earth an ever more delicious scent. Next morning the sun rises in a clear sky on a new world, transformed by that one first shower, with every colour softened yet intensified. There is a cool freshness in the air and, incredible though it sounds, the brown grass already shows a faint tinge of green. But this magical transformation at which we marvel, the native takes as quite a matter of course.

The tale might be prolonged indefinitely of the superstitious beliefs that mingle so oddly with all the religious and modern influences in this highly civilised Dutch colony. The thread of "magic" is inextricably woven into the life of the native people; and so it will doubtless remain, despite whatever changes Fate may have in store for them as helpless pawns on the chess board of human affairs.

CHAPTER NINE

For Feminists

LIFE is very real and very earnest for the Javanese woman; but the gods have endowed her with the happy faculty of carrying her heavy burdens lightly.

Unlike her brothers, she has no childhood. Everywhere you will see little boys playing and running and shouting as children do all the world over; but little girls, never. Both boys and girls are pressed early into the family service and made to do their bit; but the boys realise from the beginning that they are made of superior clay, and are treated as such; whereas girls are predestined slaves and little else from the time they can toddle.

Boys, almost without exception, go to school, gaining thereby not only the kudos attached to "learning," but all the attendant joys of rushing down the road to and from the schoolhouse; of playing games in the compound and buying "*ijs*" from the shrewd Chinese who appears outside the fence at the morning recess, carrying a fat vacuum flask from which he produces pink, yellow, and green ice-candles impaled on little bamboo sticks, at one cent each.

But to every hundred boys in any native school there will be a bare half dozen or so little girls; and even they evidently feel that they are intruders, squatting unhappily in a corner of the verandah during the play hour, never by any chance joining in the fun with the boys who are racing about outside. For the most part the Javanese girls stay at home, gravely taking their place as little women: sweeping the paths, shaking grass mats, carrying water, washing clothes; doing anything and everything in fact that a wise mother can think of to save her from doing it herself! To that mother the whole pattern of life is orderly and predestined. She married for the sole purpose of producing children, acting meanwhile as housekeeper, of course. When she has a boy, it ministers to her pride, her husband is better pleased with her, and she receives many more congratulations, but the acquisition of a son only adds to her domestic burdens. When, however, it is a girl that arrives, the achievement is much less acclaimed, and her husband is apt to give her to understand that she has let him down; but on the other hand, by way of compensation, she scores in having produced a little drudge, of whom, however kind a mother she may be, and the Javanese are almost invariably kind to children, it never occurs to her not to make the fullest use.

A Javanese baby emerges from infancy with almost the same magical speed as a butterfly from its chrysalis. One day you will see a young mother with a newly arrived baby lying curled in her *selendang*. Then, in less than no time, it will appear, still in that same useful appendage, but sitting in it like a frog, with small fat arms and legs asprawl round mother's waist and back. And before it seems possible, the little creature, if a girl, is toddling along holding on to its mother's *sarong*, its fat baby ankles, encircled with bangles, peeping out beneath a miniature *sarong* of its own. It will wear a tiny muslin jacket, and its wisp of dark hair will be screwed up into the veriest burlesque of a "bun" on the top of its head with one thick hairpin. Nine times out of ten, the toddler will have another bit of *batik* over one shoulder in exact imitation of mother's *selendang*, with perhaps a bottle or little basket in it; not, however, as sentimental tourists, ravished at the charming sight, are apt to think, dressed up "for fun." Far from it. She is learning her job already; and she will be made clearly to understand that once the precious one cent's worth of coconut oil for cooking has been bought, and is in the bottle she is carrying, it must be kept right way up, or there will be trouble! The little face will wear an expression of portentous gravity: not unhappy, but conscious of responsibility. And the lesson, thus so early and so quickly learned, will dominate the girl-child until she reaches years of indiscretion.

I stayed recently with friends who were in the habit of buying eggs from a former servant. The latter always sent them by her daughter, aged two years and three months! This comical scrap of humanity, who was turned out in faithful miniature of the market women passing up and down the road outside, would open the gate and walk up to the verandah, twist her shoulder with precisely the same gesture that all Javanese women use when taking anything from their *selendang*, and produce a small round basket containing ten eggs. She would watch gravely while they were removed and counted; then wrap the money given her in a screw of newspaper and put it in the basket, adjust basket and *selendang* to her liking, and patter away again without having said a single word.

Needless to say, little Javanese girls are expected to "mother" their younger brothers and sisters as they come along. It is quite common to see a little mite scarcely bigger than the "egg woman" described above, carrying a baby astride her hip. It would be hard to say whether the sight is more comic or pathetic; but certainly it is impossible not to smile when you meet one of these quaint little figures with its preposterous twist of hair skewered by an enormous hairpin, and the baby face with its preoccupied grown up air to match its grown up clothes.

I have seen too, in a mountain *kampong* near my home, a small girl just five years old, with bare arms and shoulders and a bit of *batik* bound round her funny little chest above her diminutive *sarong*, standing in a running stream scrubbing and soaping garments on a flat rock, while she kept a motherly eye on a naked baby brother splashing happily in the water near by.

But it is all so natural; so much all in the day's work, that, over serious though these unchildlike little girls may seem, they are quite normal young human beings when they reach the flirtatious age. They work none the less; idleness is never part of their philosophy; but they are very feminine for all that, and during the all too short time that they are marriageable and not married, they make the most of it. These slender, fine boned little creatures in their teens are often charming; and when they are, like all women worth their salt, they know it. I have seen a pretty, laughing young woman, balancing on her head a great basket of green banana and *sirih* leaves, a dead weight that I could scarcely lift off the ground, let alone carry, keeping up a spirited flow of flirtatious sallies with three smart young natives who accompanied her for the whole length of the street leading to the market. The East being the East, no embarrassment was caused on either side by the fact that the lady was carrying a heavy load while the attendant swains were unencumbered.

This flirtatious mood, like the mating plumage of birds, is worn as a rule only until it has attained its object; and once married there is no more fun with young men for the respectable Javanese woman. There are "others," of course, among the Javanese, as elsewhere. But that does not mean that she is either depressed or downtrodden. On the contrary, marriage seems to release her imprisoned spirit and, her destiny being achieved, she becomes as garrulous with her women friends as she was silent and self-contained as a child.

By European standards, her life is always a hard one, for not only is she, in the natural course of things, housekeeper, child bearer, and nurse, but she does her full share of outdoor work as well. She carries live fowls, eggs, vegetables, coconuts and other produce to market, and for sale at the houses of Europeans. Most of the ever needful weeding in the fields falls to her share, the men having their hands full with heavier work such as ploughing and watering. Most important of all, it is the Javanese woman's proud privilege to plant out the *bibit* (seedlings) of rice, thus symbolically proclaiming herself the true mother and giver of life to her race.

This rule in Java is fixed and absolute. Rice must be planted by women or it will not be fruitful. To the Javanese mind it is as unthinkable for a man to plant rice as to give birth to a baby! He may gather the *bibit* from the seed bed, he may "top" them, and set them in bunches in the shallow water and mud of the prepared field ready for the planters; but that is all. And there is no more characteristic sight than that of the rows of women planters, stooping from the waist with legs wide apart, *sarongs* kilted above their knees, ankle deep in the shining water that mirrors their every movement, setting out the slim bright green seedlings with astonishing speed in lines as straight as though every one had been marked with a cord: chattering and calling to each other, while their naked brown babies play glorious games in the warm mud and water of an as yet unplanted adjoining field, rolling and splashing like miniature baby hippos, or like our own children on a seaside holiday.

This rice planting is a communal affair, and all the available women of a *dessa* turn out together to do it. And so truly do many hands make light, or rather quick, work that you may drive in the morning along some broad valley where the *sawahs* (irrigated ricefields), as yet unplanted, shine like mirrors, reflecting every detail of the mountains that bound them as far as the eye can see; and return the same evening to find the water surfaces of the whole great area pricked with the tiny green shafts of newly planted rice.

In West Java, where the rainfall permits rice planting at any time of the year, some *sawahs* are always in process of being planted at the same time that others are being ploughed and the crop from yet others being gathered. The calls on the women's time are constant, for they reap the rice crop also; though in this they are joined by the men unless heavier work calls them elsewhere. At harvest times, every woman you meet along the country roads will have a pointed stick or bamboo, six or eight inches long, stuck in the glossy coil of her black hair. If you look closer you will see that a narrow blade, about two inches long, set in wood, is fixed half way up this handle at right angles. The little instrument is the *ani-ani*, the universally used knife with which the heads of rice are cut, one by one, by hand. The blades are sold by tens of thousands for one cent each in every *pasar*, and every countryman mounts his own in exact sizes to suit himself, his wife, and his family.

Though they all work, the lives of Javanese women differ greatly according to the various regions in which they happen to live. In the highlands of West Java, among the rich tea estates, the woman power of whole villages finds employment in picking and in the processes in the tea factories; and probably these, of all the women of Java, have the pleasantest lives. Even among them, however, tea picking must give way to rice planting when occasion demands, for this latter is an inescapable duty with which nothing can be allowed to interfere. But for the most part the lot of the tea estate hands is a pleasant one. You have only to see them to be assured of that, as they stream, laughing and chattering, to or from work, along the steep road against a background of distant mountains, looking like figures on a stage; brightly arrayed as tropic flowers, as though they had decked themselves out under the same unseen compulsion to add to the gaiety and colourfulness of the scene. Every tint of the rainbow seems to be there: the deep rich tones of native dyes in *batik sarongs*, and the lighter hues of foreign printed muslins in their jackets, and in the chiffon scarves, either tied or floating lightly round their heads and shoulders.

Some even of these bright flower-like creatures are often heavily laden. Many on their way to work will carry on their heads huge round baskets or bundles tied up in cotton stuff. These contain what is known as "*kampong* leaf," that is, tea grown and picked in natives' own small gardens, which the estate management buys from the growers up to a fixed quota. I saw a young woman one morning with a big log balanced across the bright orange scarf that covered her head, a bulky package of green leaf slung over one shoulder, and a bundle of smaller firewood tucked into the crook of her arm, gesticulating gaily with her free hand, on which there gleamed a gold bracelet and some rings, while she carried on an animated conversation with her friends in a *kampong* as she passed.

The tea pickers look more like flowers than ever as you catch glimpses of them here and there at their work among the dark bushes. But their work is skilled, for all that, and its technique must be well learned, or the picker will soon find herself among the unemployed. She must see that the shoot has four leaves (including the tip) above the tiny sepal-like leaflet that indicates a new growth, and she must pick the shoot off above the leaf immediately above this sepal. Only thus is the next new growth assured; a matter whose importance will be understood when it is remembered that a tea shoot grows at the rate of a centimetre per day, and that the same trees are "picked" at intervals of only ten days. The finest flavoured tea is not the tip, as seems to be generally supposed, but the rather larger leaves just below it, which contain more fragrance. These are those that will be found rolled up into tiny tubes by the rolling and drying process, and may be easily identified.

Picturesque though they are, the pickers do not conform altogether to the average poster-artist's conception of them, to be seen on hoardings in England and Australia, where lovely dusky figures move among the bushes with large baskets on their backs. In reality, the leaf is gathered into shapeless bulging bundles in big squares of inevitably damp and dirty cotton stuff tied up by the four corners, which are emptied into baskets dumped here and there beside the paths bordering the section that is being picked, and taken later to the factory. These dumps are the recognised meeting-places for rest and gossip, and to them come the food vendors with their portable kitchens and strange eatables, to cater for the hungry pickers, who, however, need never work longer than they choose. They are paid according to the weight of the leaf they gather, and may stop when they are tired, weigh in, and trot away home to attend to their own domestic affairs.

Much of the work inside the factories on all tea estates is done by women. When the pickers bring the leaf in, in the afternoon, it is taken up to the drying loft, a long narrow place fitted with fans at either end and a hot air apparatus in the middle, separating two sets of wire racks on which the leaf is spread at the rate of about a pound weight to the square quarter metre. Here it remains overnight, and by the next morning has lost 60 per cent. of its moisture. It is gathered up by hand and tipped down a chute to the floor below, where it is gently crushed and turned between horizontal revolving rollers like giant gramophone records; this breaks the cells and liberates the juices, as well as rolling up the leaf. It passes next into a huge tubular wire mesh container divided into three compartments, each with a different mesh. The smallest leaf that passes out through the finest of these is not put in again; but that from the others may be put back once, twice, or even three times again, each sifting an hour. Then it all goes to the fermenting room, where temperature and humidity are regulated, the latter by means of water trickling down the walls. Here the leaf, already classified into three or four grades, lies in trays about four inches deep for two and a half to three hours, while fermentation takes place. And lastly each grade of leaf is gathered up and fed into the gaping mouth of the dryer, into whose dark, hot cavern it is slowly drawn on a flat belt four or five feet wide, up to the top storey of a long tunnel which doubles upon itself in several super-imposed descending levels. Down through this the belt slowly carries its precious freight, to emerge from a chute at the

THE RICE-GODDESS ENTHRONED AT A NATIVE FESTIVAL CELEBRATING THE HARVEST.

A WOMAN PLANTING RICE. A TYPICAL SCENE.

bottom as the dry fragrant leaf so familiar to us, ready for the pot!

Though now a finished product, the tea has yet to be sorted into many more grades for commercial purposes. It goes into the sorter, a machine superhuman in its ingenuity, separating the leaf by a violent oscillating motion into seven sizes, first cutting it into diminishing lengths and then shaking it through meshes of decreasing size, ranging from "Orange Pekoe" (so called from the tiny flecks of yellow made by the tips) down to tea "dust."

This sorting process is meticulously watched by the "tea maker," and the grades thrown back again and again, until they come exactly true to type out of the separate mouths into the containers.

The big machines are served by men; but at this stage the women take complete charge once more. Hundreds of pounds of leaf are poured out in great fragrant heaps in long rows eight or ten feet apart on the spotless, polished concrete floor; and round each of these squat women and girls in multicoloured *sarongs* and quaint, tight fitting, prim little long sleeved jackets, no two of them dressed alike, picking over the sweet smelling masses of tea almost leaf by leaf, freeing it from stalks or too thick midribs, which they throw away outside the charmed circle with quick deft movements of their small hands.

Last stage of all: the leaf is gathered and swept up, each grade of course separately, and carried to the packing room, where it is poured through chutes into the cubic three-ply tea cases familiar to all of us; these being kept shaking while being filled by means of yet another ingenious device. And the whole of the transformation scene, from green, growing leaf on the bushes, to the finished product we know so well, is completed within twenty-four hours!

Women tea workers enjoy a certain prestige, and are apt to be envied by their acquaintances in less favoured occupations. Some walk long distances to the estates from surrounding *kampongs*; but many live in the quarters, forming whole large villages in themselves, built on the tea estates for their accommodation.

When the tea bushes are pruned, which is done every two

years or, on some estates, every three, the women are allowed to carry away the prunings for firewood. At these times processions of whole families are to be seen: mother bowed under an immense load, and her children laden in descending scale according to size, jogging gaily home with this valuable perquisite. The system has the advantage from the estate management's point of view that the prunings are cleared away as cleanly as though the place had been swept, at no cost at all. A newly pruned tea plantation in Java is as bare as a French vineyard in December; but with the difference that only two and a half months after pruning, the women will be hard at work again, picking from bushes as richly green as ever.

All this, and more, goes to the making of that "nice cup of tea," as dear to the heart of the Javanese woman as it is to ours.

Many women are employed on the Java rubber estates as tappers and weeders, and many more go over to Borneo and Sumatra, where labour is scarce, to work on similar plantations there. They are drawn from the most densely populated parts of Java, tempted by heaven only knows what dreams of prosperity in these, to them, distant lands. Their El Dorado, alas, soon fades in the light of reality, and many of them suffer tragically from homesickness; so much so that suicides among them are not uncommon. The incoming and outgoing streams of these humble migrants at the ports of Sumatra and Borneo are sights not easily forgotten.

The lives of women in the poorer regions of Java whence these emigrants come, notably in the Sultanates of Solo and Djokdja, are very unlike those of the bright little butterflies that flit in and out among the tea bushes of the Preanger. Their appearance too is different. The colourful clothing that elsewhere in Java is everyday wear is not for them, and they dress, except on high days and holidays, in a uniform shade of dark blue. This depressing fashion is due not so much to poverty as to politics. Indigo[1] is grown here by decree of the native rulers who, from time immemorial, have derived much profit from the dyeing industry, and their insistence upon the wearing of indigo-dyed stuffs by their

[1] See also Chapter X.

subjects is one of the few prerogatives remaining to them under Dutch rule, with lamentable results upon local colour.

Bales of cotton material of this doleful hue are exposed for sale in every shop and *pasar* in the Sultanates; and so, when poor Mrs Ah Wan or Kartjo has at last managed to save up enough to buy a new *sarong*, she is denied the innocent feminine delight of choosing among the myriad gay patterns available to other Javanese women. She has to get what poor thrill she can out of a dull deep blue that differs from her old one only in being stiff and clean: a deprivation that every woman will well understand.

Despite their rather drab appearance, however, the women of the Sultanates are cheerful enough; and if their standard of living is lower than that in other parts of Java it does not seem to worry them. Even the poorest, who hire themselves out to labour which is proportionately greater in relation to their size than we should consider reasonable loading for ponies or donkeys, never seem in the least degree depressed by it, and are always ready with a cheery smile, or to chatter with others similarly laden. But it is noticeable that youth for them is even shorter lived than among the other women of Java, and that with its passing there dies all instinct to attract. A very short time after marriage their mouths are discoloured and distorted with betel-chewing; and it is not long before appearance matters to them so little that they, as well as the older men, adopt the ugly habit of holding a whole big betel nut in their mouths instead of the usual rolled up *sirih*, and you will see them walking unconcernedly to the *pasar* with lips and cheeks distended as though by a hideously bloated cigar.

The loads that these frail-looking small women carry are unbelievable. I have seen a wizened little wisp of humanity, who must have been sixty years old, climb day after day down the side of a steep, slippery ravine, from a mountain village to the bed of a rushing stream, and plod up again carrying on her back, slung in a broad blue *selendang*, a basket, into which her own shrunken little body might have been packed several times over, filled with smooth round stones from the river bed, each the size of a man's head. She was bent double, but apparently quite undistressed, as she returned time after time with such burdens to a great pile in the compound of a village official, kept there to be drawn upon for communal building purposes. One of these stones is a dead weight that no white woman, however well nourished, would care to carry far on the level. How she would deal with a dozen of them on a steep, slippery, rock strewn climb, heaven alone knows.

Other women in these same regions hire themselves out to Chinese or Arab merchants, to carry the products of one *dessa* to the markets of another. There is much of this inter-*dessa* trade in Java, as many places have their own local industries, specialising in *batik*, basket weaving, hats, whips, pottery, and so on. The women carriers of baskets, who cross the Lawoe mountain range from Magelang on one side to Solo on the other, one of the longest and steepest passes in Java, are so completely hidden under their loads that they look like weird, shapeless moving monsters, ten or twelve feet high. But enormously bulky though these loads are, they are not so appallingly weighty as those of tiles or earthenware, which also are transported fifteen or twenty miles by scraggy little women over a road that for at least eight miles climbs relentlessly at grades that are formidable even to the mere unencumbered hiker. But they plod steadily up, swinging their thin bare arms, chattering and often even singing, as they breast the endless slopes in long single files. These women, and others who do exceptionally heavy work, wear a long piece of blue dyed cotton material called a *kain pandjang* wound tightly round the abdomen, and another round their breasts: a primitive form of stays that is probably the best ever invented. All Javanese women wear this support when they go back to work after childbirth.

Like other Oriental women, the Javanese are experts at carrying heavy loads on their heads. The secret of success in this connection is to coil a piece of an old *sarong* or a small towel into a round pad on which to perch the burden. Sometimes, after disposing of a load, they appear to forget that the pad is still in place, and will walk airily along wearing what looks like a clumsy turban. Or they will unroll the towel and use it to protect a precious Tanggerang straw hat, worn for shade occasionally in the fields, with very comical effect.

No kind of weight carrying comes amiss to Javanese women.

The enormous earthenware jars in which they fetch water from the streams for domestic purposes are slung in the ever useful *selendang* on their backs; or, failing these, they will fill a four gallon paraffin tin, of which, like white colonials, they have learned the usefulness, and carry it, brimming, uphill for a mile or more.

Needless to say, human nature being what it is, this labour that offers itself so willingly for even the heaviest of work, is fully exploited by those in a position to employ it, be they Arab, Chinese, or European. And when the labourer is so eager to earn even the small amount offered, and the employer is in genuine need of labour, it would take a wise head indeed to determine the ethics of the case.

A very different aspect of women's life in the Sultanates is that of the dancers, or *ronggeng*. They are part of the royal entourage and there are more than a thousand of these dainty little ladies in each *kraton*. This, though commonly called the Sultan's "palace," is in reality a town within a town, for an Eastern prince's entourage is a population in itself. The *kraton* at Djokdja, rebuilt about 1760, houses between 15,000 and 20,000 people, and that at Solo rather fewer. Each of the two Sultans have bodyguards of 1000 men. The Djokdja *kraton* measures about 1200 yards by 800, with an outer wall 14 feet high and 15 feet thick, and an inner wall of earth.

The royal dancers were formerly to be found also at the courts of all the now vanished Javanese princes. They are believed to be the successors of the temple dancers in Hindu times, who represented the celestial *Apsaras* so familiar in the carvings at Angkor and elsewhere.

In the days of the Javanese sultans' glory, before the Dutch set the conquered princes' houses in order, poor orphan girls became automatically the property of the reigning prince, who took the pick of them for his harem, and handed the rest over to men in his employ, who sent them out as prostitutes and collected their earnings on their royal master's behalf. From which it may be seen that the prerogatives of Javanese royalty were not always of the nicest.

The art of dancing, held in very high esteem in the great days of the native kings, came very near to extinction with their fall. A Javanese, R. A. Soerjodinnigrat, writing in

Wasita, and Dr Krom in *Hindoe-Javaansch Kunst*, both say that dancing was a national art of importance in the time of King Airlangga, about A.D. 1000. And in the reign of Sri Hayam Woeroek, who reigned over Madjapahit from 1334 to 1389, the king and his family took part with their dancers in the ballet, and also sang, and directed the *gamelan*. With the fall of Madjapahit in 1478 the Hindus faithful to the defeated régime fled to Bali, to the Tengger mountains, and to Balambangan in the extreme south east corner of Java, facing the Bali coast. In these places the old dances have survived, becoming blended in Bali, however, with those already in vogue there.

The *ronggeng* dances were of a popular order and designed to appeal to simple folk. Such themes as "the hen laying an egg," for instance, is an old favourite. But nowadays the royal families both in Djokdja and Solo are making great efforts to revive the more classical forms, particularly the once famous *Serimpi* and *Bedaya*, which are being studied under the direction of the Crown Princess. The well-known native educationist Ki Adjar Dewantoro is also taking much interest in the work.

These dances are most "select," and the performers are drawn only from among the native nobility, whose duty it is to appear on certain special occasions. Four or five girls dance the *Serimpi*; and in the *Bedaya* there are nine, representing the nine nymphs of Ratoe Kidoel, King of the South. In this latter dance, if it should happen that not enough girls of high rank are available, the parts may be taken by well-born boys in women's costumes. No words are spoken by the performers, a *dalang* (showman) speaking for them as in the *wayang*.

The school education system introduced by the Dutch, which has had so marked an effect upon the male population of Java, has affected the women but little. Life is too serious an affair to them to allow even its earliest stages to be wasted upon such fripperies as book learning; that is reserved for the Lords of Creation. There are no illusions in the Javanese woman's mind concerning her place in the scheme of human affairs, and she knows and keeps that place without the least ill feeling. Most Javanese women are lovable little people, simple and unsophisticated, grateful for the smallest gifts, and for wages that by our standards seem a pitifully small recompense for so much devoted labour. There is something very touching, too, in their easily inspired affection, and the little spontaneous gestures with which they show it.

It is the custom here to have a "wash-*baboe*" who collects your clothes of yesterday early every morning, launders and irons them, and brings them back during the day in a fresh and delectable pile, every separate item of which is an object of pride to her. If you admire her work as, if you have a heart in your body, you must, your little maid will probably show you each article, and describe with childlike pride just how she ironed this one or that, perhaps even a handkerchief carefully pressed from the wrong side so as to show up the embroidery. If for any reason you should go in search of her when she is at work, you will find her hard at it in the wash house, singing to herself or chatting to the others, up to her elbows in soapsuds, with her tight, long sleeved jacket soaked through, for Javanese women never roll up their sleeves as we do, or crouched beside her big charcoal iron, fanning it with a little bamboo *kipas*. But by the time she brings back your linen she will have changed into fresh garments, and appear spick and span and dainty, complete with gold pins and brooch, and perhaps a gold necklace and pendant.

I am quite sure to be accused of exaggerating the Javanese servant's virtues. So I had better admit at once that they are not perfect. In many respects the native maid has much the same ideas as her white prototype: as, for instance, when she "does" a room she likes to demonstrate her extreme industry by making as thorough an upheaval as possible of everything in it. She turns chairs and tables upside down, rolls up mattresses, takes cushions off the chairs and puts them on the window ledges, whence they often fall into the flower-beds, shakes mats, and does everything else she can think of to make your quiet sanctum uninhabitable. And should you happen to have a job to finish and try to carry on with it at your table, which stands like an island in the midst of a stormy sea, she is likely to assure you still further of her zeal by banging the chair seats nearest to you with her *sapoe lidi*, or even flicking the books under your very nose with a feather duster.

But the great essential wherein she differs from her opposite number in Europe is this: if you should decide that you can bear the hullabaloo no longer, and you mildly but firmly ordain that the spring cleaning shall be deferred to some more convenient time, she will acquiesce at once with a smiling "*Baik, Nyonya*" (All right, madam), and vanish swiftly from your sight without the slightest sign of rancour, leaving you to think of the thunderclouds that would gather about your defenceless head if ever you should dare to issue such a counter-order to an English housemaid.

The ordinary routine of housekeeping in Java provides the European mistress with such constant and colourful entertainment that it is never boring. She never looks up, from whatever she may happen to be doing, but some picturesque person or other is trotting up the drive bearing something eatable for her consideration. It may be a man with twin loads of green oranges, doerian, mangoes, melons, mangosteen, or sapodilla; or a woman in gaily flowered *sarong* and *badjoe*, balancing on her head a round basket from which peer the inquisitive little faces of two or three fowls, apparently greatly enjoying their last ride to eternity as they squat snugly with their legs tied together; or she may carry one under her arm, caressing it gently now and then as though it were a pet kitten, and not doomed to an early and ignominious execution. And how much pleasanter it is for the housewife to stroke the soft warm feathers while she chaffers amiably over a price, that may rise as high as sixpence for a nice roasting fowl, than to purchase it in all its trussed and chilly nakedness on an English poulterer's bench at some twelve times the price! Or perhaps to buy, for a change from more conventional vegetables, the curly, unopened fronds of wild bracken which the women of mountain *kampongs* gather and carry round in baskets for sale.

There is one duty, conscientiously performed by all Java *kampong* women, which is not likely to commend itself to persons of fastidious taste, but is a most necessary item in the routine of village life. This, not to put too fine a point upon it, is the de-lousing of their own and their daughters' long, luxuriant hair. You will often see a native mother sitting cross-legged before her house door, with her daughter's head, or that of a friend, on her knees, bending over it with intent gravity as her slender, agile fingers search for the prey. It is not a "naice" pursuit, it is true. But it does not reflect so adversely upon native standards of cleanliness as is often supposed. The Javanese are naturally clean; but not all their passion for bathing can compete with the speed with which parasites multiply in the conditions of *kampong* life. Sleeping, as these humble people do, crowded side by side on the floors of small windowless bamboo and wooden houses, in a tropical climate, the prevention of parasites is impossible, and they accordingly apply the only practical means of cure.

There is however another custom in which Javanese women are concerned which has not, so far as I know, been adopted elsewhere. The Javanese are intensely hospitable, and no passing traveller on his way through a country *dessa* is ever refused a meal and shelter for the night. Formerly, hospitality went much farther; and the really genial host did not feel that the demands of true courtesy had been fulfilled unless he also lent his wife to the guest. This custom is officially extinct in Java, except perhaps in very remote *kampongs* where old-fashioned standards of hospitality still obtain; but it is doubtless still *de rigueur* in the farther islands of the archipelago.

It is a far cry from such domestic amenities to the native wives of Europeans, about whom so much has been said and written. Of late years the Dutch authorities have facilitated more and more the marriage of even the lower ranks of their Colonial army and navy with white women; but, nevertheless, the native wives and "housekeepers" of the men have earned much praise, and the Dutch officials give them credit on the whole for an excellent influence.

Women are almost entirely responsible for the making of *batik*, the distinctive dress material of the Javanese people. This, however, is decidedly "work of national importance," and must be dealt with in another chapter.

CHAPTER TEN

Batik, *Dyeing*, & *Other Crafts*

JAVANESE *batik* cannot by any means be lightly dismissed as merely one of many native crafts and industries. It is much more than that. It is bound up in the history of the people; its classic designs embody all sorts of obscure associations with ancient legends; and there is nothing quite like it in any other part of the world. Its survival as the material of the national costume of the people in face of all foreign influences is strangely consoling. For the time and care that go to its making, the frequent repetition of drawing, dyeing, drying, re-dyeing and re-drying upon every single piece of the millions upon millions of *sarongs*, *selendangs*, and *iket kepala* in daily wear are proof positive that here at least patient and painstaking craftsmanship is still alive in a senselessly hustling hurrying world.

There are many theories about the origin of this curiously characteristic art. But the only thing that seems to be certain is that it is a true indigenous product and not an importation. The earliest known record of *batik* making dates from the year 1518 and was found at Galoeh, South Cheribon, at that time a Sultanate; but it is generally believed to have been made from much more ancient times.

The making of what must once have been the generally used foundation of *batik*, an unbleached handwoven material, is still carried on in a few very isolated places where cotton is grown by the natives; and *batik* that is dyed on this is called *lawon* or *kain ketel*. It may be easily recognised by its uneven pattern, due to the coarse weave of the stuff.

But with this exception, all the *batik* made and worn nowadays in Java is dyed on machine woven material, until recently all imported, first from Lancashire, then from Japan and India; but now increasingly the product of a newly established weaving industry in Java itself.

The Javanese use many beautiful classical designs in their *batik* which they claim are exact reproductions of patterns handed down for hundreds of years. Knowledge of these

Batik, *Dyeing*, & *Other Crafts* 139

designs is surprisingly widespread among the people; and often a simple, apparently quite uncultured countryman will recognise and put names to specimens shown to him, at first glance.

The designs are classified in groups, each with its own name, with a sort of central motif which appears in each of the well known patterns belonging to it. There is, for example, the "*Semen*" group (from *semi* = to grow), in which the same tangle of leaves and flowers threads its way here and there amid whatever else the pattern may contain. In the "*Semen Nogobisikan*" they entwine themselves about a lyre-bird; in "*Semen Redjoenowidjojo*" about multiple horns and bunches of fruit; in "*Semen Goenong*" they radiate from a mountain shaded by an umbrella; in "*Semen Groedo*" about a winged lyre and flights of birds; in "*Semen Remeng*" amid wings rising from a curious rectangular centre-piece and a maelstrom of intricate curves and twiddles, and so on. Other groups are "*Kembang Kentang*," "*Djonggrong*," "*Djlamprang*," and "*Tjakar Wok*," all of which names, and many more, fall trippingly from native lips, and sound much more musical than might be supposed from their forbidding appearance in cold type.

Easier for our European eyes to recognise is the familiar blue and white "*Kelengan*," dyed with indigo only, and much worn by Chinese ladies. It was also a favourite with Europeans up to a generation ago, when the *sarong-kebaya* (*kebaya* = a long jacket) was the prevailing feminine fashion among them in Java. The rarer "*Latar Iring*," with its black ground, which the name literally means, and a green and yellow pattern called "*Paré Anom*," young rice, are also simple ones for foreigners to distinguish from the rest.

"*Kain Pradan*," with gold leaf added to the dyed pattern, were, and still are, made only for nobles, and may cost a hundred or two hundred guilders each.

Batik making, that is to say, the method of dyeing these patterns on what the Javanese call *blanco* (plain white material: the name doubtless a legacy from the Portuguese), is probably almost exactly the same to-day as it was hundreds of years ago. The designs are drawn by hand in hot wax which is poured out of a tiny vessel called a *tjanting*, rather like a doll's teapot, in somewhat the same way as a cake is iced with sugar. The wax is warmed in a special pan called a *wadjan* over the small round charcoal cooking-stove or *anglo* used by every native. The drawing on a *sarong* of one of the intricate patterns described above is a matter of weeks; but time is nothing to the happy and sensible Javanese. It would be all the same to the *batik* maker, except for its effect on her revenue, if it took a year. Nor is she in the least dismayed at the infinite labour of "undrawing," as it were, parts of the complicated design over and over again with acid, after each dyeing, fixing in a bath of water, palm sugar, lime, and alum, and drying. The wax prevents the action of the dye upon the material, and its removal allows each successive colour to take effect. The patient, unhurrying deliberation of the whole process, so foreign to the spirit of the Western world, is almost incredible in these days. It is a home industry, and many Javanese women dye *batik* in their spare time, by way of making a little pocket money; but mostly *batik* is made in Chinese owned factories, places that do not at all resemble what the term conveys to European ears. Usually they are nothing more than rough *bilik* sheds in which the dye baths are housed, standing in a compound where the *batik* is hung out to dry after dyeing on long parallel rows of bamboo supports.

The *batik* habit is deeply ingrained in even the humblest Javanese; and to meet the poor man's demand for a cheaper quality, which is still more or less the genuine article, the pattern is printed on the material with copper stamps dipped in hot wax, instead of being drawn by hand. These are called *batik tjap-tjapan* (= printed stuff). The rest of the process is the same as in the hand drawn kind, but as a rule only two colours are used in order to keep the price down to the minimum.

Formerly all the colours came from native dyes, and a great proportion of them do so still. But aniline dyes, which the Javanese call *sepoehan*, are being used more and more. In one district, that of Pekalongan, on the north coast, they have ousted native dyes and patterns altogether, and the "Pekalongan *kain*," adorned with gay flowery patterns like those of European chintzes, are recognisable at a glance even

Batik, *Dyeing*, & *Other Crafts*

by the veriest foreign tyro in such matters. They are known to natives as *bang-bangan*, and are much in vogue among smart young Javanese men on courting bent, especially in West Java.

The predominating colours of true native design *batik* vary in every part of Java. Blue and a warm brown are the favourites in Djokja and Solo. Red is much used with brown and orange in West Java, and seldom seen in the East. But, generally speaking, the dyes are legion, and the Javanese are as full of wisdom in getting colours from innumerable different fruits, barks, leaves, and flowers as they are in the concocting of their amazing pharmacopœia of *obats*.[1]

The following are among a few of those most generally known and used. *Benkoedoe*, a bush found wild all over Java. The skin of the root produces a red dye; the fruit is edible, and also makes a popular hair shampoo. *Setjang* is another bush that grows wild and is also much planted for the red dye got from boiling the wood which, by the way, is so hard that it can be used in place of nails. *Bakoe*, or mangrove bark, yields a black dye. *Koenjit padi* is a mountain plant whose root, when cut up and infused like tea, produces a rich yellow. Other yellows are derived from the dried fruit of the huge *nangka*, from the gardenia, from *Konkoma*, a sort of crocus, and from the padding round the seeds of *kasoemba kling*, a tree easy to mistake for the well known *ramboetan*. It has a very similar red fruit which yields a red dye. This tree is much planted by the Javanese on boundaries, in decorative avenues at the entrance to *kampongs*, and formerly round coffee plantations, the belief being widespread that it was a protection from the dreaded coffee disease.

A deep red dye is also got from the familiar red *Colius*, which the Javanese call *bayam merah*, and from the red *hibiscus*. Green is made from the sap of many kinds of leaves, particularly *daoen telang* (*Clitorea*), *daoen katoek* (*Sauropus*), and *kore legi* (*Phaseolus*). The flower of *Clitorea* also yields ultramarine blue.

But most interesting of all the natural dyes used in Java is indigo, which has played a part in history that is far from

[1] Obat = medicine. Classified and illustrated in *Indische Kreuden* by Mev. J. Kloppenburg.

being suggested by its nondescript appearance. It has been known in Asia from time immemorial, and in Europe since that of the Romans, who called it *pigmentum Indicum* (Indian dye), from which, no doubt, the name "indigo" is derived. Marco Polo referred to it as "endego." Its Sanskrit name is "nili" or "nilini," meaning dark blue, which was corrupted by the Portuguese to "anil." In Java it is called *nila*, a similarity that suggests the probability that the plant was introduced here by the early Indian settlers. It was a very widespread native culture when the Dutch arrived in Java, and they were quick to see its profitable possibilities. They shipped large quantities to Europe, and the records of the Dutch East India Company mention three shiploads of it sold in 1631 for 500,000 florins.

After Roman times, indigo seems to have disappeared from European commerce until the Middle Ages, when its reappearance was greeted with violent opposition from the powerful financial interests connected with the cultivation of woad. An agitation to prevent its use was worked up; indigo was described as "Devil's Dye," and in France the death penalty was actually imposed upon anyone who dared to use it. In England, Queen Elizabeth ordered its use to be restricted; and in Germany the famous Nuremberg dyers were forced to take a solemn oath every year that they would use no other dye than woad for blue dyeing. It was not until 1737 that the use of indigo was permitted by law in France. Opposition to its use is said to have been due to ignorance of its origin for, until the beginning of the eighteenth century, it was popularly supposed to be either a dangerous mineral dye or else an animal product derived from urine! One cannot help suspecting that these notions may well have been the result of shrewd propaganda by the financial concerns interested in ousting the newcomer's unwelcome competition.

Forced culture of indigo was much increased in Java under the famous, or infamous, van den Bosch, in whose time it was grown in over one hundred large plantations in the Preanger (West Java), as well as in Middle Java. The crop was "rotated" with rice in the same manner as sugar, indigo being a plant that severely exhausts the soil. Indigo culture was bitterly hated by the Javanese because they were often forced

Batik, *Dyeing*, & *Other Crafts* 143

to work at great distances from their home *kampongs*; so much so that a saying was common among them that "they were born, married, and died in the indigo fields." They were paid nine cents (less than twopence) per day. Happily for them, sugar began to prove more profitable than indigo, and consequently indigo planting decreased as that of sugarcane increased. Indigo was finally ousted as an article of European commerce by aniline dyes; and it has now reverted to the place it occupied in pre-Dutch days as a product for native use. Even that might well have disappeared had it not been for the profit the wretched plant yields to the native princes, by whose orders it is cultivated in the Sultanates.

The seed is sown about the end of May, after the rice harvest, and planted out about a month later. It grows into a tall, weedy plant known as *tarum* or *tom*, with small oval leaves and little red flowers in bunches which produce tiny pods containing yellow seeds. The whole plant is cut, steeped, fermented, and boiled in the indispensable paraffin tin, and the dye is squeezed from the resultant pulp.

Cotton goods have been increasingly woven of late years in Java in small Chinese and native owned mills; and recently Dutch enterprise started the weaving industry on a large scale at Garoet, West Java. Here, not only white material as the basis for *batik*, but also artificial and real silk, and coloured cotton *sarongs* are woven at the rate of some half million yards per year, as well as the greenish khaki drill worn by the army. It remains to be seen whether in the fullness of time the Javanese will be weaned from their traditional *batik* and, following the example of the Indians, adopt as their national dress the ugly quasi-tartan *sarongs* like cheap tablecloths that are the product of the mills. But I doubt it. The Javanese are conservative, and tradition dies hard. Moreover it is a hopeful sign that the machine industry has already been forced to give in, in one particular, to native prejudice.

A *sarong*, as distinct from a *kain*, is sewn up into a sort of skirt, which native custom demands must be seamed up by hand. So all attempts to foist upon the populace *sarongs* with nice neat seams stitched up on a sewing-machine, or woven in one piece without any seam at all, were a complete frost. They were politely but firmly declined. The innovation was ignominiously abandoned, and in order to capture the native market some thousands of native women are now employed to sew up the seams of the factory produced *sarongs* by hand instead.

The Javanese are as conservative in their housebuilding as they are in their dress. Their national building material is bamboo, split into strips and woven into sheets of tough, stiff fabric known as *bilik*, which is mounted on a bamboo or timber framework. To anyone living in Java the sight of it is so familiar and ordinary that it is taken as much for granted as are bricks and mortar in England. But a recent London broadcast to schools announcing that "houses in Java are built of palm leaf," a piece of information by now doubtless entered in our educational archives, served as a reminder that the making of *bilik* is not appreciated by stray European visitors. It is a skilled and essentially Javanese craft; general in native housebuilding throughout Java, but little used in other parts of the archipelago.

The bamboo stems are split with a sharp *parang* (a curved and deadly native knife) into narrow strips which are laid out on an open space and interwoven, sometimes into patterns almost as intricate as that of a knitted pullover, a task by no means as easy as it looks in the hands of a skilled *bilik* maker, for the strips are often twenty or thirty feet long.

Few Java countrymen cannot make *bilik* for themselves when occasion arises, but there are, of course, experts in this as in all trades, and in many *pasars* you may see stacks of the big sheets for sale. They are carried away by the purchaser to the scene of building operations, either doubled into a huge curve inside which the bearer walks with only his feet visible, or else carried upright, lashed flat against a bamboo supported on the bearer's shoulder. Arrived at the building site it is laid on the ground, and the doorways or other openings cut out.

An allied craft is grass weaving and basket making, which seems to be instinctive in Javanese men and women. Almost any one of them will twist up a neat carrier of grass or palm leaf at any moment it may be required. But here again there are, of course, "professionals" and baskets of every sort and size for every conceivable purpose, as well as mats, hats, and fine woven cigarette cases and other such small articles, are

Batik, *Dyeing*, & *Other Crafts*

made and sold by the million. Their makers do not grow fat on the proceeds of their skill. Containers the size of an ordinary barrel, in which vegetables are packed for transport to market, are supplied by village basket makers at the rate of five cents (about a penny) each!

Pottery is a native craft throughout all the archipelago, born no doubt of practical necessity. It is mostly made, naturally, wherever good clay for the purpose happens to be found, and in Java its transport from such regions to others not so favoured make it one of the most familiar sights on the roads: loaded house high on *grobaks*, on the backs of women or pack ponies, or hung in baskets from the two ends of men's shoulder yokes.

Much of the pottery is made by women who work the potter's wheel with a cord made of *loeloep* (the bark fibre of the *waroe* tree) tied to a bamboo and operated with the foot. Among the innumerable shapes and sizes made are one or two that soon become familiar to everyone who travels the roads of Java. Most common of all is the *gendi* (also called *lantingan*), a little drinking vessel with a spout, used by every native. At the other end of the scale for size is the *gentong* or *genoek*, an enormous earthenware jar used for water storage at native houses that are some distance from a stream. They are usually buried in the ground up to the neck. They are transported in couples, one at each end of a *pikoelan*, encased in stout split bamboo baskets woven to fit them. A smaller size jar, holding about five gallons, called a *djoen*, is used by women for fetching water from a stream. These are to be seen in use a dozen times a day, either balanced on the bearer's head or slung on her back in the indispensable *selendang*. The *kendil* and *kenaron*, small and large rice pots respectively, are always much in evidence, as is the *kuali*, a cooking pot very like a French *marmite*. And the *anglo*, the bucket shaped charcoal cooking stove, is of course the most familiar and ubiquitous of all. The making of tiles is an old native craft, and not learnt from Europeans, though the style and shape has changed under modern influences. Ancient buildings at Madjapahit and elsewhere in Hindu Java were tiled with interlocking curved tiles admirably designed to carry off heavy rain.

Like the Chinese, from whom, probably, they learned the art, the Javanese are good brass workers, and their productions contribute much to the decoration of all homes in Java. The Dutch are fond of mingling brass with china in the adornment of their charming *voorgalerijs*, and though they use much of their own imported brasswork there is plenty of room for Javanese and Chinese also. The Javanese designs do not reach a very high level artistically, perhaps, but they are very pleasing. The familiar *wayang* figures are often introduced.

The best of the old luxury crafts of Java have died out with the passing of the former wealthy royal courts, whose pride it was to maintain and encourage them. The glory of the goldsmiths has departed with the rest, but their art, though very humble nowadays compared with that of former times, is preserved to some extent in the people's love of adornment which is at the same time a form of investment and of insurance against a rainy day. Every Javanese woman who can afford it, or whose husband or father can afford to give them to her, owns gold ornaments of some sort. If you happen to see your cook when she arrives in the morning, before she changes into her working clothes, she may very likely be wearing a gold chain and pendant round her neck, and her gaily coloured muslin jacket may be fastened down the front with three or four gold brooches. Another day she may appear, neat and clean as ever, but minus the necklace, and with the gold brooches replaced by ordinary safety pins. In response to inquiry she will tell you cheerfully that they are in the *Roemah Gadean*! (the pawnshop). There is nothing in the least embarrassing to her about the confession because one of the chief objects of possessing them is their usefulness as a source of cash when funds are short. No Javanese is capable of putting money aside for an emergency; but it is the understood thing that whenever there is a sudden strain on the family exchequer, the first and obvious remedy is to put the womenfolk's gold ornaments "up the spout," to be redeemed again just as naturally when the financial crisis is past.

In the big towns the Chinese have almost entirely absorbed the goldsmith's trade that this custom supports. But often in a country *dessa* you will find a tiny shop, built of *bilik*, and perhaps a bare four or five feet from the ground to the over-

Batik, *Dyeing,* & *Other Crafts* 147

hanging tiled roof, bearing the sign: TOEKANG MAS (goldsmith), with a rough painting of a ring or gold ornament. If you peep inside, you will see an old native squatted on the ground before a low bench, shaping out in the dim light the soft pale gold rings and brooches for which, even among the simple country people, there is such a constant demand.

An ancient art now adapted to modern markets is that of decorating specially prepared buffalo hide. The immensely thick leather is thinned down till it is so thin as to be almost transparent, cut and punched into lacelike patterns, and delicately coloured. Formerly used in the making of *wayang* figures, this unique and beautiful fabric is now mounted in fans, lampshades and other articles in well deserved demand by Europeans.

At the other end of the scale in leather work is the rather rough and ready saddlery worn by Java's countless ponies. It is no uncommon sight to see a country saddler at work by the roadside in some out of the way *kampong* carrying out an order for a local client. His leather is tanned as a rule with the bark of an acacia called *pilang*, or of two sorts of *cassia*, the *tangoeli* and *boengboengdelan*. *Mimosa* (the "wattle" of Australia) is used for better class work; and *gambir*, which is more expensive than any of the others, only for the very best.

Javanese craftsmen have discovered in the buffalo's horns, as well as in its hide, a material full of possibilities for the making of saleable articles. He seldom leaves what to him is the beaten track in the matter of design: birds, *wayang* figures, and the *kris* are his favourites; but for all their lack of originality the results are always characteristic and sometimes charming.

One of many local industries, confined to their own particular region, is the making of the immensely long tapering whips that are the pride of the *sado*-drivers of East Java. These are made in the Kediri district, from finely split *rotan* (rattan), plaited together and bound at intervals of a few inches with narrow bands of metal. The longer the slender whip that sways, gracefully as a young bamboo, above the little two wheeled carriage with its quick-trotting pony, the smarter feels the driver and his fare. The final touch is often added with a posy of flowers or ribbon at the tip.

148 Batik, *Dyeing*, & *Other Crafts*

Recently the Javanese have adopted a craft hitherto entirely a monopoly of the Chinese: that of making oiled paper umbrellas. In this country of sudden showers they are carried by every man, woman, and child during the wet monsoon, so that the industry is an important one. The old familiar Chinese *payong* is still to be bought in most village shops at the modest price of one *tali* (25 cents = 5*d*.); but the Javanese article, which is still cheaper, is becoming more and more popular, especially in East Java, where they are mostly made.

The making of *gapjak* (wooden sandals sold for two cents per pair) is so simple that it should perhaps scarcely be classed as a craft; but the sight of them, piled high on *grobaks* drawn by two big oxen, is so familiar that it deserves mention. They are to be seen, too, in twin man-high loads with their bearer squatted between them, at street corners and at the entrance of many *pasars*. The puzzle to the casual observer is to guess when all these enormous quantities of *gapjak* can be worn, for it is rare indeed to see a Javanese of the humbler class anything other than barefooted. They buy them, nevertheless, and the Chinese also. Among Europeans they are popular as bath sandals.

The superlative skill that went to the making of the famous bas-reliefs at Boroboedoer has not been bequeathed to the people of Java, any more than the art of the Khmers has come down to the Cambodians. A universal instinct for carving seems to be the fortunate monopoly of the natives of Bali. But the Javanese respond quickly to training in woodcarving, and they turn out work that would attract more attention if it had not to suffer comparison with that of their Balinese neighbours. Like the French in Indo-China, though on a lesser scale, the Dutch are now encouraging this and other almost vanished native arts, which are taught in schools at Djokja and elsewhere, and the work finds a ready sale.

True native carving has survived in West Java in the making of the wooden puppets or *golek* used in the *wayang* shows that are the accompaniment to every native ceremony. There are few villages of any size where you will not find a carver of these grotesque, jolly little figures, of which some fifty or sixty, all different, and so meticulously correct in every particular that they are easily recognisable to any native, are used in one performance. The finished figures are painted in gay colours, and dressed in *sarongs* of *batik*, into some of which a diminutive *kris* is stuck.

An allied art is the painting of these same classical figures on black woven material, to be hung as wall decorations. They are offered for sale at prices that can barely cover the cost of the paints and goldleaf used.

In recent years natives who possess artistic talent have been taking more and more to painting in European style, and they produce often really charming sketches of the lovely Java landscape in both watercolour and oils. There is no false pride about these humble artists, and their pictures are hawked about the streets, either by the blushing artist himself or by a coolie, as unaffectedly as though they were mangoes or haberdashery. The pioneers of this kind of art, who had the good fortune to make their appearance during the after the Great War boom, used to be able to ask, and often get, ten or twelve guilders for their pictures. But so many natives turned their artistic facility to account in the hope of making these quick and handsome profits that over production was the inevitable result; and nowadays you will be offered your choice of dozens of charming little watercolours at a fixed price of fifty cents, or oils at one guilder. I have often tried to imagine what would be the reactions of some of our best "arty" circles if they could see one of these least of their brethren carefully propping up his pictures on tables and chairs or against verandah posts for your inspection, and then standing back humbly, hoping for sales at a flat rate of tenpence per masterpiece. I have many of their little pictures in my possession, and they do more to call up memories of the lovely land of their origin than all the hundreds of photographs I ever took.

The Javanese artist not only sells his pot boilers at prices to suit the times but, like his more distinguished *confrères* elsewhere, he has a keen business sense, and is not above making a bit "on the side." If you buy paintings to-day the news travels so swiftly through the appropriate channels that there will certainly appear to-morrow, apparently by the merest coincidence, another neat little native equipped with mitre, mounts, mouldings, glass, and all the rest of the picture framing paraphernalia. He will frame your purchases for you, skilfully and neatly as in any London shop, squatted on the path in your front garden, all for a modest guilder apiece.

The true assessment of a work of art in terms of cash is always difficult. And quite apart from Old Masters and suchlike, why should you be able to buy a delightful little landscape from a Javanese for one guilder and be asked twenty pounds for one that pleases you no better by a European visiting artist? The explanation is beyond me; but my native house-boy had no doubts as to how the proper price of a painting should be arrived at. Inspecting critically one that I had just bought from a Javanese hawker, old *kartjo* asked how much I had paid for it. I told him, a guilder and a half. He shook his head sadly. "It was too much," he said. "It is not worth it. The paint on it did not cost nearly all that!"

The pathetically low price of all native made articles makes the contrast with those asked in European shops in Java all the more startling. Accustomed to the endless variety of ingenious and charming toys sold in every native *pasar*, little birds made of painted shells nodding their heads on an inch of wire spring, quaint tiny *wayang* figures with jointed arms, and the like, at prices never above a penny, I picked up one day in a European "fancy shop" a little egg cosy, thinking it would do to post home in a letter to a child. I put it down again hurriedly when I learned that the privilege of being knitted by white fingers raised the value of the trifle to eighty-five cents, though any native could have copied and improved upon it, and would have sold it gladly for five!

CHAPTER ELEVEN

A Word about Eurasians

THE sweeping assertions commonly made about "natives" are surpassed, if anything, by the clichés so glibly quoted by Europeans on the subject of Eurasians. To most British people the very word is anathema; but many of them are as ignorant of the subject as their prejudice is strong, and they seem never to make the slightest effort to repair it. Superior persons obviously feel that the last word on the subject has been said when they remark with an omniscient air that "Eurasians always combine the worst qualities of both races," and leave it at that. But the matter of "crossing" two human racial types is far too complex and important to be so lightly dismissed; and nowhere less so than in this corner of Asia, where persons of mixed blood are so numerous that they form an anything but negligible part of the community. We seem prone to forget, moreover, that mankind has been "crossing" since the beginning of history; and that such a thing as a "pure" human type, if indeed it exists outside the lowest and most isolated of human strata, must be a rarity indeed.

Such careless thinking and ignorance of essential facts is all the more remarkable in view of the study that is given to the matter of types and quality when the breeding of cattle and other domestic animals is in question. In their case it is taken for granted that a good cross will be produced when both parties are of good quality, and that failing this the result will be a poor one. So, obviously, it is with the blending of human types that go to the making of the Eurasian. Given poor stock in both European and Asiatic, say, for instance, a hobbledehoy Dutch trooper and some immature native *kampong* girl, one of the sort that is drawn as by a magnet to garrison towns, what hope can there be that the offspring will be of any better quality than the parents?

But by no means all Eurasians belong to this category, though admittedly there are some. Dutchmen have been in Java for more than three centuries, and it was generations before the women of their own country came out in any numbers to join them. So they had no choice but to seek their domestic partners on the spot, as the rank and file of the Army do to this day. And though many, if not most, of the old East India Company's men were rough and brutal, there was, at least, a leaven of the better sort, and these sought wives among the upper class Javanese. The highest native circles of all, the families and connections of the Javanese princes who had ruled over the kingdoms into which the country was divided, were forbidden to the white conquerors, for the proud defeated aristocrats would have nothing to do with them. But there were plenty of natives of good family—shipowners, merchants, and others—who, accepting the inevitable, and looking at the situation from a business point of view, just as their forebears had done a thousand years earlier on the coming of the Indian conquerors, saw in the newcomers desirable *partis* for their daughters.

It was these marriages, with good blood on both sides, that founded some of the fine old "Indo" families of Java, with traditions of their own as proud and ancient as those of many pure-bred Europeans, and much more so than most. Others, bearing French names, trace their origins back to the early nineteenth century, when French armies under French officers fought side by side with the Hollanders against the English, and left behind them not only the families they founded, but also French words and expressions that are now a part of the language.

These families are true "gentlefolk," living proofs of a racial blend that happily combines the instinctive courtesy and hospitality of the Javanese with all that is best in the European. If the cavilling critic at this point contends that such people are rare compared with the numbers of the cruder sort of half caste whom he insists upon regarding as typical, is not the obvious retort the sad fact that in any community, of whatever race, the best are inevitably and always in the minority?

The social status of the Eurasian in Java, and elsewhere in the Dutch Indies, is quite different from their position in British colonies. In British Malaya, for instance, they have their own tennis, cricket, and other clubs, and live their lives more completely insulated from the European community than do the Chinese. For such is our peculiar snobbery that, in the case of a Chinese, wealth proves a passport to "select" British circles from which Eurasians are irrevocably barred.

The Dutch, however, unlike the British, are realists, and approach the matter in a more practical way. They recognise the absurdity of treating as a "minority" with unequal rights a section of the population which has existed in Java almost as long as the Dutch have been there themselves. The "Indos," therefore, possess full European status. And it has been estimated by some statisticians that as many as 75 per cent. of the population officially classed as "European" have native blood in their veins. Nor is there any rank, not excepting even that of Governor, from which they are debarred.

Those persons who ignorantly damn all Eurasians out of hand as "a poor lot" would be embarrassed indeed if it were their privilege to come in contact with some of the cultured, charming, and often highly intellectual descendants of the old "Indo" families. The women especially are notably gifted with poise and dignity, and dispense hospitality with an old-fashioned grace as rare in our time as it is charming. A few of these ladies, nowadays, alas! very few, too individual and too wise to be slaves of modern fashion, still wear in the country that most effective dress the *sarong* and *kebaya* which, a generation ago, was worn throughout Java by European, Chinese, and Javanese women alike. White women have now abandoned it entirely, and the "Indos" almost so. The few who are still faithful to it are those with the good taste to realise how extremely becoming this costume is to brown or brownish skins. Among the Chinese it is still the accepted feminine mode; and it is devoutly to be hoped that some day the cycle of time may bring the fashion into general favour again.

The difference in the appearance of "Indo" ladies when dressed in the *sarong* and *kebaya* that sets them off so well, and the same ladies wearing European styles, which presumably most of them feel more consistent with their official status, is unbelievable.

There are some, of course, in whom the European strain

predominates so strongly that Western dress suits them just as well as it does the "volbloed." But whenever the Javanese strain is apparent, often to great advantage, conferring fineness of bone, slender wrists and ankles, and long fingered shapely hands, the olive skin that goes with these assets, though not unpleasing in itself, is at once affected adversely when set off by a smart European frock. This, however, is a matter of degree. The well bred "Indo" lady usually has such excellent taste that when occasion demands that she shall wear European dress she chooses quiet styles and tones that suit her colouring. But others of humbler origin are apt to display a predilection for crude colours and extreme fashions that have the effect of vulgarising them completely.

Rather pathetic figures they are, though they wouldn't thank you to say so, these ultra smart young women with their shingled hair, their too bright, too tight frocks, and three inch heels! It would be interesting, if it were only possible, to find out what human ingredients can have contributed to the make up of some of them. Now, for instance, place the forebears of two attractive young creatures spending a holiday in a mountain resort, who appeared each day in different and ever smarter frocks, daintily smoking cigarettes in long holders, and were greatly concerned to preserve their dark brown skins from sunburn! "Just *look* at my arms, how burnt they are!" one would cry, holding out for inspection a shapely arm about the colour of a good willow calf shoe, on which the sun would have his work cut out to make the least impression. Carrying sunshades to shield equally brown faces, these two would set out for walks in high-heeled sandals and such skimpy skirts that to climb a bank on which to pose for a photograph was an affair of real difficulty; and they tired so soon that a rest seemed to be necessary at very short intervals, while past them plodded the tireless native women in an endless procession, steadily climbing the steep slopes, bowed almost double under the preposterous loads on their backs. Is it possible that such as these can really have been the ancestors, on one side, of the backboneless "young ladies" lolling limply on the bank?

The official recognition of all Eurasians as Europeans has certainly proved a sound policy from the national point of

A Word about Eurasians

view in modern times. For whatever may have been the case earlier in the colony's history, there can be no doubt nowadays of the Eurasians' dyed-in-the-wool "Dutchness," particularly in the case of the type represented by those two decorative young women. Needless to say, Dutch is their accepted mother tongue, and when they are proficient in native languages, it is considered as much a matter of scholarship for them as for us. There is no suggestion of any reason why they should possess any special facility.

Yet, now and then, even in the most ultra European, the other side of the mixed ancestry will show itself. I have seen a seductive young creature, dressed in all respects, save one, like a fashion plate, sitting at a well appointed hotel luncheon table, suddenly drop the sandals off her bare feet, and tuck up her legs under her chair in characteristic native fashion exactly as though she were squatting on her heels! But for that one odd lapse she could have held her own with the best at Ascot.

But even to those who are not quite the cream of the Eurasian population, the usual careless judgment does not apply. The "worst" qualities of a people are by no means confined to its humbler classes. And the children and children's children of poor parents on both European and native sides present a combination rather of the little peculiarities natural to people of humble station than of any "bad" qualities. The tastes and manners of the Dutch working class are no more "refined" than those of their opposite numbers elsewhere, and they share the same somewhat crude sartorial standards, whether those of Brixton or Broadway.

There is nothing "bad" about the "snoepen" habit, that is, of eating all sorts of strange snacks at all hours of the day: jelly, soup, cakes, corn-cobs, cold poached eggs, or any other tasty morsel that happens to be handy, which is prevalent among these innocent children of European colonisation and policy. It is simply the logical outcome of two strong characteristics transmitted side by side. The Dutch, not to put too fine a point upon it, are frankly fond of food. So are the Javanese; even the poorest of them go to endless trouble to provide astounding varieties of highly flavoured embellishments to the daily rice. The conditions that govern the lives of most of them, working out of doors from dawn to sunset, has made it habitual to them to eat snacks at all times and seasons, buying them from the countless itinerant food vendors who exist to supply this very demand. So what more natural than that two such elements should combine to produce the famous "snoepen" habit?

It is so fatally easy to criticise and to "smile superior." The habit of entering nothing but debits to the Eurasian account is so engrained that the possibility of credits is overlooked. Once rid your mind of borrowed, second hand generalisations and you are apt to be shamed by the example of these much maligned people. It could, for instance, only have been philosophy derived from the native side of their ancestry that enabled a Eurasian family of my acquaintance who fell on evil times to weather the lean period by cutting down a lavish European style commissariat to the simplest of native fare costing some twopence per head per day without reducing in the least their Dutch standard of perfection in an immaculately swept and garnished house. As another example, the windows of my home in Soerabaya looked out upon a tennis-court where a Eurasian four used not only to start play daily with the earliest light of dawn, but would play also, and a very high standard tennis too, all through the stifling afternoon hours of the *kentering* months (October and November) at the end of the East Monsoon. The heat at sea level in East Java during those months prostrates many even of those Europeans long accustomed to the tropics; hours when white women retire to their rooms and lie limp and effortless till the *djongos* brings tea, and the evening, relief; while white men, sweating and cursing, go about their business only because they must. During those same sweltering hours, those young Eurasians would be running, leaping, and smashing their hardest, obviously for the sheer joy of the thing, as oblivious to the temperature as though they were at Wimbledon.

It is rare to see a white woman walking in the town except in the cool of the evening. But the admixture of native endurance in the Eurasian endows her with greater energy, and it is by no means unusual to see Eurasian housewives on

A Word about Eurasians

their way home after doing their morning marketing at the *pasar*, walking along in the shade of the great trees beside the river, usually wearing sandals and carrying a sunshade, followed by one or more native women with baskets on their heads or hips containing the day's provisions.

It has often seemed to me that there is much to be said for a "cross" that blends the sporting energy and keenness of the European with the physical endurance of the Javanese that is their heritage from countless generations of ancestors with a superhuman capacity for toil. It sets one wondering whether, after all, by other standards than those we Europeans have come to accept as absolute, people combining the best, not the worst, qualities of European and Asiatic, may not prove in the fullness of time to be best fitted to guide the destinies of tropical countries and coloured populations.

CHAPTER TWELVE

Beasts of Burden & "Pets"

THE taxi of the town dwelling Javanese is the *sado*, a small two-wheeled trap drawn by a pony; and the clatter of fast-trotting hoofs, most familiar of all sounds in the Java towns, makes a delightfully gay impression upon the visitor, enhanced as it is by the cheery jingle of the bells with which the ponies' harness is adorned. But jolly though the effect may be upon the hearer, the gaiety begins and ends there as far as the ponies are concerned. Java has been well named a tropic paradise, but it is no paradise for domestic animals. Not because the Javanese is deliberately cruel, but because animals to him are not sentient creatures at all; they are merely machines which exist for his convenience. Hence the lot of those commonest and cheapest of his slaves, the ponies, is not a happy one.

There is another note in the merry sounding tunes played unceasingly in the streets by those small twinkling hoofs with their gay accompaniment of bells, and that is the sound of the long supple whip, falling flail like on flanks and sides: a combination of sound that becomes as familiar after a time as that of the instruments in an orchestra playing some well known air.

Sometimes the driver plies his whip mechanically in perfect time to the pony's trot, and the "thwack, thwack" mingles rhythmically with the tapping hoofs and jingling bells. At others, the tune is more varied, starting as the *sado* comes within earshot with the quick "tip-tap" of the trot, into which there break three or four swishing cuts of whip on flesh, changing the rhythm of the trotting hoofs to the "ti-tappat, ti-tappat" of a smart canter, soon to change down again to a trot as the pony tires; then the whip again, and then the canter, and so repeated *ad libitum*, *ad nauseam*, and for the pony, *ad damnaum*, till the sounds pass beyond your hearing. Our convention of driving a harness horse at the trot does not exist for the Javanese. If the pony can be made to go faster, make him! And with that end in view he plies his whip as mechanically as he jerks eternally on the bit in the sagging, ever dribbling mouth, totally unconscious of cruelty, and only doing what is equivalent in the native mind to pressing the accelerator of a motor car. As a result of this ceaseless pulling at the bit, it is seldom you will see a pony that has not tucked up the tip of a pink tongue against his cracked and bleeding mouth to ease the pain.

It is rare to see a pony whose knees do not show unmistakable marks of having been "down." The beautifully surfaced roads of whose upkeep the Dutch are so justly proud are a joy to the motorist, but they take a heavy toll of the gallant little trotters with their slippery shod hoofs, in conjunction with the universal bad driving.

The ponies are fed on the same principle that they are driven: simply to keep them going. The grass-sellers, whom you will see near every *pasar* and *sado* stand, and here and there along the streets, squatted beside baskets full of green grass in neat bundles which they keep fresh by sprinkling with a cigarette-tin of water now and then, are the "filling stations" for the little beasts that supply the motive power of Java's cheap transport. The average *sado* driver will feed his pony as it stands with sweating, heaving sides in a short respite between fares, shoving grass into the little creature's mouth without removing the bit, just as a motorist might put a "drop of juice" in his tank to carry him on for a few miles. The simile is strengthened by the custom of buying a supply of grass bundles and stowing them under the seat like a spare tin to give more fuel to the engine as required.

Whole families of natives or Chinese are often to be seen packed into one of these little carriages, looking as though at any moment the weight must swing the pony off the ground with its legs dangling in the air; and the fares paid are so low, anything from a cent (about a farthing) up to a penny or two, that profits are small; and it is perhaps not surprising that in the poorer parts of Java the ponies' food ration is cut down to the irreducible minimum that will keep them alive and moving.

In West Java, though the drivers are no better and have no more sentiment for their animals than the rest, they are more prosperous, and the appearance of their turn-outs is a matter of great pride, with the result that the ponies are better fed and cared for. They are well groomed, and many of them even sleek and fat; the *sadoes* are smart and bright with polished brass, the harness encrusted with glistening metal plaques, and the whip often adorned with a large muslin bow.

The grass, which is the principal feed, is cut by hand, often by children, on such little uncultivated land as there is, on roadside banks and the boundaries between ricefields. Not a blade is wasted, and the tightly packed double *pikoelan* loads are carried immense distances into the towns for sale. As a supplementary feed the ponies are given wet meal-mash which, especially in East Java where appearance is not considered, they must eat as they do their grass, at odd times between fares with bit in mouth, so that bits are nearly always clogged with the dirty remnants of a hundred such hasty meals, and the pony's nose, like a slum child's, badly in need of wiping! It never occurs to an East Javanese driver to remove the bit and give his pony a feed in peace, as we give a horse a nosebag; and though the Batavian driver does so, he is more influenced by a mixture of vanity and laziness than by consideration for the pony. He wants his turn-out to look smart because otherwise his fellow drivers will look down on him, and also do better business; and he has discovered that it is less trouble to take a bit out of a horse's mouth than to clean it.

Draught oxen, *sapis* as the native calls them, are fed at odd times in the same way, but being of more phlegmatic temperament they appear to accept the snacks offered to them with perfect equanimity. Anywhere along the roadside you may see a *grobak* driver squatting in front of his quietly munching pair of beasts as he feeds them with stalks of *glagah* (wild sugarcane) or *djagong* (maize). But these drivers jerk as unthinkingly on the ropes threaded through the sensitive quivering nostrils as do the pony drivers on reins and bit; and there is never a *sapi* whose flanks and sides are not scored with a network of whip-weals.

Oxen, so small as to look absurdly out of proportion to the huge clumsy *grobaks*, can pull an enormously heavy load once it is on the move; but sometimes to start it is beyond their power, especially if a wheel has sunk deep into asphalt softened by the hot sun. It is then that the native shows to advantage.

Beasts of Burden & "Pets"

The driver and a dozen passers-by will push and pull at the great wooden wheels, in diameter more than the height of a man, to help the gentle little cream coloured oxen as they sink to their knees in the effort to get the load started. Then they go swinging quietly off again with the big bells round their necks softly clinking, while the driver's mate stoops to pick up one of the leather shoes, worn by the beasts tied over their hooves with a thong, that has been lost in the struggle. This is a far pleasanter scene than some I have seen in white countries, merciless thrashings of willing horses in France, struggling to drag the deadweight of a great load of coal out of deep mud; Australian stockmen viciously kicking their mounts in the belly in sheer rage at some mishap; a "sportsman" at Singapore doing the same; exhibitions of brutality that you will never see in a lifetime among the Javanese. When the native is cruel it is due to lack of imagination, and to the impossibility of bringing home to him the idea that animals can suffer. At the bottom of the garden one day I found our cook who had been told to kill a goose for dinner. He was singing softly to himself as he sat in a shady corner with the bird held between his knees, sawing patiently away at its neck with a blunt old knife that would scarcely have cut cheese. When, horrified, I remonstrated and told him to dispatch the unfortunate bird quickly, he smiled gently and said in a reassuring tone: "*Saya, Toean*. It is all right. There is no hurry. This knife will kill it presently. It is not to be cooked until the evening!"

Very noticeable among the draught oxen are some, light chestnut in colour, with large white patches on the buttocks. These patches are the distinguishing marks of the *banteng* (the wild ox of the islands) now tamed and crossed with other breeds. They are perfectly docile, but will sometimes escape and run wild again if used in places within reach of the forests.

The lowest caste of the Java ponies are the pack ponies, much used in mountainous regions. In the densely populated Sultanates the fate of these stunted, inbred, underfed little slaves is a miserable one indeed. Often they are mere walking skeletons on to whose sharp-ridged narrow backs immense loads of stone, cement, chalk, pottery, manure, lime, and so on are piled in twin baskets balanced across rough pads of sacking, and secured with girths and cruppers of bark rope; and if you should chance to see them when the packs are removed, their hides are a patchwork of open and half healed sores. Yet it must not be forgotten that in those regions where these pitiful little beasts call for most sympathy the people inflict upon themselves as merciless a slavery as they do upon their pack animals, and carry loads just as outrageous, if not more so.

At the other extreme end of the scale are the saddle ponies ridden by well to do native countrymen, to whom, as to the Australian bushman, riding is the everyday mode of transport. It is an accepted convention among Europeans that the Javanese is no horseman, and judged by their driving they certainly are not. But some of the smartly turned out mountain riders, astride the fast *koré* that are their pride, have as pretty a seat as any horseman could desire.

It would be as difficult to imagine Java without its ponies as without its mountains, but it is doubtful whether the ponies were originally natives. Their ancestors are generally believed to have been imported by immigrants, anything from a thousand to two thousand years ago, so that there has been plenty of time for their increase. They breed now in countless numbers in most of the East Indian islands; and in some, where the human population is not large, as in Timor and South Celebes, they have become completely wild animals. The well known "Sandalwoods," from Soemba (Sandalwood) Island, are the best of the breeds, and for many years thousands of these handsome and very powerful ponies have been brought across annually to Java. The inter-island steamers are equipped with special accommodation for them and for those from the neighbouring island of Soembawa. The Sandalwood breed is the proud possessor of a stud-book and a very ancient ancestry. Native legend records that the ponies ridden by the ruling prince of this island were always killed when he died, so that their spirits might go with his to the holy forest of Parai Merapoe in the Massoe mountains, for his use after death. To this day natives of Soemba will tell you that in those mountains there are wild horses that no one ever tries to catch, though they are finer than any others:

the spirit-horses of the long-dead Sultans. Ponies were killed, and eaten too, at the death of all important persons in many of the outer islands in olden times.

Ponies were bred in Java for some time under government supervision for the army and post services from about 1820 onwards at Tjipanas and Tjiandjoer. The records say that only one stallion was kept "in the Resident's stable to prevent misuse"; but the natives replied to this restriction by refusing to part with their mares, and the scheme ended in failure. Another attempt was made with more success in Timor in the seventies, which no doubt accounts for "Timor ponies" being so generally known.

If the Javanese has a soft spot for any animal, it is for the *kerbau*, or water buffalo; though his solicitude is more likely to be due to the fact that the beast is a valuable and very costly asset than to any sentiment. Whatever the reason, he takes immense care of the great lumbering brute, never fails to scrub it from horns to heels in the river every day when its work in the fields is done, and houses it, every bit as snugly as he does himself and his family, in a *bilik* stable that is, as often as not, a part of his own home.

Until recently no native householder felt his establishment complete without a dog. Often they were quite good looking ones, but possessed of an ineradicable dislike of Europeans, inherited perhaps from the days when their ancestors barked hopeless defiance at the invaders who came to destroy their masters' homes. These *kampong* dogs are certainly many degrees higher in the canine scale than the wretched pariahs of India, or the swarming mongrels of Bali. But it is doubtful whether their lives were or are particularly enviable; and therefore their recent virtual extermination as the result of a dog tax is probably as humane a measure to the dogs as it is a blessing to those of us who take our walks abroad round about their former haunts. A year or two ago, as you walked through a *kampong*, the wretched brutes would tear out, barking furiously from each and every native house in turn, only to rush inside again, tail between legs, the moment you approached nearer, or clicked your fingers in an attempt to establish friendly relations. Nowadays, except in places far off the beaten track, you rarely see more than an odd one or so, owned by the local head man perhaps; for cents are worth more than dogs to the native, and the tax, at first ten cents per dog, was soon raised to twenty-five cents, and later in many places to a guilder or more.

Now and then you may come across a queer exception to the typical snapping, barking *kampong* dog in one that has been owned and petted by a white man, probably some lonely bachelor planter, and abandoned (in the humane European way!) or given to a native house-servant on leaving the district or the country. You will find yourself being shyly followed at a respectful distance by a dog of breeding just as dubious as the rest, but unlike them in his pitiful eagerness to make friends, coming to you at once if you speak to him, wagging a deprecating tail and imploring you with eloquent eyes to let him follow you home. If you give him the chance he will curl himself up on the mat at your door or, better still, at your feet, with a sigh of utter content; reminding you that it is not only the native who forgets that animals have feelings and affections.

It is the fashion among the Dutch in Java to keep a dog; but why they should do so, except as guardians, is a mystery, for they rarely take them out themselves, leaving them to be exercised by servants as impersonally as though they were racehorses in training. Big dogs such as Alsatians (much bred on the high plateaux, and very popular) are taken out by the house-boy, and you will see them in the cool of morning or evening solemnly pacing up and down with them on a chain. Small ones are taken for their airings by the *baboe* (maid), and you may even see these pampered pets being amused by her in the garden as though they were children. I saw a Pekingese one morning that had been provided by its ingenious native nursemaid with a plaything in the shape of a living rhinoceros-beetle, a big black creature that inhabits and destroys the coconut-palm, tied to the end of a string of fine grass. The little dog was enjoying the game immensely, making furious rushes at his toy, but never quite daring to seize it in his mouth.

European dog-owners do, however, occasionally exercise their own pets when on holiday in the mountains, and I once saw one who made a picture I have never forgotten. It was a tall, stout, perfectly bald Dutch gentleman, gazing out through his spectacles upon our simple village ways with the bland superior air of a townsman in the country, and leading two probably priceless boarhounds on a double chain. He was obviously quite unaware that twenty paces or so behind him was a native leading a pair of shaggy goats and that, to the casual glance, the two pairs of animals being much of a size, there was very little to choose between them!

The Dutch in Java have a weakness for deer as well as for dogs, the result perhaps of nostalgic memories of the charming deerparks in their homeland. In such surroundings as the park at Buitenzorg nothing could be more charming; but these animals do seem rather out of place in small, dusty wired-in enclosures like hen-runs, in the backyards of hotels, where they are often to be seen.

It may be that they give the same sort of satisfaction to their owners as do the caged doves, without which the native householder feels his home lacks the final cachet of respectability. It is his first duty in the morning, especially in East and Middle Java, as the sun pours its earliest rays over the mountain-tops, to hoist the dove in its gaily painted cage to the top of a lofty bamboo, as if it were a Royal Ensign to show that the Sovereign is in residence. At Banjoewangi the sight of hundreds of these cages silhouetted against the sky, high above the roofs of the native town that straggles along the estuary, is an amazing one, easily to be mistaken for a plantation of some weird growth such as *agave* in flower. In West Java the natives also keep doves, but they are more often hung on trees or house walls. At the home of a village head man in the Preanger I saw a row of nine gaily painted cages hung along the verandah, and one on a post at each end, by way of adding tone to the establishment.

There are "S.P.C.A.s" in the Java towns, and they do their best; but it is hard to see how any organisation could ever cope with so vast a field of genuinely unconscious cruelty, and where, moreover, so much of it, as for instance in the handling of poultry, is condoned. Mevrouw sends her cook to the *pasar* to buy "kippen" (fowls), the mainstay of all Java menus, and welcomes her back quite unmoved by the sight of two or three wretched birds hanging head downwards as they are carried in a bunch by the legs, feebly cackling their last protest to an unkind world before they receive the *coup de grâce*.

Veterinary clinics are provided by the authorities in Soerabaya and Batavia for the treatment of sick animals, to which the natives are encouraged to bring their ponies and *sapis*. These do excellent work, but it may be imagined that the number it is possible to treat is a mere drop in the ocean of the thousands that would benefit if the work could be organised on a bigger scale, and if the conservative native would make more use of them. Veterinary inspection of cattle is, however, rigorously carried out, and often on *pasar* days in the country you may see, on the grass by the roadside or in the space where the *sapis* are tied to bamboo stakes awaiting attention, a big teak armchair, looking oddly out of place in such surroundings, but representing the natives' idea of hospitality to the visiting inspector.

The Javanese may not be sentimental as we are about animals, but at least he is not a hypocrite. He is simply a realist. Working animals are there to work; others are there to provide food and must therefore be killed; that is all there is to it. He sees no reason to camouflage, as we do because we "can't bear to think about it," the unpleasant stages that intervene between the charming picture of contented grazing cattle and the meat we eat at table; and he leads to the slaughter a petted calf that has been his children's playmate and almost a member of the family for a year or so, with no more feeling than he markets a basket of cabbages from his garden.

A young calf is a favourite investment of the Javanese countryman, and a gentle little golden-buff *sapi* tied to a bamboo stake in the corner of the compound is to be seen outside many a native house. There the animal grows from calfhood to maturity, fed by the children on grass cut far away on the roadsides or hillsides, and carried down, perhaps by "mother," bent double by the damp green mass on her back: a devotion that would be touching if it were performed out of affection, as the stranger is apt to suppose. The calf soon becomes to all appearance as much a beloved household pet as any dog in a European family. He lies peacefully chewing the cud while the children play around him, climb over him and sit on his back, or feed him with stray morsels of sugar-cane; and he has also the companionship of the older beasts used for ploughing, which spend their leisure hours tied to stakes in the compound, doubtless envying him as a spoilt young idler who does not have to go out into the fields to bear the burden and heat of the day, or have a rough cruel guide-rope pushed through a cut in the cartilage of his nose. Instead, he is led out with a rope round his neck by the children in the cool of the evening, to graze by the roadside or in the *sawahs* where the crop has been cut.

The days and months drift thus peacefully by, until presently the calf has grown by imperceptible stages to be a sleek young steer of something like full size, though a modest one at that, for these island cattle are only pocket editions by European standards.

Then there comes a day when, to the animal's mild surprise, it is aroused from its sleepy cud-chewing at an unusual hour, in the middle of the morning, to see the master of the house who stands looking at him in conversation with a friend. They give him a friendly prod or two in his now well-covered glossy sides and flanks, which he accepts, as he has accepted everything that has come his way during his pleasant uneventful existence, as a well-meant harmless gesture. Then, still vaguely surprised at the unusual attention, he is led forth on to the street by the master himself with his friend or friends in attendance, administering encouragement from behind with a thin bamboo. But that troubles him not at all. Animals are perforce philosophers accustomed to take the rough with the smooth, and he trots confidingly along, snuffling and nuzzling in friendly fashion at the hand of any chance met passer-by in the hope it might offer him a mouthful of something nice to eat.

Poor trustful affectionate little martyr, so basely betrayed by those he has always believed to be his friends! What has he ever done to deserve a worse fate than the one we deal out to our vilest criminals? He meanders on down the road, heartened now and then by a hand slapping his flank, reminding him that friends are near, or so he thinks. Right through the village they go, pausing here and there while the master exchanges a word or two with acquaintances, and the velvet nose and eager tongue make more contacts on their own account; until at last the little cavalcade turns in beside the *pasar*, and makes its way along a narrow path between high hedges towards a small, immaculately whitewashed building bearing the word "SLAGTERIJ."

It is at this point, I think, that the first stab of fear must touch that gentle heart; for on the stream that runs beside the path there is carried, faint but unmistakable, the sharp acrid smell of blood from the constantly washed concrete floor, bearing a message to this latest victim that he is to be added to the long list of martyrs that have been butchered here, innocent sacrifices to the appetites of Man.

Now, for the first time, poor Si Ali (or whatever his name may be; he is sure to have one) pulls back on the headrope, and digs his small pointed hoofs into the ground in a desperate attempt to escape. Surely his own friends, the master who has so often sat beside him, squatted on his heels in characteristic native pose, humming a little song as he pushed mouthful after mouthful of succulent grass or maize-top between the greedy lips, will not desert him now? Surely, surely, he will deliver him from this horrible danger that has so suddenly challenged his affrighted, quivering nostrils? But no. The master's is the very hand that now drags him ruthlessly towards it, jerking cruelly on the rope so that it tightens round his throat, almost choking him; while from behind, someone is belabouring his flanks and legs. Terror seizes him. He is suffocating. His eyes bulge from their sockets. His tongue lolls out. But his groans of terror and despair are strangled by the ever tightening rope. Someone twists his tail, his feet are dragging, but somehow, against his will, they still carry him up the low concrete steps and on to the wet slippery floor of the secret little building with its awful sinister smell of blood. It may be that by now the mists of fear and pain have gathered too thickly for him to know much more, or to feel the last searing agony of the knife that ends them all. One can only hope it may be so; and hope, too, that the murder of the gentle household pet is soon over; for the Javanese, despite his many good qualities, is quite incapable of realising that it should be so.

Sometimes the torture is prolonged for a second or third

victim while the first is being done to death in the Chamber of Horrors; and the next predestined sacrifices are dragged and driven into the nice clean hygienic concrete stalls adjoining, there to hear and smell all that is going on only a few feet away, with plenty of time to think suitable thoughts for the dying. While the loving masters of those about to die calculate their profit, or shrug their shoulders over the necessity to forgo it, if the meat be intended for a wedding-feast, and bewail the hard fate that in either case they are obliged to hand out the four hard-earned *roepea* (guilders) that are the fixed price of the killing.

Later, you will be lucky if you do not meet your late friend on his return journey, either as a limp shapeless mass covered with grass mats hung across a stout bamboo supported on the shoulders of two men, leaving a trail of bloodstains along the road; or else in a sort of wooden cradle in which are piled the still bleeding "joints," covered with banana leaves, while another carrier brings up the rear carrying on his shoulder a basket in which you recognise the pretty head that stretched out to lick your hand an hour or so ago, now all dabbled hideously with blood. As likely as not, too, the boys whose duty it is to carry home the hide will stop outside your gate to refold it in the middle of the road, and tie it up more securely with grass; and in this limp, slippery horror you will know the velvet coat you have so often stroked. There is not one whit more cruelty in all this than in the butchering of our "prime cuts" in England. The only difference is that the Javanese is less squeamish, and perhaps more honest, than we are.

At least, however, it is to be hoped that no such horror as one brought home to some Madoerese cattle vendors a year or so ago could ever happen in England. Whether Javanese would have been capable of it I cannot say, but there is no reason to believe that the ordinary people of Madoera are any more cruel than those of Java. It is the custom to bring live cattle by ferry at night across the strait from Madoera to Soerabaya, where they are sold the following morning by live weight before they are killed. Some fiend among the Madoerese owners originated the idea of increasing the weight of the cattle by forcing a bamboo tube down their throats and pouring through it quantities of water, so that the poor brutes passed their last hours of life in agony, with lacerated throats and distended stomachs. When the disgusting torture was discovered, after it had been going on for some time, and the market overseer reprimanded for having failed to report it, his excuse was that he had not dared, for fear of reprisals!

CHAPTER THIRTEEN

"*The Glory of the Garden*"

ABLE though he is in so many other avocations, it is above all as a cultivator that the Javanese native excels. It is this quality of his, linked with an incomparably fertile soil, that has made of Java one great garden from end to end.

Many English people seem to imagine that although an "eternal summer" may be pleasant enough in its way, it is bound to be rather monotonous, and that a country which enjoys such a climate will lack all the charm of seasonal changes. It is true that Java has none of the violent contrasts in temperature that must be endured in Europe; but of monotony there is none. The monsoons bring variations just as great in their way, but far pleasanter; and the diversity of crops borne by the rich soil move through as orderly a progression as do the wheat and oats and barley that struggle from seedtime to harvest in, say, the stony fields of Buckinghamshire.

Not even the contrast between July and December in those English fields is greater than that between the silver mirrors of the flooded ricefields before planting, and the same fields green as the sea with waving rice; or, on the wide flats of East Java after the rice harvest, when the rich dark soil is cut into deep, lance-straight water trenches fifteen feet or so apart in preparation for sugar planting; work for which huge spades are used in place of the otherwise universal *patjoel*. Among many other seasonal transformation scenes is that when the sugarcane comes into flower, and the sun lights up the silky sheen of the great creamy plumes as they wave high above the tall cane, looking from the heights above like forests of pampas grass.

To a visitor who shares the average Englishman's passion for "growing things" the interest of this Java-wide garden is enthralling. But at the same time the puzzlement aroused by the bewildering diversity of novel growth that greets him at every turn soon grows well nigh unbearable. He may have arrived in Java possessed of a gratifying sense of superiority over his town dwelling friends, founded on his ability to distinguish, with luck, between wheat, oats, barley, beans, and "root crops." He may even perhaps have a nodding acquaintance with lucerne in Australia and South Africa. So that it is wounding in the extreme to his agricultural *amour propre* to find himself unable to put a name to any of the thousand and one plants, trees, and crops that are to be seen on any road or rail journey in this intensively cultivated land.

At first, perhaps, all had been well. The Java landscape is so dominated by ricefields and in some areas by the "big" crops, sugar, rubber, tea, coffee, teak, and tobacco, that for a time they distract the attention from all else. But that phase soon passes. If the newcomer travels by train, he finds himself being swept past field after field planted with different crops: some close to the ground like thick green carpets; others tall and slender; groves of shrubby trees with big white flowers and others with small yellow ones; climbers trained on trellises; and dozens more, which flash past the windows and vanish into the distance before there is time to register a clear impression of them, so that any hope of describing them later in an attempt to discover their names and uses is slight indeed. Nor is that the end of the troubles that beset the seeker after this kind of knowledge; for there is scarcely a plant, a fruit, or a tree that has not an entirely different name in East, West or Middle Java, to say nothing of innumerable local variations. But it is a fascinating game for all that.

The harvesting of many of these infinitely varied lesser crops of Java brings each of them into prominence in turn. One that will certainly attract the attention of a newcomer is that of the groundnuts, or pea-nuts (*arachis*), which are grown in enormous quantities in areas where the water supply available during the dry East Monsoon is insufficient for rice growing. Such areas are most numerous in East Java, where the effect of this monsoon is most marked.

In mountain regions in this part of Java these so called "nuts," which, in actual fact, are not nuts at all, but beans, are often interplanted with potatoes or maize, according to a system of planting and interplanting which keeps the soil almost continuously productive. This the Javanese

"The Glory of the Garden"

calls *terus-menurus*, an untranslatable word denoting ceaseless progress, or the rotation of crops without pause or interruption.

The planting of the nuts is timed so that the crop is ready to gather in November in order that the land they have occupied can be broken up and prepared for rice planting when the rains start in December. The "nuts" are the easiest of all crops to gather, for the whole plant, top, roots and all, with the so called nuts hanging among the root fibres, comes up with one pull of the stem. For this reason, one of the plant's many native names is *katjang broel*, meaning "all-together bean." All along the roadsides at harvest time you will see them in great heaps, just as they were pulled, awaiting transport, and everywhere you will meet men jogging along between twin loads of them, and *grobaks* piled twelve feet high with the fading green mass. They may be taken to their native owner's house, where the children pull off the damp, earth covered nuts and strew them to dry on the ground of the compound, or along the roadside in front of shops or houses where no one seems ever to interfere with them. Sometimes a Chinese or Arab merchant will buy the crop and it is taken to a bigger depot. But wherever it may be, you will see the nubbly, shabby little nuts looking like rather coarse gravel all over the ground, and even perhaps find yourself treading on them unawares as you enter some small village shop.

This *arachis*, one of the many varieties grown in most tropical and sub-tropical countries, is a native of South America, and the nuts are not, as they appear to be, attached to the root fibres. Soon after blooming, the bunches of small yellow flowers borne by the plant droop downwards and gradually creep underground, where the pods mature. The plant itself, after these have been removed, is used as a manure, especially for sugarcane.

The popularity of the nuts, fried either in coconut oil or in the oil produced from the nuts themselves (an important industry), is country wide, and the consumption of them enormous. They are eaten daily by natives with their rice, and accompany every European *rijsttafel*. The cry "*katjang goreng!*" (fried beans) is one of the most familiar of sounds in every town and village, where they are sold in the streets in small conical newspaper packets for one cent a packet, and are almost as popular with Europeans, at all events among their children, as they are with natives. They are often called *katjang tjina*, being said to have been introduced by the Chinese.

Another crop greatly in evidence during the East Monsoon is *katella*, better known to English speaking people as sweet potato, and to the French as *patate*. In Middle and East Java it replaces rice during the dry season over immense areas, and covers miles of country like a thick green carpet. The Javanese have adopted it as their very own, and mostly call it *oebi Java*, i.e. "Java potato," for, after rice, it is one of the most important items in their dietary. Several different varieties are cultivated in Java, all growing low to the ground with very dense foliage. Like the ground nuts, the crop is gathered just before the rains come, and the roots are spread out on every available space to dry. Europeans in Java very seldom eat *katella*. Having myself had to make this singularly uninspiring vegetable my staple diet during a lean period in the Australian Bush, I must say I do not wonder!

The *kapok* harvest must surely be the oddest harvest in the world. Towards the end of the dry season, in October and November, the big torpedo shaped green pods begin to shrivel and turn brown; and then, here, there, and everywhere, you will see bamboo ladders being reared against the stiffly outstretched horizontal branches of the queer ungainly trees, so unlike any other tree that grows that, once seen, no one can ever fail to recognise them. The pods gathered, they are carried in split bamboo baskets of enormous size, on the backs of women or of ponies, or by men with their *pikoelans*, to wherever it is to be shelled; perhaps to some big depot where the pods are spread out in the sunshine on an open space paved with concrete until they are hard and dry; after which, if they do not split of themselves, as they often do, they are split open by hand, the soft fluffy white cotton pulled out and its seeds removed. Sometimes it may be only the product of a couple of trees, or even of one; and even then it is not to be despised, for the yield of each tree is almost incredible; in such a case it may go, perhaps, to its owner's

"The Glory of the Garden"

home to be dried and opened, either for sale or for his own family's use.

Anyone who has ever handled *kapok*, even to the extent of filling a cushion, and thus knows its uncanny capacity to spread itself all over a room, will easily imagine that at big *kapok* depots, or so called factories, the road, the trees, and indeed the whole scene, for hundreds of yards around, is white and fluffy with the clinging stuff, as though it had been through a heavy stage snowstorm. And all the people who have handled it, or have even been anywhere near it, look as though they had been pushing their way through a barrage of cobwebs. So, too, if you linger long, you will yourself, especially if curiosity should prompt you to peep inside a shelling shed, where, through a tangible fog that tickles your nose and clings to your hair and eyelashes, you will see the bursting pods piled roof high.

Because of its extreme lightness, the size of the loads in which the *kapok* goes on the next stage of its journey is simply enormous. Sometimes it is packed in immense sacks, lashed together four upright and two across their tops, and one such load roped at each end of the bearer's *pikoelan*; or in two vast square packs similarly carried, dwarfing the man who jogs cheerfully between them, bearing their weight on his shoulder, to pygmy proportions by comparison. Sometimes one such pack is carried on a little old woman's back, or they may be piled on pack ponies into loads so wide and so high that all you can see is a jerkily moving mass supported on four absurdly inadequate looking legs, with sometimes the tip of a protruding nose. And from each and all of the loads, however carried, the breeze blows back frail fluffy little puffs of white cloud.

In this order the *kapok* comes to the factory, where the remaining seeds are removed and the cotton is pressed, like Australian wool, into square standard bales for export. Thereafter you may see it piled high on motor lorries, or on barges being slowly poled down the river on its way to the docks, where, if you care to follow it so far, you can walk between mountains of it as though along the feet of cliffs.

Immense though the quantity of *kapok* is that is supplied by Java to the outside world, by no means all of it is exported.

The local demand is also great, for the reason that this beneficent tree produces its luxurious mattress stuffing to all intents and purposes ready made, so that it is remarkably cheap, and therefore *kapok* mattresses are as universally popular among Chinese and Javanese as among Europeans. Made by Chinese workmen, these mattresses are superlatively good; and many a former Java resident bemoans the fact that nothing like them is to be obtained in Europe.

And, finally, if you should wish to fill a new cushion here in Java and unless you are living at a great distance from a town, you need never trouble to go shopping to buy your *kapok*. It is seldom that a day passes without a *kapok* seller wandering by, a bamboo across his shoulders with a bunch at each end of fat, dangling, sausage shaped blue, red, green, purple or yellow oiled paper bags, each holding about enough for your purpose, and at the same time adding their quota to the general colourfulness of the scene.

The Javanese never waste an inch of cultivable earth if they can avoid it; and the narrow earth banks that intersect and hold water in the rice-*sawahs*, serving also as paths, are often planted as well. Climbing plants of all sorts are favourites for this purpose, mostly beans of various kinds, all neatly trained on slender bamboos, as we grow exhibition sweetpeas in England. The list of *katjang* (bean) varieties grown in Java fills several pages in agricultural publications, and includes all sorts and sizes from the giant *paté* with its foot long pod containing seeds nearly as big as table-tennis balls, and which are chopped up and eaten as a relish with rice, down to the diminutive *taugé* which is allowed to sprout in the dark after being gathered, so that a dish of the tiny half-opened beans with an inch of curling white stem looks not unlike our mustard, of the "mustard and cress" partnership. The Dutch have aptly named them *kommajes* (little commas).

The famous soya bean should be mentioned among the many sorts that are grown and flourish here. It is rather a nondescript looking plant and not very easy to recognise. It has small oval leaves and purplish flowers like a vetch, and grows best on the warm low levels, though it is also to be seen in the mountain districts up to about 3000 feet.

A NATIVE HOUSEWIFE AND A FIREWOOD-SELLER. THEY DID NOT SUCCEED IN COMING TO TERMS!

DRYING AND STORING MAIZE COBS AT THE HOUSE OF A KAMPONG HEADMAN.

"The Glory of the Garden"

Spinach, and a green vegetable rather like it, called *kankoeng*, cover hundreds of acres. Peas, including a miniature variety eaten with the pods, are largely grown for European consumption, as are potatoes, tomatoes, and many other vegetable crops. Onions do particularly well, and a tiny pink kind is a great favourite with native growers.

A characteristic sight in East and Middle Java is a small leaved leguminous bush bearing yellow flowers, which is much planted on the earth banks between ricefields. This is *crotelaria*, known variously to the natives as *entjing-entjing*, *orok-orok*, or *kakatjangan*: it enriches the soil and provides a useful fibre. Other varieties, called *goedeh* and *widgen sesam*, have small white blossoms and edible seeds which are added to the *sayoor asem*, a sort of pickle used by natives; another member of the same family is the much larger *tori* bearing handsome white blossoms which are crushed and eaten with rice. The branches and prunings of all these are a useful source of firewood.

A beautiful crop to be seen here and there in Middle and East Java, where it is being planted experimentally, is *rosella*, a member of the large *hibiscus* family. It is a very tall slender lance-straight reddish cane, with narrow leaves and a large single white flower. It produces a valuable fibre, and it is hoped to cultivate it profitably on land formerly occupied by sugarcane, the planting of which has been so drastically reduced since the slump in this commodity.

Sugarcane has been cultivated in Java since early in the sixteenth century under the control of Arabs. The Dutch on their arrival were quick to follow so profitable an example, and by 1620 some twenty mills were in operation round about Batavia. It was destined to become the most important of all the European cultural enterprises in Java.

At first it was a forced culture, but later, as a private enterprise, sugar became a source of prosperity to the whole native population of East Java as well as to Europeans. Huge fortunes were made through it in the Great War, as well as in coffee, quinine, and other products, and Java cane crops were sometimes sold three or four times over before they were cut, with staggering rises of price on each transaction. But in recent years the industry suffered the greatest *débâcle* in the colony's history.

Up to 1931 Java was producing from her 179 mills about 3,000,000 tons of sugar a year: one fifth of the world's sugar supply, and was only second in her output to Cuba. But for years powerful native financial interests in India had been working for the establishment of sugar culture in their own country; and in 1931 the Indian Government imposed a high tariff on imported sugar under which mills sprang up like mushrooms. In the first season there were thirty of them, producing 158,000 tons between them; three years later 135 mills were working, with an output of 650,000 tons, which rose still further the following year. With the result that Java, which in 1931 sent nearly a million tons of sugar to India, by 1936 sent scarcely a ton. And Japan, formerly also a big customer, had in the meantime become self-supporting through its development of sugar culture in Formosa.

The Java industry was desperately hard hit, and for some years the dislocation and distress was extreme. Dozens of the great mills stood idle and empty, their machinery having in some cases been bought and reinstalled in the very mills in India that had ruined those in Java. The offices were closed, and desolation reigned in the sugar towns that the mills had brought into being. Pretty bungalows formerly so gay with flowers and ferns and polished brass, with bright silk lampshades and blue Dutch china, were shuttered and forsaken; their once trim gardens a wilderness, and boards bearing the words "Te Huur" or "Te Koop" greeted the traveller on every side, while many of the canefields that formerly lined the roads for miles were replanted with rice and other crops.

Formerly the Java sugar industry had competed in the world's market without subsidy; but now the Government took a hand, and by guaranteeing a fixed minimum price for a proportion of the output, together with the growers' success in reducing production costs, some sort of stability has been attained, and the hope that Java will be able to produce and dispose of about half her former output. The population is adapting itself to changed conditions, and the signs of distress that followed the sudden slump are now happily disappearing.

Sugar is grown in Java by natives as well as on the grand scale by Europeans, and small plots planted by Javanese are to be seen here and there surrounded by other crops. The cane, of course, is the same in appearance whoever owns it; but you will see no lordly sugar mill with tall tapering white spire dominating the scene of these modest native holdings. The cane grown on them is crushed in a primitive stone or concrete contraption worked by a bullock marching monotonously round and round, and the resultant juice is boiled in paraffin tins, those faithful friends of both Orientals and white Colonials in modern times. The sugar is made up into little tapering packets of standard size, wrapped in palm leaf, and is one of the countless items that soon became a familiar sight in every *pasar* and village shop. These native sugar enterprises, humble though they are, have at least the advantage that they are quite unaffected by the disastrous *malaise* that has closed down so many of their more pretentious cousins. Their numbers and activity are as great as ever they were, for the Javanese has a sweet tooth, and loves sugar in any form when he can afford it.

Several sorts of wild sugarcane are native to Java. The most familiar is *glagah*, which is easily mistaken for the coarse *alang-alang* grass formerly much used for roofing. *Glagah* is often planted on native holdings, and either crushed to obtain the sweet juice, or the young shoots eaten as a vegetable. The native practice of applying the same name to all sorts of rough grasses, as well as to a small red fish eaten with rice, is very confusing to strangers.

No one who has ever seen a plantation of *agave*, a kind of aloe, from which sisal hemp is produced, will be likely to forget it. The stiff, spiky, symmetrical rows with their tall "candelabra" of flowers stretch away in unbroken ranks to the horizon, weirdly silhouetted against the sky, for this crop is cultivated on flat areas. This crop is one that no visitor will have difficulty in recognising, for it is utterly unlike any other in Java, and looks as though it would be more at home in the arid wastes of Mexico than amid the gracious fertility of the East Indian islands.

Vanilla, which is really an orchid, is much grown in Java. It grows wild in the South American forests; and when the

Spaniards conquered Mexico they found the Aztecs there flavouring chocolate with it just as chocolate manufacturers do to this day. There is no record of when it was first brought to Java, but as a Spanish writer sang the praises of its "remarkable flavour" as early as 1608, one may suppose its fame reached the East India Company and that they thought it would be a profitable culture. It is an uncannily vigorous climber, with thick fleshy stems and leaves that bring to mind the story of Jack and the Beanstalk, for if it is allowed its own way it will climb straight up the trunk of a tree on one perfectly vertical stem, to dizzy heights far out of sight and reach among the highest branches.

When grown commercially vanilla is trained on bamboo trellises or on small trees kept lopped to prevent it from growing out of reach. In the latter case horizontal bamboos are fixed from tree to tree. A drawback to its cultivation is the necessity to fertilise the flowers artificially. Opinions differ as to whether in its wild state the plant is fertilised by insects or by humming birds; but whatever the agent may be in its native land, it is not present in Java, and the grower must apply the pollen by hand.

Many other climbing plants besides vanilla excite the stranger's interest in almost any native garden in Java. Their name is legion and, with the exception of pepper, their uses are for the most part hidden from the mere European. Some add their contribution to strange native dishes, and most, you will be told if you ask, yield *obat* (medicine) for all sorts and conditions of illnesses. But there is one, the *sirih*, looking at first sight like a very handsome bean, with shiny elongated heartshaped leaves, which is one of the most important items in Javanese native life, as it is in that of many other Oriental peoples. It is one of the thousand or so members of the pepper family which grow wild all over the East Indies and South East Asia, and were the first cause of the annexation of all these lands by European powers, the spice trade having been the genesis of the East India Companies.

The leaves of the *sirih* are the principal ingredient in the "chew" without which no Javanese would find life endurable. They are a familiar sight even to town dwellers, for there is scarcely a street corner at which you will not see a native squatted beside a basket of them, piled up in neat brilliant green bundles, which he keeps fresh by sprinkling them every now and then from a little tin of water. For although the other ingredients of the "chew" can be kept almost indefinitely, the *sirih* leaves must be used perfectly fresh.

To make his chew, the native takes one of the slightly scented, bitter, red juiced leaves, smooths it on his knee, and snicks off the stalk. Then he smears it with a little fine chalk, and lays on it a tiny bit of *gambir*, or sometimes, in remote places where *gambir* is not obtainable, a bit of the *sirih* catkin, and a piece of betel nut, which he breaks off with a nutcracker. (Betel nut, by the way, is only another name for areca nut, and is called by Malays and Javanese *pinang* or *penang*.) The *sirih* chewer then folds all this up into a small packet in the *sirih* leaf and puts it in his mouth.

A chew lasts about a quarter of an hour. Hence the Javanese word for "a quarter of an hour" is *sapanginang*, meaning literally the length of a *pinang*, much as we might say "the length of a cigarette." The *sirih* chew is supposed to have healing properties, and is sometimes spat out on to wounds in the course of their treatment by a *doekoen* (a native doctor and magic maker).

The Javanese like a good ripe old betel nut in their chew, and if that is not strong enough for a hardened palate they will put a wad of tobacco in the other cheek at the same time. Malays prefer a milder flavour and choose young, immature nuts for their *sirih*. Old Javanese men and women, especially the very poor in the Sultanates, often suck a whole nut, known as *pinang merah*, instead of the mixed chew. The areca palm is grown all over Java and the East Indies, and its abundance on Penang gave that island its name.

The other ingredient, *gambir*, is the product of a bush much seen in native gardens: in its natural state a climber, but "topped" under cultivation to increase the production of leaves from which the extract is made by long boiling. The syrupy substance so obtained sets quite firmly and, after drying, is cut into the tiny yellow brown cubes in which it is sold, and which are among the most familiar sights in all markets. It is the same extract as that used for tanning, well known as *catechu*.

The *sirih* box in a Javanese household is as important an item as the teapot in ours, if not more so. Called *tempat sirih* or *pakinangan* (*kinang* is the Javanese word for the prepared mixture), the box contains compartments with two tiny covered boxes for *gambir* and tobacco, one uncovered for betel nut, and a little pot for lime. *Sirih* boxes are made of many different materials: brass, wood, silver, or even gold, and are often very beautiful. It is a strict rule of Javanese hospitality to offer the *sirih* box to a guest, and it is an equally strict rule of courtesy to help yourself from it when thus offered to you. It may play a part in courtship; if it is proffered by a simple maiden to a diffident swain, it is a hint that his advances will not be unwelcome. Being of the superior sex, he is under no obligation to accept unless he is inclined; but if he should do so, the young lady may hope for the best!

The cinnamon bush grows wild in Java, and its bark is used by natives to flavour their tiny tapering cigarettes. The cultivated variety was brought here from Ceylon when that island was in the hands of the Dutch East India Company. It was one of the forced cultures imposed on the natives in both places.

Many colourful plants are used for hedging. *Coleus*, of which countless sorts grow wild, is a prime favourite, as it roots from any sprig stuck in the ground, and grows fast and with great luxuriance. The common crimson variety, which the Javanese call *bayam merah* (red spinach), is specially prolific, and you may often see a glowing mass of the lovely thing warming the shadows on the fringes of a mountain forest.

Caladium of many kinds is to be found in such places also.

Lantana, though so abundant as to be a pest in places, is none the less beautiful for that. *Crotons*, of which many varieties are native to Java, are everywhere, and a garden in which they do not appear is rare. Usually they, too, are planted as hedges, and the brilliance of colour they lend to the roadsides is a delight to see. *Acalyphas* are equally popular as hedges and bushes, specially striking varieties with big coloured catkins being in high favour. The most curious of these is aptly called *ekor koetjing* (cat's tail), and bear thick reddish velvety catkins a good foot long. The *hosea, eixora,* and *tenoma,* all bearing brilliantly coloured flowers, are common in all gardens, and so is the *gardenia,* or *katjang piring.*

The hibiscus flourishes everywhere; not only the common red sort, beloved of South Sea novelists, but a great variety of others, including a delicate rose pink, and one whose blooms are finely fringed. The Javanese call the red one *kembang sepatoe,* the shoe flower; not, so old time Dutch planters say, with any reference to its shape, but because, in the days before improved transport made the small amenities of life so easily obtainable, native servants discovered that the squashed blooms made an excellent polish for their masters' boots and shoes.

In mountain regions there are miles upon miles of thick green hedges ablaze with big yellow sunflowers, or as the Javanese naturally call them: *kembang mata hari.* The Dutch, however, call them "Marygold" after a certain Mary Gould, the daughter of a rich American, who, so the story goes, saw it growing wild when travelling with her father in South America some fifty or sixty years ago, and took seeds back to the United States. There it was widely cultivated, and from thence was introduced to Java by Dr Junghuhn, famous for his introduction of cinchona, among other plants designed to prevent erosion of mountain sides and for the enrichment of the soil.

Another hedge much planted at high altitudes is the *poinsettia,* which, like so many other plants in this genial climate, will root and grow without fail from the roughest of cuttings stuck in the ground.

The lovely pale gold *alamanda,* which we grow with care in English hothouses, glorifies many Java hedgerows. It clambers over trellises and arbours, and hangs down in heavy masses over garden walls as prodigally as does the Mesembryanthemum in Devon and Cornwall. The gorgeous flame coloured *bignonia,* which the Dutch for some reason often call "stephanotis," is also a popular favourite.

Gardening is altogether too easy in Java! Not only can you grow a fine new hedge almost overnight by sticking in a row of twigs, but your very gateposts will burst into life if you let them, throwing out a crown of branches like those of a pollarded tree. These are a common sight in native *kampongs*. Sometimes the prudent native householder, having evidently an eye for future profit as well as for pleasing appearance, has put in gateposts of *kapok* wood, so that he rejoices not only in a living archway over the entrance to his little demesne, but gathers therefrom a useful crop. How very pleasant it would be if only our staid suburban British gateposts would develop the same virile qualities!

CHAPTER FOURTEEN

On Trees

THE trees of Java have earned a whole literature to themselves. Forestry experts estimate the numbers of distinct sorts at anything between five and ten thousand. But without presuming to attempt to approach them on so devastatingly grand a scale, the few that the ordinary layman succeeds in identifying are quite interesting enough. Heading the list for sheer breathtaking magnificence is the *Poinciana*, well named by the French, in its native land of Madagascar, the "Flamboyant," and by the English "Flame of the Forest," for this tree in full flower must surely be nature's supreme achievement in the realm of colour. Bare in the dry East Monsoon, the branches break suddenly at the change of season into a dazzling blaze of scarlet blossom which spreads day by day until it is a mass of flaming glory almost too blinding for human eyes to bear. Then, as quickly, the foliage appears in feathery sprays, supplying a perfect setting to the flaming masses of bloom. For a month or six weeks the show displays itself daily in all its glory in an ever increasing luxuriance of foliage, until at last there begin the gentle showers of falling blossoms that cover the ground under the trees with a brilliant carpet, swept up with meticulous care daily; for these trees are mostly planted to form avenues along important roads in the large towns. And then, slowly and imperceptibly, for the process takes some weeks, the scarlet seems to melt away as the green foliage thickens, as though it had been submerged and drowned by the rising green tide. And at last, "flamboyant" no longer, the *Poinciana* enters upon another phase as a gracious and lovely shade tree.

Only second to it in brilliance is the *cassia*, which bears masses of yellow blossoms like those of our laburnum, and is called *hoedjan mas* (golden rain) by the natives. Another beautiful tree is one they call *daoen koepoe-koepoe* (butterfly leaf) bearing dainty clusters of frail pink and white blooms like flights of butterflies; and the *tamarind*, a native of tropical

Africa, with red streaked yellow flowers is also a familiar roadside tree. It has a practical as well as an æsthetic value, its pods making a delicious jam and a popular syrup known as *stroop asem*.

Two other red blossomed trees which visitors sometimes confuse with the *Poinciana* are the *sepatoe dea*, or Forest Tulip, and the *dadap*. The former is a native tree planted along the roadsides at high altitudes too cool for the heat loving Flamboyant. It bears flowers which grow singly, high among the topmost branches, and are only visible as splashes of brilliant colour against the sky. It is only when they fall that the beauty of these strange blossoms can be seen. They are not unlike immense sealing-wax red sweetpeas, and are as big as a native woman's hand. The *dadap* has an equally bright red flower of similar shape but quite small. It also is a native tree, and is much planted for shade in coffee plantations, as it grows quickly and does not exhaust the soil. Its seeds contain a valuable alkaloid, and the bark of one variety, known as *dadap bong*, yields the poison *erythrinine*. Several sorts of *Albizzia* are also planted as shade trees with coffee or tea; and so is *koveel toro*, from whose light, flexible wood walking-sticks are made.

Hundreds upon hundreds of miles of country roads, as well as those in the towns, have been converted into avenues in Java by the planting of shade trees. The favourite, and most familiar, is the stately *Kenari*, which grows to a great size, and whose nuts are much sought after by the Javanese, who eat them with their rice and also extract oil from them. The *Sana* is another the sight of which soon grows familiar, for it is easily recognised in its so called "wintering" period when, like the teak, it sheds its leaves and stands looking strangely naked and forlorn against the background of rich tropic foliage. The timber from this tree is a beautiful reddish hardwood known as *lenggoa*, and trees sometimes attain such a size that table tops five or six feet in diameter have been cut from a single cross section of its trunk. Nor is its timber its only product. The Javanese make fish nets and rope from its bark fibre, and use its sap, which they call *getah angsana*, for tanning leather and as a healing ointment. Native women make an infusion of the leaves and use it as a shampoo, and the men crush and dry them for snuff.

Another remarkable and beautiful tree is the "Rain Tree," a native of South America, and another of the many importations Java owes to Dr Junghuhn. It bears delicate fluffy pale pink flowers with very long, fine stamens, and it has the peculiar habit of folding up its small oval leaves at sunset: for which reason the Javanese call it *daoen tidor* (sleeping leaves). By an association of ideas very characteristic of native mentality, they have great faith in a sleeping draught made from an infusion of these leaves.

The native teak of Java, called *djati*, is much planted for shade and decoration in gardens, as well as in forests for its invaluable timber. It is the easiest of all trees to recognise, for its leaves are bigger than dinner plates and its great trusses of creamy blossoms are strikingly beautiful.

The Java chestnut or *sarangan*, which has given its name to one of Java's best known mountain resorts, grows wild in most mountain forests. Its nut is not unlike its European namesake, and is in great demand in native markets from September till the end of the year.

The *casuarina*, here called *tjimara*, is common in East Java, but not in the West; and the *pandanus* is to be found at many places on the coast.

An "India rubber plant," in a pot, was almost as indispensable as an aspidistra in respectable British households in Victorian times, and English visitors who are old enough to remember it may recognise this old friend in much glorified form in Java gardens as the *karet* or *ficus elastica*. This is the original "India rubber tree," a native of Java, Malaya, and elsewhere in the East Indies, and has a curious history. An early navigator saw a native boy playing with a ball that "bounced in a surprising manner," and was told on inquiry that it was made of the dried sap of this tree. He took samples back to Europe and before long the product was being imported as "guttapercha." An Englishman, one Prestly, discovered in 1770 that it would rub out pencil marks, and for over half a century that was its chief use, until experiments in America led to the discovery that it could be vulcanised by the use of sulphur.

Plantations of *ficus elastica* were started and improvements and developments with "guttapercha," or "caoutchouc" as it was also called, continued until the superiority of the rubber yielded by the Brazilian *hevea* was discovered. The cultivation of *hevea*, started at Kew Gardens in 1876 from seed smuggled from Brazil, put an end to the importance of *ficus elastica*, and was the beginning of the rubber industry as we know it to-day. The tree, however, remains to beautify many gardens; it grows to great size, and it is difficult to realise that the stately tree that spreads a welcome shade above your head, and frames the distant lovely view with its great branches, is in fact the same humble "India rubber plant" of suburban sitting rooms, which its fat, pink, rolled up leafbuds and smooth thick leaves recall to mind.

Years of familiarity have never quite robbed me of astonishment at the sight of the *nangka*, or *soekoen* as it is called in some parts of Java. Its cousin the Breadfruit is startling enough, but it at least is shapely as you would expect a giant fruit to be, and grows in a seemly way on a handsome tree whose large and decorative leaves are a becoming setting for it. The *nangka* tree is a scraggy, nondescript affair, standing awkwardly as a nervous schoolgirl, as though embarrassed by the monstrous, shapeless, scratchy, dirty green fruits that poke or hang untidily at all angles from its trunk and branches, inadequately protected by a rather sparse supply of leaves far too small to be in proportion. It would be a small *nangka* that was less than a foot long; many are double that, and their weight, needless to say, is terrific.

The *nangka* is a native of Java and common in some districts; it passes unnoticed all through the year until December, when, laden as outrageously as a coolie, but with its own offspring, it is one of the sights of the regions it inhabits, at altitudes above 3000 feet. The fruit, which in shape is often rather like a collapsed half-empty sack that has sagged in the middle, is in evidence everywhere in its season by the roadsides, in the *pasars*, on the tops of buses, loaded on *grobaks* and *pikoelans*; and wherever natives congregate it is cut into hunks, exposing its pale yellow pulp and large seeds, and eagerly bought. The Breadfruit, to which this monstrosity of a fruit is related, is also much planted in Java, though less than the *nangka*. It is an importation from the South Sea Islands, and the tree is as handsome as the *nangka* is the reverse. It is easily recognised by its large, symmetrical, deeply indented leaves. The Javanese names for it are *soekoen bidji* and *kaloewieh*.

In their characteristically irrational way, the Javanese have given the misleading name of *nangka belanda* (Dutch *nangka*) to the American "Soursop" (*anona muricata*) or, as the Dutch call it, "Zuurzak." A more inappropriate name could scarcely be imagined as the tree is little more than a shrub, and the only resemblance borne by the fruit to the *nangka* is its colour and irregular shape, an average specimen being only about six to eight inches long.

It is easy enough to recognise the bamboo, but not to distinguish between its many varieties. The giant of the species, bamboo *bitoeng* or *pitoeng*, growing in great groves on the sides of deep gorges among the mountains, is a glorious sight. It grows to amazing heights, often attains ten inches or more in diameter, and is incredibly strong for all building purposes. Bridges built of it will safely carry the clumsy teak *grobaks* or *tjikars*, whose registered weight is over 1000 lb., and even motor cars.

Bamboo *taki* and bamboo *watoe* are the kinds most used for splitting into the house building material called *bilik*, described in a previous chapter. The slender bamboo *apoes* provides fibre from which is made a strong cord used to bind the framework of buildings together. The bamboos *andong*, *gombong*, and *soerat* are also used in building, as well as cut in sections to form natural containers for carrying water or collecting palm juice.

Small Chinese and Japanese varieties are also sometimes planted. These are mostly grown for export.

Methods of propagating the bamboo are simple and effective, and often to be seen on a country walk. A stem, or part of one, is buried just under the surface of the ground; holes are cut in the upper side between each of the joints, and the sections filled with water. New sprouts and roots then grow from each joint. Another method is to stick a two section piece of bamboo in the ground at an angle of about forty-five degrees, and fill the protruding section with water like a cup, when the joint, one side of which should be just under the surface of the ground, will sprout as in the first method.

Big untidy masses of what appear to be pine needles or small dry sticks, jammed in among the highest stems, which are sometimes to be seen in bamboo groves, are often taken for some kind of giant birds' nests; but they are in reality the flower of this strange tree. It often further puzzles the passer-by with the eerie rasping groans it emits as its immensely tall and heavy stems rub against one another when they are swayed by the breeze among their tops.

Palms are as familiar a feature of the Java landscape as the bamboo, and are almost, if not quite, as indispensable to the Javanese people. There are many varieties. The coconut, which grows to great heights and often lives to eighty or a hundred years, is everywhere, and serves many purposes beside its primary one of producing nuts. The midrib of its leaves, tied in bunches, is the ubiquitous *lidi*, with which all nations do their sweeping; its sap yields sugar "toddy"; its fibre makes mats; and when its day is done, its trunk is used for the inside framework of houses, to make footbridges, a row of the trunks being laid side by side, and another set on the top of them at right angles to the first.

The sago palm provides an important addition to the native dietary which, however, involves felling the tree at fourteen or fifteen years old. The trunk is cut into logs six or eight feet long, which may often be seen as they are trundled along the roads by a rope attached to an improvised axle fixed in the ends of the log. The sago is prepared by chopping the log open on a mat-floored washing place with a trough beneath it, built out over a stream. The soft heart of the trunk, a fine meal-like substance called *serampin*, is scraped out, water is poured over it, and it is kneaded with the feet in the trough into a paste. This is packed in long cylindrical palm leaf baskets, and often floated down river in its own scraped out trunk, the native being nothing if not practical. As well as that consumed by the natives, much is also converted into the pearl sago of commerce, made by the simple process of hanging it up in mats rolled cornerwise and repeatedly shaken till small lumps are formed. These are then gently baked. The process is much the same as that followed in making tapioca from *cassava*.

The *aren* palm also produces sago when its life is over; but in the meantime it has an important mission to perform, for it is the sugar and toddy producer *par excellence*. As much as 1800 litres of the so called "Java sugar" can be tapped from a single tree. The sap, which is called *toeak*, is caught in a bamboo section bound to the stem; then boiled in an iron pot till it is syrupy, and transferred to another where it crystallises. It is then cut into round cakes with a cutter formed of the round end of a large bamboo section. The fermented toddy is called *toeak kras*, and is also used as yeast. As well as the *aren* and coconut palms, the *lontar* and *nipa* yield the same sugary sap, but in less abundance. The *aren* palm also provides the native with a particularly strong fibre much in favour for rope-making, so tough that it can even be used for anchor cables.

The midrib of the sago palm fronds, laid in parallel rows, takes the place of *bilik* for house walls in other parts of the East Indies but is seldom to be seen in Java. It is known as *gaba-gaba*. Palm leaf, preferably of the *nipa* palm when available, provides the *atap* roofing that was very generally used before the Dutch ordained that tiles should replace it as a precaution against plague-bearing rats, to which *atap* offered too attractive a harbourage. *Atap* is, however, still used on all temporary buildings: notably those of the annual *Pasar Gambar*, and before and after this great fair loads of the picturesque roof material, done up in bundles of twenty-five, are a familiar sight on all the roads and canals of Batavia.

Except for the "oerwoud" (that is, the primeval jungle that clothes the highest peaks: seldom seen by Europeans save where passes have been made across the ranges) the mountain forests too are part of Java's immense cultivated garden. There is nothing at first sight in the appearance of these lovely woodlands to suggest that they are not as "wild" as the jungle above them; but the discovery of Australian eucalyptus rubbing shoulders with native *djati* and *ipé*, and mimosa cheek by jowl with *dammar* and tree ferns under the shade of big gloomy pines, sets up doubts in the visitor's mind as to whether they can really be as natural as they seem; especially when he finds himself in a real pine wood bare of undergrowth and carpeted with slippery pine needles whose sweet, sharp scent transports him in a moment from the tropics to Bournemouth or Japan.

The answer to the riddle is the Forestry Service, whose tree nurseries are often to be seen in the course of a mountain ramble. Hidden as they are in the very heart of the woods, hemmed in on all sides by towering trees, these forests in miniature are a charming sight such as Gulliver might have seen in the land of Lilliput. The fairy glades of baby pines and "gums," mimosa and many other foreign varieties, are raised from seed brought from all over the world, and supply the young trees now interplanted with the indigenous growth in countless mountain forests all over Java.

The Forestry Service was originally concerned only with the preservation and replanting of the rich natural *djati* forests which had been depleted almost to the point of extinction by the East India Company's *blandong* system. Under this the native regents were forced to supply huge quantities of the timber, and the forests were ruthlessly cut, making vast profits for all concerned, except, of course, the poor coolies who actually cut them. It was not long before the coastal forests, especially fine round about Rembang, and always renowned for the building of native *prahaus*, were cut out, and the *blandong* cutters were forced to go farther and farther inland for supplies to meet the Company's insatiable demands. All their wharves, godowns, and ships were built of this magnificent hardwood, and immense quantities were exported. It was for this reason that *djati* woods began to be planted under Company control. The *blandong* system was continued with variations up to about 1865, by which time the planted forests were becoming productive.

The first forestry experts had been brought to Java in 1849, and the first forestry inspector was appointed in 1858, in a great measure to repair the ravages of the long Java war, when miles of forests were chopped down by the Dutch to deprive the natives of cover, so that their resistance might be finally subdued. Since the last decade of the nineteenth century, the Forestry Service has steadily grown, and now controls not only the many planted *djati* woods, but the original "wild" forests also, which are regularly inspected, thinned, and replanted in the best interests of timber and firewood supply, the latter a vital matter in this densely populated country. In many places whole hillsides have been reafforested, often under an ingenious system whereby the Forestry Department allows the use of the land free for three years to farmers from Madoera for the cultivation of maize, in return for their care of the young trees between which the maize is planted. In this way, as well as assuring the welfare of the embryo forests, the Madoerese are encouraged to settle in these non-irrigable areas, less uncongenial to them than the Javanese, accustomed from time immemorial to irrigated land.

For many years Java exported large quantities of *djati* and soft woods for paper making, the latter to Japan. But in late years Japan's financial difficulties have reduced these exports to a minimum. Increased exports of *djati* to Europe have to some extent made up for other losses; but a new paper mill is Java's chosen solution to reduced sales of "pulping" wood. This new mill is to make a stouter kind of paper than that hitherto produced at the two existing mills, at Probolingo and Padalarang, where rice straw is the material used.

The planting and care of the trees that form avenues beside hundreds of miles of Java roads are also the concern of the Forestry Service.

CHAPTER FIFTEEN

The "Kweekerij"

THERE is no pleasanter way to live in the great garden of Java than to have a garden of your own: a "Kweekerij" as the Dutch call it. The word means "nursery"; but there is little or no resemblance between a Java *kweekerij* and its opposite number in England, beyond the bare fact that flowers are cultivated in both of them.

For however much beauty a British nursery may achieve through sheer mass production of colour, there is never any possibility of mistaking its commercial object. The painfully practical layout of an English nursery would make that clear, even if the fact were not shouted at us from giant signboards; and not all the glory of the flowers in even the best of such places can ever make it in the true sense a "garden."

In Java it is quite otherwise. Though why it should be so is hard to say. The Dutch are commercial minded enough, heaven knows, and they are experts in the flower business from A to Z. Nevertheless, though a Java mountain *kweekerij* may be just as much a business venture as if it were a shop, there is nothing in its appearance to suggest that it has been planted for any other purpose than the pleasure of its owners, and to add yet more colour and beauty to the wealth of both with which it is surrounded.

Of course the nature of those surroundings has much to do with it. You must go high up among the mountains, at 3000 or 4000 feet, to plant a nursery, for here the climate is that of a perennial perfect European summer, where spring, summer, and autumn flowers flourish side by side all the year round. No garden can look "commercial," or other than beautiful, when it is planted up hill and down dale on steep terraced hillsides and winding valleys, and watered by sparkling streams running under bridges of woven bamboo, between banks thick with maidenhair fern: and it is in country such as this that most of the Java nursery gardens are to be found.

No blatant signboards spoil the picture here. Only a flush of pink or crimson on the mountainside, as you turn a corner of the steep winding track, or a blur of many colours like the pattern of an old Persian carpet, set amid the vivid green of the rice terraces, announce themselves as a source of supply of some of the roses and asters always to be found in the flower shops that form such delicious oases of scent and sweetness in the hot city streets below.

It was to be expected that the Dutch, the world's greatest horticulturists, should establish flower culture and a flower trade on the grand scale in a colony whose climate and conditions were so ideal for the purpose. For many years the business was a lucrative one; and then, as with so many other crops (that of rubber is the most notable instance), its very success was its undoing. More and more Europeans planted flowers for profit; and when the Javanese began to follow suit, the familiar bugbears of over production and low prices were the result, and to-day the profits of a *bloemkweekerij* are extremely modest. In places there are actually acres of glorious roses, which look like Regent's Park rose gardens strayed on to a Java mountainside, blooming unnoticed and ungathered, because it does not pay to pick them.

Although flower growing in Java is no longer as lucrative as of old, it is still carried on. The expenses are relatively low, compared, that is, with the costs involved in Europe. A native gardener's wages are about twenty-five cents per day, and that of a woman employed in weeding, picking, or packing, twenty cents. The trade remains a large one, and the demand for flowers is great, but it is far more profitable to the retailer than to the grower, and the gap between the prices charged in the shops and those earned by the grower is ludicrously wide. The national love of flowers, or perhaps it would be more correct to say the fashion of "saying it with flowers," is very much alive in the Colonial Dutch; and every sort of occasion, whether it be arrival or departure, a wedding, a birthday, or a funeral, is marked by gifts of baskets or bouquets of flowers, for which the town florists charge luxury prices much the same as those paid for similar tokens in Europe, if not even higher.

The luckless grower, however, as a rule only gets a flat

rate all round of about thirty cents per large bunch of roses, carnations, asters, lilies, or whatever it may be, a price which has to cover all his costs of growing, gathering, packing, and transport. Native cultivators undersell even this low rate. They like to offer, and often sell, the flowers they grow to European planters in their neighbourhood, to save themselves the time and trouble of transport to market. Failing this method of disposal, they carry great loads of lovely blossoms down from their gardens to the towns far below, journeys that take many hours, and sell them for next to nothing in the streets. For the Javanese is content to accept a very small return for a very great deal of labour.

However serious the competition of these native growers may be, it would be hard not to forgive them when you see the gorgeous splashes of colour they contribute to the scene: as for instance on the *aloon-aloon* at Malang, East Java, most beautiful of all the grassy town centres in the whole island. Here, under the far flung shade of an immense old *waringen* tree which dominates the centre of the great space of close cropped turf, the native flower sellers congregate every morning in the midst of a crowded mass of multicoloured blossoms shimmering like rainbows in their setting of green, against a background made up of glimpses between the *waringens* that stand sentinel all round the *aloon-aloon*, of white walled, brown tiled houses; and above and beyond them the serene distant beauty of the Ardjoeno mountains, on whose slopes these very flowers have grown.

Thanks to the indispensable bamboo, this wealth of flowers is always fresh. They stand in water in deep "vases" easily made by sawing off sections of its immense hollow stems.

On many European owned *kweekerijs* the culture of flowers is combined with that of oranges, coffee, vegetables, vanilla, and other crops. And some of the town flower shops have their own gardens in the mountains where they cultivate their supplies. The best flower growing climates being at altitudes that are delightfully cool and healthy to live in, the owners and managers of these nurseries naturally make them their homes, adding still further to their informal and welcoming appearance. They seem to apply the same principle to them as the Frenchman does to the matter of food, when he argues

The "Kweekerij"

that since we must eat and drink to live, we may as well make it as enjoyable a process as possible. So the nursery gardener in Java sees no earthly reason why the garden that supports him and his family, albeit modestly, should not be a place that will give them pleasure as well as profit. He not only plants rectangular blocks of flowers, so far as the probably irregular contours of his land permit, in true Dutch style, and others of oranges, coffee, strawberries, or anything else that happens to suit his taste and his business, but makes among them grass paths and rockeries, with orange and pommelo and mimosa trees here and there for shade and decoration. He will have beds of begonias and pansies and violets and nasturtiums; and pergolas and arbours covered with deep red bougainvillea, golden alamanda, clambering roses, or fluffy pink Honolulu creeper. In shady corners there will be banks covered with maidenhair fern of every kind, from the giant that in England is seen only at Kew, to one so fine it seems made for fairy bouquets; and rare gold and silver ferns and many others, all to be found wild in abundance in these mountains, and brought home and planted here, most likely, by members of the family from country walks.

Not that the "business" part of such a garden is any less lovely in its way than the rest. There are trim rectangles of yellow, red, and white roses; of pink, cream, yellow, and red gerberas which grow to even greater perfection in this climate than in their native land of Africa; of hydrangeas, dahlias, carnations, chrysanthemums, asters, marigolds, coreopsis, gladiolas, cannas, blue and white agapanthus, tall crimson, orange, or white lilies, blood-red orchids from Borneo, and many more; most of them surrounded by broad belts of zinnias of every brilliant hue imaginable, which grow here to giant size, and serve in their sturdy perfection as a windbreak for less robust flowers, while themselves adding to the glory of the garden with their gorgeous masses of colour. In the same way the clumps of gerberas of every shade, of coreopsis, marigolds, and dwarf zinnias lining both sides of the grass paths serve the double purpose of beautifying it and adding to the supplies of those flowers for the market.

The delicately scented mimosa, known in its Australian homeland as wattle, blooms here all the year round and is as much in demand in Batavia and Soerabaya florists' shops as it is in England and France. And these graceful trees render even more valuable service when they throw their feathery shade over the bamboo seats beside the shaven turf path that runs between carpets of colour melting in the distance into the dark shadows of a coffee plantation and the misty blue of the far off mountains.

Work on a *kweekerij*, as on all tropical plantations, starts at daybreak, and both Mijnheer and Mevrouw are pretty sure to be out soon after setting the gardeners to their various jobs. Some will be preparing beds with the *patjoel*, or *changkul*, as the Malays call it, almost the only tool used by the field worker in these parts. It is shaped like a narrow spade, with the difference that it is set at an angle of about thirty degrees to the handle,[1] the edge of the blade pointing back towards the user: the perfect instrument for working soft rich stoneless soil, into which it cuts as though it were cheese, as the gardener drops it with much the same action as a man using a pick. The *patjoel* is the inseparable outdoor companion of its native owner, who cares for it like the true craftsman he is, and keeps it always bright and keen. It is said that he never sharpens it, and that his custom of leaving it to soak all night in a stream or tank is the correct way to keep it in good order.

Other gardeners will be taking rose, carnation, or chrysanthemum cuttings, or planting them out by hundreds; and others, again, transplanting seedlings, sowing seeds, or weeding; or perhaps cutting, with the faithful *patjoel*, channels to lead water from a stream running through the garden, to irrigate one or other of the flower crops.

To a British visitor accustomed to measure the work that can be accomplished in a garden in terms of one pair of hands, all this seems like a miracle. The plans that have matured in the minds of Mijnheer and Mevrouw during the night watches are translated into fact with no more labour, to them, than that of directing it. Cool and clear come the instructions, gently uttered, in fluent Javanese; and Soemo and Kardjo and Matradji and the rest, who know their work, and know that those in command do so too, buckle-to with a will; and

[1] The Provençal peasant, working in his stony soil, uses a two- or three-pronged fork set at exactly the same curious angle.

in a few minutes, by magic as it seems, a big perfectly symmetrical bed has been prepared, banked up, holes punched at measured intervals, and a couple of hundred cuttings set out and already looking quite at home. "Ach ja!" says Mevrouw with a smile. "When you garden here in Java, you use your own brains and other people's hands and muscles. It is much better so, *nietwaar?*"

It certainly is. And it is not only abundance of labour, but of labour that is both willing and efficient, that makes gardening in Java so doubly pleasant. There are no glum looks, no grumbles, and no arguments. The Javanese is a born cultivator, and as a rule he is as eager to carry out instructions as his employer is to give them.

You need not wait here, as in England, to transplant roses or other shrubs at the "proper time" in spring or autumn. Any time is proper in Java. If you should decide that a rose bush would look more effective in some other part of the garden than in its present place, you have only to call one of the gardeners, give instructions, and the thing is done. That perfect tool the *patjoel* releases the roots without damaging them, and prepares their new bed. The good earth makes them welcome; and though the young shoots may wilt for a few days, in a week, at most, the tree is perfectly settled down and goes on flowering as though nothing had happened.

A section of the garden devoted to the cultivation of large specimen chrysanthemums, such as we grow in glasshouses, is typical of the patient devoted labour so willingly given by the Javanese gardener. Every plant, with its one perfect bloom, is shaded by a small conical hat made of split bamboo, held over it like an umbrella on a stick stuck in the ground; and the effect at a distance is exactly as though rows of men were standing stiffly at attention between the plants.

Early every morning the important business of picking the flowers for market is done by native women; and a pretty sight it is to see them in their brightly coloured *sarongs*, for once in a way kilted to the knee, for the ground is often wet, from irrigation in the dry monsoon or heavy showers in the wet one. They move, always stooping, between the rows of plants, picking or cutting with mechanical speed and skill, and a complete lack of sentiment; they always carry the flowers head downwards!

Prettiest of all is to see one of them returning from some distant part of the estate carrying on her head, like a huge beflowered hat, the carnations and asters and sweetpeas she has picked, piled up on a round bamboo tray a yard across. The slim upright little figure in its gay red, green, and yellow *sarong*, and maroon *badjoe*, and serious young brown face shaded by the wide flower laden tray, is one that artists might search the world for in vain, as she tops a little rise, and pauses for a moment silhouetted against the vague blue of the distant mountains, and then sways easily down the grass path between the squares of red and pink roses and flaring belts of zinnias, with one hand, on which a couple of pale gold rings gleam softly, raised in an unconsciously classic pose to steady the lovely burden on her head. Unsmiling, and apparently deep in thought, she passes from the bright sunshine into the luminous shade of the mimosas and out again, to disappear at last under the pommelo trees laden with their great golden globes, in the direction of the packing-sheds.

Carefully separated into bunches of different sorts and colours, the flowers are put in to be watered in bamboo section pots, in the big, cool "godown," where they stand in battalions, making lovely dim, vague blots of colour in the sweet scented half darkness until the time comes to pack them for transport to town.

The baskets, if they can be so called, in which they are sent to market are bucket shaped and about the size of an ordinary wine cask. They are mere skeletons made of strips of split bamboo about six inches apart, but wonderfully strong and perfectly rigid. A huge pile of them appears every day or so at the entrance of the "godown," moving apparently of its own volition, so entirely hidden beneath them is the old man who makes and delivers them, for one penny each! They are lined with banana leaf, and the flower bunches tied one by one all round inside, so that the effect of the finished package before the lid is put on is that of a giant bouquet with a space in the middle. Finally they are sprayed; the round top, also lined with banana leaf, is tied on, and the big baskets stand in a row in the shade to await the special motor lorry that calls for them daily.

Man cannot live by flowers alone in Java nowadays, and other crops have to be pressed into the service if a *kweekerij* is to pay its way. Fortunately the mountain climate so favourable for flowers is equally well suited to all kinds of vegetables, for which there is an immense demand; but here again the story of the flower industry has to a great extent been repeated, and prices have fallen too low to bring much profit. And when you drive through one of the fertile mountain districts and see the huge piles of magnificent cabbages from native gardens awaiting the transport lorry at close intervals along the roadside you can only marvel that there can possibly be enough people in Java to buy and eat them, or that they bring in even the low prices that they do.

And what would the London housewife say if she could buy lovely asparagus, fresh picked from the garden, for threepence or fourpence per lb?

The vegetables are packed in another shed or "godown," in stouter baskets, varying in price from two to five cents according to size. Like the flower baskets, they are made of the white inner layer of the bamboo, with one strip of the dark green *koelit* (the skin, or outside layer), not, as might be supposed, for decoration, but for strength. Many people in the towns place orders with the mountain growers for regular supplies of vegetables two or three times per week; and very attractive these baskets look, with their assortments of firm fresh cabbage and lettuce, carrots, silver beet, asparagus, etc., with always, in season, a dozen or two of the rich dark green oranges in insatiable demand for the making of cool drinks. The skin of these oranges never turns yellow, but remains a rich dark green when the fruit is sweet and ripe.

While the packing is going on, the two great pale buff oxen who will presently draw the huge creaking *grobak* with its load of vegetables down the long steep winding mountain road to the railway, twenty miles away, lie dozing in the shade of their *bilik* shed near by, lazily chewing maize husks and leaves, until the baskets are loaded, the big gentle beasts yoked, and they set off with softly clanking bells on their slow all night journey; a cheap and admirable mode of transport when speed is not the essence of the contract, as in the case of flowers.

Oranges are grown successfully anywhere in the Java highlands, but they thrive best in the centre and east of the island where the dry season is more marked. On the rich plateaux of Batoe and Poedjon, above Malang, they have found their ideal climate, and not only are there many European plantations of them in this region, usually in conjunction with flowers and other crops, but few native gardens are without a few trees. The prime favourite is the delicious *djeroek manis*, a very sweet, juicy variety; and though great quantities of these are grown on the *kweekerij*, the demand for them in the towns is so great that the natives are encouraged to bring the crops from their trees to supplement the supply, so that the orders for them may be fulfilled. As with their flowers, the local Javanese are delighted to sell on the spot and save themselves the long trip on foot down the mountain; so at all hours of the day in the orange season there are pretty sure to be one or two picturesque figures squatting contentedly between their twin loads beside the verandah, smoking their tiny cigarettes and chatting in low voices, until such time as Mevrouw shall appear and offer them, as is most probable if their fruit is sound, the ruling price of Fl. 1.25 to Fl. 1.75 per 100, according to size, for *djeroek manis*, and Fl. 1 per 100 for so called "sour" oranges, which are also very juicy and make very refreshing drinks. (The Dutch Florin or Guilder—the names are used interchangeably—is worth, at par, 1*s*. 8*d*. sterling.)

The enormous pommelo, known as *djeroek Bali*, is also a favourite in native gardens, though the demand for the fruit is not great and they make little profit from them. The fruit is, however, a useful contribution to the native commissariat, and it is for this reason that the pommelo tree is to be seen here and there among the trees that line the roads, according to the admirable custom throughout the island, on these high plateaux. During the last century, when the Dutch were still engaged in opening up the country and making roads farther and farther into the hinterlands, the Government adopted the excellent plan of planting at intervals along those roads trees that would bear fruit to feed the ever plodding natives who would travel along them to carry their produce to market. The pommelo and the *nangka* were among the trees chosen for this purpose at the elevations that suited them, and although nowadays there are *kampongs* and *waroengs* (small shops) and itinerant food vendors everywhere along the highroads to cater for travelling natives, and the food bearing trees are no longer needed for their original purpose, many still remain among the ranks of shade trees as evidence of a practical and kindly consideration that is rare indeed in Government departments.

This *djeroek Bali* is truly magnificent, and makes the finest of oranges look like a poor relation. The tree grows to a height well above the roof of an ordinary house, and the sight of one laden with bunches of the huge golden balls, bigger than a child's head, often six or seven in a bunch, from the topmost branch down almost to the ground, interspersed with great clusters of outsize blossom, is a thing never to be forgotten. Like all the citrous family of trees in this generous climate, the pommelo is in bloom almost all the year round, and the scent of its wonderful flower, like orange-blossom many times magnified, fills the air even when the crop is ripening; and the fat creamy buds and thick petalled blossoms fall on the grass at your feet as you reach up to gather the giant fruit.

The *djeroek kaprok*, a sort of mandarin, is widely grown as a "side line" or for decoration in European and native gardens. This fruit finds a ready sale in Java as elsewhere. Another small variety no bigger than a mandarin but with the tight skin of the true orange, variously named, but generally called by the Javanese *djeroek sambalan*, being used chiefly, like lemon, as a relish, is extraordinarily prolific, and on the *kweekerij* was found to be an excellent substitute for the Seville orange for marmalade making. The tree, planted for shade and ornament, is a lovely sight indeed in the fruit season, for it bears so heavily that it is almost covered with small golden balls, and in the distance looks as though laden with masses of yellow flowers. And there was surely never marmalade made under such pleasant conditions as when we picked the ripe fruit which fell, too, in thousands and carpeted the ground for yards around, washed them in a handy stream, and cut them up, sitting amid the scent and under the shade of the tree that bore them; stirring them later over a little earthenware *anglo*, while a Javanese girl, squatted on her heels, gently fanned the charcoal to a glow.

Other so called choice varieties of orange, such as the Valencia and Washington navel, are grown in many plantations and are in great demand. These, however, have not so good a flavour as those grown in dryer climates and in latitudes where a cold winter allows the tree to rest.

An interesting method of increasing the vitality of trees, rather on the monkey gland principle, is much practised by Java orange growers. The tops of three or four well rooted seedlings of sturdy "rough orange" or lemon stock are planted close round the tree it is desired to tonic, and the tops of the seedlings grafted into its trunk. The effect is somewhat that of living "flying buttresses." The tree thus stimulated quickly draws new life from the strong young seedlings, and its crop is usually much increased by the very next season.

A quicker and easier method of getting new trees than by raising them from seed is common among both European and native orange growers. A convenient branch is ring-barked, earth is bound round the gap in palm leaf and kept damp until the roots are formed. The rooted branch, called a *tjangkokan*, is then cut off and planted. Trees started in this way are usually to be recognised by their rather lopsided shape.

The coffee grown on the *kweekerij* is a survival from the time when the whole of the surrounding country was planted with this crop by order of the Government; and to-day there is scarcely a native front garden in the district in which dark leaved coffee bushes do not rub shoulders with orange trees. The network of good paths or by-roads, too, which nowadays are the delight of visitors on mountain holidays, are another good legacy from those bad old days.

Happily native memories are short, and their records scanty; and the bitter hatreds of the days of forced coffee culture on these same peaceful hillsides and plateaux are now long forgotten.

Arabica coffee, introduced by the Company from Arabia early in the seventeenth century, was carried on as a forced culture by them and by the Government that succeeded them until early in the twentieth century. According to records 45 million trees were planted by Daendel's orders. Raffles made the culture free during his short interregnum; and when the Dutch resumed control it remained nominally so, but the plantations were hired out to the *dessas*, whose populations had to pay for them at the rate of half, or sometimes one third, of the crop. In practice this meant that the unfortunate natives worked for nothing, as they had no means of selling the balance of the crop, and so simply turned it over with the rest to their taskmasters. In 1830 the notorious De Bosch tightened the screw still further, and all coffee grown had to be sold to the Government at the latter's own price, after two fifths had been taken off for rent and transport. Whole *dessa* populations were called up willy-nilly to work the huge plantations, no matter how far away they might be from their homes. News of the oppression filtered through to Holland and aroused a wave of indignation at what was described as the virtual slavery of the natives. After this the scheme was modified by degrees, until by 1872 most of the plantations had been broken up into small gardens of 50 or 100 trees round about the native *kampongs*.

Early in the twentieth century the dreaded "Coffee disease" which had appeared previously in Ceylon attacked the crops. It was a kind of mildew which formed in orange coloured spots on the undersides of the leaves of coffee and other members of the *rubiaceæ* family of plants. It ravaged and almost entirely wiped out the *arabica* coffee plantations of Java; and incidentally was the cause of the very great increase in the cultivation of tea, which was planted in its place.

When at last coffee growing was resumed many years later by private planters, it was the sturdy, big leaved *robusta* from the Congo that they selected. And it is this, with its white starry blossom growing in thick double rows along the stem, half hidden by the glossy dark leaves, that is nowadays mostly to be seen. But here and there you will see a bush of *arabica*, easily recognisable by its much smaller leaves and general slenderness; and now that the disease has disappeared, *arabica* is being grafted on *robusta* stock and planted once more. Very misleadingly, *arabica* is always called "Java coffee" by the Dutch planters.

A grey wild cat, common in mountain districts, and called the *loewak*, is a scourge to coffee growers; for not only is it, like all its kind, a robber of hen roosts, but has an insatiable predilection for the sweet, reddish ripe coffee berries, which it strips off the branches and swallows in dozens. The brute's taste is unerring, and it may be relied upon to choose the very best. But things are seldom so bad that they might not be worse; the twin seeds of the coffee berry are too hard to dissolve, and pass unscathed through the animal's digestive system. They are carefully collected by the native coolies, roasted and ground in the ordinary way, and called "*loewak* coffee"! According to many people, both native and European, such coffee has a more delicious fragrance than any other.

The *loewak's* lair, or the hide out whence it makes its nightly raids, will often announce itself unmistakably from a patch of thick cover on a mountain walk, with a whiff of pungent, horrible wild-beast smell that transports you in a moment, in imagination, to the lions' house at the Zoo. But the *loewak* itself is never to be seen in the daytime.

Worn-out coffee bushes serve a last useful purpose as charcoal—the staple cooking fuel of the native population. When the great Government plantations were ordered to be grubbed up, charcoal burners were everywhere encouraged, in order to use up the wood and clear the land. But nowadays, the industry being a lucrative one, natives who carry it on may not do so without a Government licence, and in some places are obliged to sell only to Government depots.

The favourite wood for the purpose is tamarind. But on the *kweekerij*, for a time at least, our charcoal was home grown; a plantation of old coffee bushes having been condemned and dug up, a native charcoal burner was sent for from his home in the forest, and we were able to watch the process from start to finish on the premises.

The old man and his assistants first dug a shallow hole some eight or ten feet square, in which a fire was laid ready for lighting. Over this they built a strong platform of green wood, covered with several layers of fresh green banana leaves, and on them were piled the coffee roots and chopped up bushes destined to be turned into charcoal. Then, over a bamboo framework, they constructed a sort of hut made of clods of grass and mud, leaving an opening as a chimney for the smoke. The fire was then lighted, and kept smouldering for three or four days. At the end of that time the queer edifice was dismantled, and the charcoal laboriously picked out bit by bit from the pit, where the men and their wives, who by this time had joined the party, squatted chatting or singing softly in the midst of a charred, sodden mass made up of charcoal, damp brown leaves and branches, and muddy clods. They were paid by results: at the rate of thirty cents per *pikoel*, one *pikoel* filling two big baskets.

Charcoal is a very important item indeed in the domestic economy of life in Java. Not only do all native women cook with it, but it is used in the kitchens of all, or nearly all, European country households. At first sight it would seem impossible that any but the simplest sort of cooking could be done on the queer little bucket shaped *anglo*, with its ridiculously tiny charcoal fire kept glowing by fanning at intervals with a small split bamboo fan, sold for a farthing in any *pasar*. But the most elaborate meals, including the myriad dishes of a complete *nasi*, or *rijsttafel*, are cooked as a matter of course on two or three of the primitive little stoves standing in a row on a concrete slab. Even baked dishes present no difficulty, for charcoal piled on the top of an iron pot on the fire produces exactly the same results as an oven, in the hands of a good native cook.

None of the inconveniences usually associated with housekeeping in remote country places trouble the mistress of a Java *kweekerij* or plantation. For not only are supplies of all kinds brought to the door without even the trouble of ordering them, or if by chance they are not, a native servant can always be sent to the *pasar* or the nearest *kampong*, but her domestic staff can be increased at a moment's notice to meet any emergency.

Friends perhaps turn up unexpectedly, and she invites them to stay for the week end, but no domestic upheaval follows the invitation. She confers with her cook; and presently, as though by magic, there will appear a smart *djongos* (house-boy) in clean starched white jacket and neat *batik sarong* and headdress, accompanied, perhaps, by a demure little *baboe* (maidservant). Within a few minutes they will have joined forces with the other servants, and everything is working as smoothly as though they had been part of the regular domestic staff for years. Yet in all probability they are just ordinary *dessa* folk, relations, very likely, of the servants regularly employed, whom you would see at any other time, if you happened to pass their homes, busy with their own simple affairs. The spick-and-span *djongos* who waited so deftly on your guests on Saturday and Sunday will probably be found in his garden on Monday, splitting bamboo or planting maize, or breaking up land with a *patjoel*, clad only in a pair of black shorts; and the *baboe* may be winnowing rice or weeding in the fields.

Why there should be this unfailing supply of quite reasonably efficient house servants among the inhabitants of so many country *dessas* is a mystery. Asked where they learned housework, they will often reply that at some time or other they have "followed" a white master as a personal servant; or they may have picked up what they know of European domestic ways from parents who have been called in as extra kitchen hands at holiday times in mountain hotels. But whatever the reason, there they are: so many degrees higher in cleanliness and efficiency than the average European "daily" as not to come into the same category at all.

Insect pests are not nearly so bad in Java as many people seem to imagine. There is none, for instance, to compare with that horror the English earwig, with its uncanny faculty of materialising out of thin air, and vanishing when you attempt to kill it, to reappear crawling on your sleeve or your neck or in your hair. It is only in England's so called summer that you find this vile insect in your sponge, on your bath towel, emerging with an obscene leer from the binding of every book you take from your shelves, under your pillow, and in the tea cosy, dropping from your toothbrush, or even committing suicide in the mustard!

But though this scourge has no counterpart in Java there is one that is cursed high and low by housewife and cultivator alike, and that is the ant. Not the destructive white ant, with its occasional visitations in its winged stage as the *laron* at the beginning of the wet monsoon; nor even the smaller flying varieties, though they are bad enough; but those innocent

A CLOSE-UP OF THE BRIDEGROOM AND HIS STEED, WITH THEIR ATTENDANTS.

EUROPEAN CHILDREN CARRIED UP A STEEP MOUNTAIN ROAD TO SCHOOL IN NATIVE SEDAN-CHAIRS OR *TANDOES*.

THE EVER-USEFUL PETROL-TIN.
WATER SUPPLIES BEING FETCHED FROM A
STREAM FOR A NATIVE GARDEN.

A MOUNTAIN PATHWAY.

SUNSET ON THE LAKE SARANGAN.

looking little hypocrites, the tiny black and brown ants that appear from nowhere if sugar, fruit, or anything else to their taste is left on the table.

Indoors they are a pest, but out of doors they are a menace. To the planter they are dangerous and insidious enemies. Swarming up the trunks of sturdy orange or other fruit trees in countless hordes, they eat every young shoot, covering whole branches with a black sticky mass composed of millions of their bodies, and reduce the trees to impotence. Against copper sulphate, however, they are powerless, and repeated sprayings of a strong solution will eventually vanquish them. But an attack on them is not an easy or a pleasant job, for they fall like rain on to anyone standing below the branches, and make fierce counter forays into his hair and ears and under his clothing, biting venomously as they go.

There is a *kweekerij* of a special kind at Nagrok, in the Preanger, where orchids are cultivated on the grand scale. They are propagated by seed in culture tubes on a chemical glucose mixture: a process taking several months, though it is possible to see within two or three days whether the seed is germinating. The fairylike seedlings are transferred to pear shaped bulbs like electric lamps for a further two months or so, and then to a tiny pot. Most orchids take three years to attain maturity and to flower, so the business is one of infinite patience. This Dutch specialist has some hundreds of new hybrids to his credit, and does business with all parts of the world. The orchid houses at this nursery are ingeniously designed to reproduce natural conditions. Some are in shade houses with soft constantly dug earth floors, copiously watered to give off a damp heat like that of forest undergrowth. Tree growers, on the other hand, are provided with branches high above the ground in open, cool, wire-netted houses roofed with tiles, where the breezes are as refreshing as in the tree tops.

Prices for these pampered gems of tropical beauty are very high, and the profits from a nursery of this kind far greater than those of an ordinary *kweekerij*.

The running water supply of Java country homes, as described in an earlier chapter, is usually assured without difficulty from natural sources. But it must be confessed that the

British visitor or resident accustomed to the staid conservatism of streams at home may be apt to get some odd surprises. In England, it is a thousand to one that a brook remembered from childhood will still be trickling along in the same place if you should revisit it half a lifetime later. But here in Java the handling of water is so much a commonplace that a stream which is here to-day is just as likely to be gone to-morrow. You may perhaps have leased a house and land that possessed among its attractions a stream that bustled merrily through the garden, not only adding immeasurably to its charm, but also playing the beneficent part of rubbish remover, and even, as is often the case, of sewerage system.

The horror of the householder may be imagined when one morning in the dry monsoon he awakens to an unwonted silence to find the pleasant music of laughing water that had lulled him to sleep no longer agreeably assailing his ears. When this happens there is nothing to be done except possess the soul in patience. Water, in this intricately irrigated land, serves nobler purposes than mere hygiene. Your stream has been diverted to play its necessary part in watering the crops elsewhere in the *dessa*, and will return to you when its more urgent work for the general community is done.

It is not only flowers and fruit that give colour to country life in Java. Contrary to what seems to be the general belief, Java is rich in bird life; especially on the rich plateaux far above sea level. In these regions the chorus of bird song is gayer than that of an English spring, and many of the birds wear plumage as brilliant as their voices. King of them all is the gorgeous *kepodang* (*oriolus indicus*), brighter in colour than any canary, and big as a missel thrush, with glossy black head and wing markings. And when he flashes like a sunbeam across the carpet of colour in a mountain flower garden, to perch in a *pommelo* tree loaded with great golden fruit, or among the dark foliage of a "mountain tulip," near one of its flaming scarlet blossoms, he looks like a flower that has been miraculously endowed with wings. His rich mellow unmistakable call of "wieliwaal," by which name the Dutch call him, usually brings his mate to perch on a neighbouring tree; but never in the same one, a rule so invariable as to arouse the suspicion that the *kepodang's* character is less beautiful than his appearance, and that his spouse prefers him at a discreet distance!

Parrots also contribute much to the colour of the mountain country scene. They are vivid green with pinkish orange breasts and, like their Australian cousins, they take the air in large companies. Like them, too, their beauty, from the gardener's point of view, is only feather deep, for they are most destructive and extremely greedy. But all the same, much must be forgiven them in return for the lovely gleaming pattern that they paint as a big flight of them rises and wheels in a gleaming shaft of emerald across the field that they have just ravished.

Less decorative, but far more companionable, is the *djalak*, another link with the bird life of Australia, where he is familiar to all bush dwellers by the inappropriate name of "soldier-bird." Happily a bird by any other name whistles just as sweetly, and his cheery, encouraging note is as pleasant to the ear in one country as in the other. The Java *djalak* however has an immense advantage over his Australian relations in numbers, owing to the much greater abundance of food he finds in the rich, cultivated volcanic soil. He is as tame and friendly when you work in your garden in Java as the robin is in England; and for this reason the Dutch call him "makker," meaning comrade or mate.

Another very common bird is the *gelatik*, known to most English people as the Java sparrow, or rice sparrow. He is a most charming little fellow in appearance, with his red beak and smart white wing facings, but he is a greedy pest, and by no means beloved of farmers or gardeners. These little birds gather in flocks like the common sparrow and are just as impudent and easily tamed. Given the slightest encouragement in the way of scattered grain, a colony of them will only too willingly adopt your garden as their own, selecting some special tree as their roosting place, to the delight of that shrewd tactician the family cat, who soon learns that his supper awaits him nightly among the packed ranks of sleepy birds in the branches, without the trouble of hunting for it. A fluttering, and a few startled twitters announce the tiny tragedy, whose regular recurrence fails entirely to teach these perky but silly little birds the elements of wisdom.

An occasional visitor to mountain gardens is a *bosch-hahn*, one of the wild brown jungle fowl with which the forests abound. They might easily be mistaken for our domestic bantam, of which they are probably the prototype. It is always startling to hear one of these little cocks crowing in the depths of the forest; and still more so to see so domestic looking a bird rise and disappear high on the wing among the great branches overhead.

The great white rice bird, which the Javanese call *tjanga oelor*, a member of the heron family, will sometimes honour a mountain garden by coming to roost in a *pommelo* tree for the night. He is a welcome guest as well as a beautiful one, for his sharp eyes seldom miss a snake, especially the slender black and cream banded variety that sometimes finds its way in from the maize fields: a titbit of which he is very fond.

At the other end of the scale in size are the tiny honey-eaters, of which Java has many varieties. One of the most charming of these birds is pale delicate grey green in colour, so that when a flight of the fragile little creatures settle, as they will, amid the feathery foliage of a mimosa tree after rain, they would be perfectly invisible if it were not for their quick nervous movements. Another kind is black and scarlet; and when a flock of these settles on a tree in your garden, the effect is as though it had burst miraculously into flower.

These dainty birds are so tiny, and some of Java's wealth of butterflies and moths are so large, that it is often difficult to be sure which it is, as these exquisite fragments of living colour flit to and fro among the flowers. The butterflies of the East Indies are world famous, and Java has its full share. Their colour and brilliance are as astonishing as their size; and so is their capacity for flight. They will fly out to a ship lying far off the shore, flutter all round as though making observations, and then return to land without having made the least attempt to settle. The smaller butterflies are often to be seen in great numbers on the banks of streams in sheltered mountain places, half hidden among the grass like flowers, or rising as you approach, in clouds of sky blue, white, or yellow. And you may often see a single specimen, enjoying the sunshine with outspread wings on a warm smooth stone in the middle of a mountain pathway, a quivering jewel of electric blue or green set in an intricate pattern of velvety black.

The only drawback to this wealth of lovely butterflies, from the *kweekerij* point of view, is the inevitable corresponding abundance of caterpillars which do an immense amount of damage to flower and vegetable crops.

Dragonflies, "glasmakers" as the Dutch call them, of all sorts and sizes, are to be seen in thousands, especially in the high plateaux towards the end of the East Monsoon, adding yet more brilliance to the scene with their sudden gleaming flashes of blue, red, or gold. And at night, as in all tropic countries, fireflies are everywhere.

In spite of all this wealth of lovely living flying things with which nature has filled the air about and above them, it would seem that the Javanese are still not satisfied, and must needs make more contributions of their own. So it is that as a final touch you will often see what appear to be super giant butterflies moving rather jerkily high in the breeze against the blue mountain background; they are the gay coloured paper kites that are the pride of the highland villagers, made and often flown with as much enthusiasm by grandfathers and fathers of families as by their young sons.

CHAPTER SIXTEEN

The Great Post Road

THE "Great Post Road" of Java, which runs up hill and down dale for a thousand kilometres from Anjer on the coast of Bantam, the extreme westerly point of the island, to Panaroekan, a few miles from the coast at the eastern end, is a legacy to the colony from the ruthless but efficient Governor Daendels, founder of the beautifully planned town of Weltevreden. Originally, and for some decades, the only road by which wheeled traffic could travel, it remains to-day the backbone of the remarkable road system that has gradually stretched out to give easy access to every smallest and most remote hamlet in Java.

The building of this road was an extraordinary achievement. The conditions in Java when Daendels arrived there in the early years of the nineteenth century were so bad, in regard both to the health of the community and its finances, that it is more than doubtful whether so stupendous an undertaking would ever have been attempted in the existing conditions by a governor less determined or more squeamish. Daendels, however, was hampered by none of the ordinary man's conscience in regard to human life and suffering. It is true that his concern to create a healthier town for the people of Batavia was of immense public benefit. But the end in view was practical rather than humane.

And so it was with the Great Post Road. In Daendels's opinion a main "through" road was necessary in the first place as a military measure to facilitate troop movements in case of enemy attack, and in the second to provide speedier transport for the coffee and other cultures that he was inaugurating on the grand scale. This decision once arrived at, a road he must have at all costs; and to carry out his plan he set in motion all the untrammelled powers at his command, on a scale that even in the East India Company's heyday had never been attempted before.

The fiat went forth. Word was sent to the head men of all the hundreds of *dessas* through which the road was to pass,

The Great Post Road

from one end of Java to the other. A route was worked out, following, where practicable, the narrow footpaths and rough cart-tracks that had been used by the people from time immemorial. For hundreds of miles the way ran through primeval jungle where the giant tree trunks of colossal girth rose from dense forests of lesser growth, all woven together by vines and creepers into an impenetrable tangle that defied the puny efforts of man to violate it. Breathless, steamy, full of mysterious sounds and the hum of myriads of insects, the haunt of tiger and panther, the rich earth with its lush wet grass alive with leeches, a forbidding scene indeed as the setting of a main road! And as though all this were not enough in itself when on the level, there were innumerable mountain ranges to be negotiated, so that to the already almost insurmountable difficulties of cutting a way through the forests was added that of doing so amid a labyrinth of steep and often precipitous slopes, and of finding passes where none was to be seen.

Of rivers too there were plenty to be crossed. But these, rapid and rock-filled, and in some cases liable to flood, as they are, for the most part are neither wide nor very deep, and by comparison presented only minor difficulties.

At all events the apparently impossible was tackled. European overseers were sent to various points along the route that had been approximately worked out. The man power of every district, with its oxen and buffaloes, was mustered, and set to work: felling jungle giants against whose massive boles their puny axes seemed no more than importunate flies, yet crashed to their doom at last; chopping and cutting and crashing their way through the bewildering undergrowth, their straining limbs covered with leeches; digging and dragging with the combined strength of scores of men to remove rocks and huge stones; collapsing from exhaustion and fever and dying like flies, their tired-out bodies pushed aside with no more thought than those of the leeches they themselves had crushed by dozens. A terrible price it was in flesh and blood and human misery that had to be paid for the Great Post Road. Seldom in the annals of road building, even in the East, can the ancient convention of human sacrifice have been better obeyed, or human bodies more lavishly buried among the foundations of any building enterprise, than under this lovely motor highway that is nowadays the delight of every traveller in Java.

The road was actually completed for traffic in about a year; nothing less than a miracle of achievement in such country. And now for the first time Java was to begin to take on the complexion of one big Dutch colony instead of a collection of colonies as distinct almost as those scattered throughout the farther islands, for hitherto the only practical means of communication had been by sea.

A journey overland from east to west, or *vice versa* (if anyone should be rash enough to attempt it), in the days before 1808 was estimated to take about six weeks, not, of course, allowing for the breakdowns and washaways that might delay the traveller still more. But on Daendels's Great Post Road it was possible to travel from one end of Java to the other in six days.

Daendels wasted no time in establishing communications. The road was no sooner through as far as Buitenzorg, about forty miles from Batavia, than a horse post was started, described as "from Batavia along the Great Road to Buitenzorg and more distant places," the service being extended to those places as the road reached them. The road had been started in 1808, and by 1809 a post and passenger service was already running regularly between Batavia and Soerabaya. The fare from Batavia to Buitenzorg by post coach was five rex dollars per passenger, or a special private coach for four passengers might be hired for eighteen rex dollars (1 rex = 4s. 2d.). There were five stages at which horses, or rather ponies, had to be changed on this forty mile section, which gives an indication of what the road surface must have been like, for this part of the route is not mountainous.

When the post service was started, Daendels issued orders to the native regents of the districts all along the route to supply relays of ponies and to erect *bilik* shelters at given points. The coaches set off twice a week from both ends of the route, drawn by four or six horses according to the steepness of the stage, from each of which also two extra horses were always sent on ahead of the coach in case of accidents, which appear to have been numerous.

The Great Post Road

On the route between Batavia and Soerabaya there were twelve principal stopping places with good inns where passengers could put up for the night if they so desired. Each of these inns had six or eight bedrooms, stables, and outhouses. The charge per day, which included "two good hot meals, morning tea or coffee, breakfast, and afternoon tea or coffee," was Fl. 2.55. So that in those days, as in ours, Dutch hotels evidently offered generous hospitality at a modest charge. These inns were obliged by the terms of their licence to keep available for hire two post chaises for six persons with the necessary ponies, and two riding ponies for any persons who did not wish to use the regular coach.

There were at many other less important places along the route, rest houses or *pasang-grahans*: probably very much the same as those in remote places to-day. At these the traveller could always get a bed and a meal of some sort.

A seat in a long distance post coach cost the passenger 5 stuivers (a stuiver = about one penny) silver per *paal* (1500 metres: roughly one mile); and a span of four ponies for a private chaise, 16 stuivers per *paal*. A good riding pony, called *koeda aloes*, cost the hirer half a silver florin or guilder per three *paal*; but a pony good enough for a native servant to ride (a *koeda gladag*[1]) might be had for no more than 4½ stuivers per three *paal*; and it is only too easy to imagine the pitiful walking skeleton it would probably be.

Travel by the post coaches must have been most select, and "naice" passengers ran little risk of making undesirable acquaintances. For, according to the old regulations, "no vile or mean person" was allowed to ride in them, and it was emphasised that "passengers must be of a certain style, quality, and good condition." It is sincerely to be hoped that the passengers were always able to live up to the desired standard; but the doubt is apt to intrude itself as to whether a perfectly ladylike or gentlemanly "style" may not have fallen off a trifle when the coach was bogged, or even perhaps capsized, and its occupants were obliged to turn out in the mud and drenching downpour of one of Java's terrific mountain storms.

---

[1] *Gladag* is the place outside the north gate of a Kraton (the royal palace) where a Java sultan's transport ponies, carts, and coolies must always be in waiting. Hence *koeda gladag* means an ordinary service pony.

It was half a century before the Javanese people themselves were allowed to use the road that their fathers had died in thousands to build. The Great Post Road was known to them as the "Herenweg" (the road of lords and gentlemen) whose sacred surface might not be profaned by the clumsy native *grobaks*. These they had to drive as best they could through mud and stones and rivers on rough tracks following as nearly as might be the course of the Great Post Road, so that this lordly thoroughfare might not be damaged by their weight. It was not until 1857 that the main roads, until then reserved for Europeans and for the post services, were opened to native traffic, and the making of supplementary rough tracks for this was discontinued.

The vehicles in use as coaches and post chaises were modelled more or less on the lines of those in Europe at the time, but there were many others peculiar to Java itself. The light two wheeled pony-carriage known as a *sado*, rather resembling what used in England to be called a governess cart, but with the addition of a top to shade it from the sun, the most generally used passenger vehicle in Java, appears to have been a native design; but its name is a corruption of "dos-à-dos" (back-to-back) and dates from the period of French domination just before the English conquest. The name is firmly established in West Java; but farther East the little carriage is called a *dokkert*, possibly from the English dogcart.

A hundred years ago you could not only hire a "dos-à-dos" or a post chaise, but a high two wheeled carriage drawn by a trotting bullock, like those still used in parts of India to-day. They were doubtless introduced to Java by Indian immigrants, and were called in Java *plankin-sapi*.

The most conservative places in Java are the two remaining Sultanates, and here, especially in the royal towns of Soerakarta and Djokdjakarta, a type of vehicle long extinct elsewhere is still in use. This is the *andong*, a large four wheeled pony chaise with a flat canopy and a box for the driver, who wears a uniform consisting of a black sailor jacket with white braided collar and cuffs, white trousers, and *batik* headdress. These jehus flourish long whips plaited round with coloured cord: often to be seen in the making under the shady trees bordering the streets. With these an endless tattoo is kept up on the shaggy hides of pairs of miserable ponies that are a disgrace to the Sultanates and all others concerned. The *andongs* entirely replace the *sado* in the two royal capitals. Another vehicle peculiar to these parts is a sort of barouche drawn by fat white ponies and driven by men wearing the uniform and odd tapering top hat of the Kraton. These carriages are used by inmates of the Kraton only.

Another relic of old time transport, but of a later date, is the *kossong*. It is what in England used to be known as a "Victoria," and was fashionable among Dutch as well as English ladies when they took the air in pre-motor days.

In Java its name, which means "empty," is a survival of the times when these vehicles plied for hire as cabs in the streets of all the towns, and the drivers, ever on the hunt for fares, as their successors the native taxi drivers are to-day, used to shout "*kossong! kossong!*" as they gaily cracked their whips and raced their smart pairs of ponies at a gallop to secure a likely passenger. Nowadays a few still jog sadly about the streets of Soerabaya, but all pretensions to smartness have long since departed. They have arrived at the last stages of shabbiness and are drawn by the poorest of ponies; regarded by natives as many degrees lower in the transport scale than the ubiquitous *sado*, the *kossongs* are hired only by those who are too poor to pay even the few cents fare asked by *sado* drivers.

Here is one glimpse we get of European travel in Java in the days before the Great Post Road was thought of. In 1747 there had been a very serious epidemic of fever in Batavia, where health conditions at that time were fast deteriorating. The town records state that in consequence of this, many sick persons were carried at their own cost from Batavia to the Tjipanas hot springs by buffalo cart. For their convenience a number of halts were established at which food was obtainable at fixed prices, and a change of draught animals was kept. The price of a buffalo cart from one of these halts to the next was five-eighths of a rex dollar (about half a crown). The interest of this lies in the fact that nowadays a run up to the Tjipanas bathing pool for a swim in the morning, or between tea and dinner, is a popular diversion with the motoring public of Batavia.

For a time the Great Post Road remained the only highway in Java on which it was possible to travel in comfort, and all points not served by it could only be reached by means differing little from those in vogue a century earlier. But Daendels's example had not been lost on the rest of the white population, either in the matter of road making or in the means to get them made. The revolutionary change in the conditions of life in the colony brought about by the post road had opened their eyes to limitless possibilities, and once the English interregnum was over, "herendienst" (forced labour) was revived in full force, and an orgy of road making set in all over the country. Not only were roads cut through from town to town, but to serve the interests of private individuals and make their particular way, to wheresoever their business or pleasure might take them, as easy and pleasant as possible. So notorious did this become that in 1835 the Government issued a decree that no more new roads might be made, or old paths or byways widened, without the consent in writing of the Governor-General. It is to this earlier virtually unrestricted use of free labour that Java owes to-day much of its extraordinary wealth of roads and byroads.

The perfection of these roads, and especially their banked curves in mountainous regions, makes them a pattern to other lands. The volume of motor traffic on them outside the towns is not great, and motoring in Java is still the joy it was in England years ago, before it degenerated into mere speeding. Here in Java you may still drive at your own pace as a means of enjoying the beauty of the countryside, which was the primary purpose for which the motor car was invented.

Perfect upkeep involves constant repair, of course; and big red lettered "wegherstelling" signs are as frequent on your drives as "Road under Repair" in England. But the scene is more picturesque; especially when, as so often on the carefully graded mountain roads, a theodolite is in use. Then a wide oiled-paper Chinese umbrella is held over the instrument and its operator by an underling, and you are apt to think at first glance that it is some stray sultan taking a walk abroad that you are overtaking.

The settings of the roads are as well groomed as their surfaces. The grass banks and verges are so trimly shaven

The Great Post Road

and shorn that they might be in a private park, but the local councils have no need, as in England, to employ men to keep them tidy. Draught animals are too many, and food too dear, to let any grass go to waste, and everywhere men, women, and children are to be seen busy cutting it with their sharp curved knives, and filling the twin bamboo baskets through which the ends of the *pikoelan* are pushed. More roads than not are avenues, and often clumps of rich red *acalypha* make glorious blots of colour in their shade on the cool green grass.

A new section of road came into being recently following a volcanic tremor which emptied the lake at Sindanglaya, West Java, a few years ago,[1] and provides an interesting example of Dutch engineering skill. The lake, which lay in a deep depression between two mountainsides, was bordered at one end by a road, and this was swept away by the weight of water as the lake burst its bounds, leaving two clean cut ends of tarred surface separated by a chasm some 200 feet deep and several hundred yards wide, broadening out into the empty basin of the former lake. The day after the occurrence, I had to make a detour of nearly ten miles to reach the point opposite; but now the narrow footpath along which amorous couples used to wander round the dreamy waters in the moonlight, or stop at the boat house to hire a skiff, has been transformed into a magnificent road, sweeping in a noble curve round a great gorge veiled in ferns and vegetation which was once the bed of the lake. The new road slopes easily down to the former lakehead, there to cross a bridge and curve up again to meet the farther end of the broken highway. If you stop your car at the point where the road bears away from its original route, and walk to the edge of the gorge, you can still find the broken ragged edge of the old tarred surface showing through the tangle of growth that has covered it. A stream meanders gently down the middle of the lake bed, whose sides are now as thickly clothed in green as though it had been as it is now since the beginning of time; so closely resembling, too, countless other such lovely mountain gorges that you are reminded how often the face of this volcanic land must have changed in the course of the centuries. A native house and garden now occupy the space left free between the broken end

[1] See *Java Pageant*.

of the old road and the curve of the new; so a line of brightly coloured washing hangs, banana leaves rustle, and naked brown children play on the grass where once the motor buses roared along the main road from Bandoeng to Buitenzorg.

In 1870 the first railway was opened, connecting Semarang and Solo; and thereafter, like the road system, gradually extended its tentacles to serve all the principal places in Java. There are about 2000 miles of 3 feet 6 inch gauge track; and what is more remarkable, as indicating the difficult nature of the country with which the engineers had to contend, more than 5000 bridges, many of them spanning deep gorges at giddy heights, whose length altogether totals over thirty miles.

Strangely enough, there were many modern residents of Java who knew nothing of the railways except from the distance, until the "depression" transformed the commonplace convenience of yesterday into too costly luxuries and suggested, among other economies, the possibility of travelling by train instead of by car. In Java the price of petrol is more than doubled by the petrol tax; and when, in the case of British residents, this was aggravated by the fall of the pound sterling from its par value of twelve guilders or florins to less than eight, it was obvious that motoring could no longer be taken quite so lightheartedly for granted as of old.

But every cloud has its silver lining. And in this case it was the discovery that even after years of familiarity with Java its acquaintance yet remained to be made from an entirely novel point of view. And had it not been for the "daling van de pond" (fall of the pound: a phrase that soon became hatefully familiar) it is probable that the unique panorama to be seen from the windows of the Java State Railways would have remained unknown to me for ever.

The names of the "*Eendaagsche*" (one day train) and the Java "*Nachtexpres*" (night express) had both become household words in Java since these much advertised trains *de luxe* had replaced the former slow, strictly daylight service. The latter restriction had been in deference to native engine drivers' reluctance to risk offending the spirits that walk in darkness; for a man may be a first class mechanic and driver and yet remain faithful to the beliefs of his forefathers. But education can achieve wonders; and now, so the posters of the *Staatsspoorwegen* proclaimed on all sides, travel on either the day or night express compared more than favourably with any in the world.

I was sceptical about the attractions of railway travel in Java. But needs must when the devil drives. I had survived long railway journeys in other hot climates, and reflected that at worst it could hardly be as bad as a summer trip across Queensland. And so one fresh delicious morning, just as the eastern sky was changing from silver to primrose, I took my place in a second class compartment of the famous "*Eendaagsche*," and saw the sun rise as we ran smoothly through the sweet scented gardens of the outer suburbs of Batavia.

I soon wasted no more regrets that for the first time I was not setting out across Java in the car. Far from it. The long airy compartment with the passageway down its centre was almost empty, and I had my end of it entirely to myself; so pleasant was it that a very few minutes served to convert me to this, to me, new mode of Java travel. I knew the Great Post Road from end to end, and hundreds of miles of it and other lovely Java highways and byways were far more familiar to me than any in England. But it became apparent at once that the panorama to be seen from this railway carriage was a revelation to one who had hitherto only travelled the country at the wheel of a motor car. No longer was I a part of the tangled pattern of life upon the roads, forced to thread my way among *sadoes*, *grobaks*, bicycles, cars, buses, handcarts, stray cattle, goats, dogs, fowls, ducks, buffaloes, and foot passengers, ever watchful to adjust my pace to their vagaries. All these terrestrial anxieties troubled me no more. I had removed to another plane, whence, godlike and unassailable, I could ride at my ease and survey the ever changing scene as we raced along, high above crowded roads and villages, houses and gay gardens, and the chequer board of ricefields, on embankments that seemed to have been designed for no other purpose than to provide the best of all possible observation points. The Javanese call an ordinary train *kereta api* (fire carriage); but they have aptly amended the name to *kereta api sambong*, the *proud* fire carriage, to describe these fast trains that disdain to stop at any but the largest stations, roaring past contemptuously unmindful of the humble human atoms toiling far below, instead of ambling quietly along like the ordinary trains, stopping to pick them up and carry them for a few cents from one wayside halt to the next.

It was harvest time on the rice plains of northwest Java when I made that first railway journey; and often as I had watched the scene before, I felt that I was now seeing it properly for the first time. As the sun rose, it lighted up scenes of unimaginable colour among the golden rice crops. We looked down as we passed above hundreds of men, women, and children, dressed in every conceivable shade of red, blue, green, pink, yellow, and lilac, streaming in single file along the narrow earth banks separating the *sawahs*, on their way to work; and on hundreds more already busy among the crops, cutting, as we knew, but of course could not distinguish at that distance, the heads of grain one by one with the odd little knife they call *ani-ani*. The men mostly wore flattish pointed straw hats, painted in all sorts of bright colours, and the women's heads were adorned with floating veils of equally gay and varied tints. Mile after mile the colourful pageant of the rice harvest was displayed: the same, yet ever shifting and regrouping itself against its eternal but always different mountain background.

We passed through countless *kampongs*, still on our high embankment, so that we had a thousand intimate bird's-eye glimpses of a simple people's home life that imprinted themselves like snapshots on the memory: a woman stirring a cooking pot; another winnowing rice; an old man in his garden splitting bamboo; a tiny girl very solemnly sweeping the path; a mother with a child's long black hair spread like a shawl over her knees as she searches for parasites: little pictures all set against backgrounds of *bilik* houses, and gardens gay with flowering shrubs and colourful *sarongs* hung out to dry in the sun dappled shade of palms and bamboo.

Presently, leaving the lowlands, we began to wind our way among rocky foothills, sometimes running close beside the banks of wildly foaming torrents, the music of whose waters mingled with the clatter of the train; climbing steadily, all sense of direction lost, as the sunshine poured in now from this side and now from that, and we twisted and turned bewilderingly through a maze of mountain scenery where every corner was a revelation, or so it seemed, of even greater beauty than the last; not the cold austere beauty of the Alps, but the green living beauty that clothes these tropic ranges to their very summits with forest and grassland and, wherever the hand of man can reach, with patches of bright green rice or shimmering water on tiny, precariously perched terraces. On and on, crossing bridges and viaducts from whose dizzy heights we looked down on to magnificent gorges with silver threads of waterfalls tumbling through the dense foliage that covered their sides; until these too were left behind as the line crept like a snake in among the higher ranges and out at last upon a broad plateau bounded in the distance by yet more mountains.

Not one of the countless rivers and streams that we had crossed but had its parties of bathers, for the Javanese can never see a stream without wanting to get into it, and not one of the groups but included a delightful brown baby or so, splashing water solemnly over its small fat naked person. Here and there, too, would be three or four water buffalo lying immersed with only eyes and ears and nose tip above the surface, and others being scrubbed as they stood in the sparkling water, obviously enjoying their bath at the hands of naked brown boys. By the roadside at a river's edge the driver of a buffalo cart was sometimes to be seen dipping water and throwing it over his patient weary beast; and always, wherever there was a river, there were women washing and spreading out red, brown, and blue *sarongs* to dry on the rocks.

All this was repeated over and over again with endless variations as the train descended once more to lower levels and we came into the sugar lands. Here for mile after mile the line, now on ground level, ran between high walls of sugarcane, just now in full flower, all crowned with heavy cream coloured feathery plumes. And then, for a change, came teak, or *djati*, forests, where the line took to the embankment again, as though on purpose to give train passengers a chance to look from above at the extraordinary giant foliage of these trees and their masses of creamy buff blossom, and at the "nurseries" of baby trees here and there among their elders, looking ridiculously top heavy under their crowns of enormous leaves much bigger than dinner plates.

Next, this obliging train took us through the tobacco lands which, too, took on quite a new aspect as seen from the "*Eendaagsche.*" The railway embankments allow a much more extensive view of them than the motorist sees from the road, and at one point near Djokdjakarta ten of the great drying houses were in sight at once. The line passed many more of these, distributed over a wide area; most of them standing at this time of year, in the way that is so puzzling to strangers, not in the midst of the tobacco that they are there to dry, but surrounded by ricefields: the simple explanation being that the two crops are alternated to prevent soil exhaustion.

Rice was being harvested in the fields of the Sultanates, through which the line passes, but the scene was a very different one from that we had watched in the morning: a contrast much more noticeable to the traveller by train, who sees both within a few hours, than to the motorist who usually traverses the length of Java leisurely in several days. Instead of the gay and varied throng of the West Java people in their *batik* garments and painted hats, the workers here in Middle Java were all clad in dingy blue, dyed with indigo grown by order of the native rulers.

The passing show to be seen from the carriage windows had been so enthralling that I had scarcely noticed the internal arrangements of this admirable train. I still had the long coach almost to myself, and so could stretch my legs or change my seat as often as I wished in search of shade when, in our shifting course among the mountains, the sun had made it too hot for comfort on one side or the other. There was no doubt that the train deserved all the praise that had been lavished upon it. Electric fans hummed steadily to keep the heat at bay. The split bamboo seats were as comfortable as they were pleasing to the eye, and the best for coolness and comfort that could possibly be designed for tropic use. Exploration further afield did certainly reveal one flaw, but not in the second class by which I was travelling; instead of the cool clean bamboo here, and also in the "third," the seats in the first class had the very doubtful distinction of being upholstered in shiny black American cloth: with the lamentable result that many passengers who travelled "first" paid the penalty of their exclusiveness by sticking to the seat, and emerging at their destination with indelible traces of select travel written on the nether portions of white drill trousers or silk summer frock!

The conductor of the train was a wizened, cheery little old native, a most companionable person, with none of the haughty airs of conductors on European expresses. He seemed to spend the entire journey wandering from one end of the long train to the other, wiping dust off seats, windows, and woodwork: an admirable idea, by the way, that might well be adopted on railways elsewhere. Of the meals served in the restaurant car I cannot speak at first hand; but the air of bland repletion on the faces of the passengers who passed through my compartment on the way back from lunch suggested that its standard had been well up to the general excellence of the train. At all events the iced coffee which, on the friendly old conductor's recommendation, I ordered many times throughout the day from the *djongos* who made periodical pilgrimages through the train, was delicious. Served in a tall glass, in which tinkled a big silvery chunk of ice, they cost about twopence each.

My fellow passengers were few, but just enough to provide an occasional diversion. An elderly Javanese, obviously of the upper class, smartly dressed in European white suit and native *batik* headdress, sat opposite to me for a time, and conversed with animation on the affairs of Europe and China, regarding which he was at least as well informed as the average Englishman or Dutchman, if not better. On descending at his station he was met by two low bowing servants and greeted with the utmost deference by the native stationmaster, past whom he walked with a truly Oriental air of arrogance and climbed into a smart *sado* with a uniformed driver.

Two dignified grey haired Chinese ladies, immaculately clean and tidy in the becoming *sarong-kebaya* costume, were also my companions for a short time; and so, less pleasantly, was a fat Hollander, by all the tokens a "drummer," smoking a most pungent cigar, who boarded the train at a Mid-Java station, followed by a skinny little porter loaded with four bulging and obviously very heavy portmanteaux. These safely stowed, the owner took out his purse and carefully counted out three copper cents (less than three farthings) into the man's hand, receiving in return a deep bow and an apparently grateful "*Terima kaseh banyak, Toean*" (Thank you very much, sir).

Two European ladies who travelled with me through some of the loveliest of the mountain scenery were interesting as examples of the oddly diverse preoccupations that blind human eyes to the beauty of the world around them. One of them, turning her back squarely on the window, took a Bible from her bag, and never, so far as I noticed, raised her eyes from its pages till she reached her station. The other, an elaborately dressed matron of generous build, concentrated with equal devotion on a fashion journal: seeing visions no doubt, in her mind's eye, of the creations that would presently adorn her majestic proportions.

I was to travel often on the Java railways after that first experience, and to make the acquaintance of many stations on its lines. Many of these display one very odd inconsistency. Their waiting rooms are delightful, and a greater contrast between them and those in Europe it is hard to imagine. Sitting in a big, cool, comfortable easy-chair, looking round at an airy, pleasant room with tall jars of cannas and gladiolas, and small tables covered with gay cotton cloths, each with its bowl of roses, it is amusing to recall the discomforts of waiting in the dingy, soot begrimed, cheerless equivalent at an English or French junction, trying to warm yourself at the dead ashes of a fire that looks as though it had been out for weeks. But on the other hand, though so mindful of their passengers' comfort in the waiting rooms, the Java railway authorities abandon them to their fate on the platform, and seldom or never provide seats of any sort. So that if, as is usually the case, passengers have luggage that they do not care to leave unguarded, they are condemned either to stand, or to pace up and down like a lion in a cage.

The station and railway employees are all natives, but the differences in status among them are made obvious even to European eyes. Stationmasters appear at each stop, resplendent in freshly starched white uniform, red and gold peaked cap, and laced shoes: manifestly dressed up specially for the arrival of the "*Eendaagsche*," the great event of the day. This functionary's wand of office is a little bat made of split bamboo about the size of a ping pong racquet, painted white with a green centre, with which he signals to the driver of the train. Ticket collectors wear blue drill suits, peaked caps perched on the top of their *batik* headdress, which "grows" on the male Javanese head almost as inseparably as his hair, and leather sandals: these last indicating a certain status upon which all those entitled to wear them are very insistent. Porters wear black jackets and shorts, and go barefoot; but they too wear a *batik* headdress.

The trains are not the only modes of transport with which the ex-motorist in Java may make acquaintance. The old post coaches have their successors in the motor bus services of which hundreds now scour the roads from end to end. In these the post coach restrictions as to the "style, quality, and condition" of the passengers find a modification to suit the times in the division of the seats into first and second class. Europeans, Chinese, and natives all use the buses, and the only "style" anybody worries about nowadays is their ability to pay the difference in fare. Europeans, however, usually sit in the front first class seats as a matter of course, leaving the relatively "vile or mean persons" behind to sort themselves out according to their own ideas of social station. Fares, even in the first class, are very low: on an average about half those on English buses. But even cheaper transport is available for humbler folk in shabby old small car taxis, into which these "vilest and meanest" pack themselves like sardines and travel perhaps fifty miles for a few cents.

The main route motor buses are fine modern vehicles, and the services excellent. Especially so are the "*sneldienst*": road-expresses stopping only at certain fixed points. These can only be appreciated to the full when travelling by one of the ordinary services which stop wherever they may happen to be hailed. A native who is waiting to board one will never dream of walking twenty or thirty yards back if he should see it stop to pick up or drop another passenger before it reaches him; he will stand where he is, watching it stop, start, and get slowly under way; and then, just as the heavy car begins to pick up speed, he will calmly wave to the driver to stop again. The Javanese, happy man, is never in a hurry, and he cannot possibly imagine why anyone else should be. Nor, since he has been told that the bus will stop wherever it is hailed, does he see why it should not do so half a dozen times within a hundred yards, if it saves him trouble.

Although persons of impatient temperament will be well advised to use the "*sneldienst*," others with time to spare will get plenty of amusement from watching their fellow passengers' chafferings with the vendors of queer eatables, of lurid hued syrups, and fruit of all kinds in cleverly made grass carriers, who swarm like flies round the car at every stop. Even more entertaining is the amazing variety of baggage that is piled on to the top of the long suffering omnibus; for much of the popularity of this method of transport is due to the fact that there is no limit to the amount of luggage that may be taken, and free of charge. Tin trunks, bulging suitcases, bundles and baskets, barrels, bicycles, agricultural tools, crates of fowls and vegetables, planks, iron sheeting, tiles, garden seats, perambulators, and the rest, are swung deftly up and roped into place by the conductor-general-factotum, who spends most of his time scrambling up and down the iron ladder, loading or unloading, and by a miracle, as it seems, disentangling unerringly from the heterogeneous collection the correct property of each owner as he arrives at his destination. This generous policy in the matter of baggage greatly simplifies bus travel also for the European. There is nothing to prevent him from taking all his belongings with him if he wishes, as at any point where he may alight he will always find plenty of willing hands waiting and ready to handle it for him in return for a very few cents.

There are, of course, exceptions to every rule, in Java as elsewhere; and the exceptions to the general excellence of the motor bus services have the "Heath Robinson" touch. A good example of these is in a long suffering mountain district which is dependent upon the erratic transport provided by a Chinese owned veteran which, by some oversight on the part of the authorities, has been granted a licence to carry mail and passengers. This fact, however, is no deterrent to its proprietors, if profitable occasion should arise, to hiring the ancient vehicle out to a picnic party, leaving the postbag to wait until to-morrow to be called for, and its lawful passengers stranded at its official starting place. When it does run, the last ten miles or so of the journey up a steady but not steep incline has to be done with a furiously boiling radiator which is filled at least a dozen times on the way from roadside streams, and the bonnet propped open, rattling wildly, to keep the engine cool. Despite these slight drawbacks the bus is always crowded, and is to be relied upon at least in one respect—which is to cover its passengers' hands and clothes with dirt, oil, and grease.

Times change fast; it was a far cry from Daendels's post coaches to the so called "steam trams" that, until a few years ago, used to tear through the streets of the chief Java towns, with bells clanging and whistles screaming, like runaway trains in a nightmare. But now they too have vanished into the limbo of the past; they have been electrified as befits the fine modern towns they serve, and the queer bulbous compressed steam engines that drew them are no more seen. The trams themselves, however, remain, with their old fashioned first, second, and third class compartments, and trucks barred like wild beasts' cages in a travelling menagerie, in which every conceivable kind of merchandise is carried, with the bearers squatting beside their loads. Their progress is still fairly sensational: probably because it has been found that the long familiar noisy warnings are the only sure and certain means of inducing the native population to get off the rails. So the modernised trams, particularly in Batavia, scour the town to the accompaniment of the same shrieking whistles and clanging bells as of old.

The trams are popular with all races and classes: even the Dutch, who are happily exempt from the snobbishness that prevents the average Singaporean from using public conveyances. Dutch business men and *mevrouws* with shopping bags mingle in the first class with Chinese and Eurasians; a somewhat lower strata of the two latter, and better class natives, travel second; and the coolie working class go third: a scale of social gradation that seems to have been arrived at by common consent. Fares even in the first class are extremely cheap; they are collected by a barefooted native conductor in khaki or dark blue uniform and *batik* headdress, who salutes as he approaches and hands over the ticket with a polite bow. I happened one day to find on boarding a tram that I had no money; but the courteous little conductor confidingly gave me a ticket, telling me his number, and saying that if I would give the fare to the conductor of any other tram he would be sure to get it, as, happening to meet him again a few days later, I learned that he had.

These polite little people, however, are less trusted than they are trusting. They are always closely followed on their rounds by a native inspector whose superior rank is indicated by his European shoes and a peaked uniform cap worn over his *batik kepala*; and, lest perchance you should not have noticed these insignia of authority, he often tries to impress the passengers by chivvying his underling.

The financial depression brought to the roads of Java some new forms of cheap transport. The hard times were felt more acutely in the densely populated eastern half of the island where, in addition to the general malaise, the brunt of the *débâcle* in the sugar industry, in which was bound up most of its prosperity, had to be borne. The closing down of so many sugar estates and mills disorganised the whole region by throwing out of employment not only hundreds of Europeans, but also thousands of natives, and so reduced spending power to the minimum. Soerabaya, Malang, and other East Java towns rose with practical common sense to the occasion, and there appeared on the streets dozens of little three wheeled taxis ("*amcos*," as they soon came to be called) in which an astounding distance could be travelled for about twopence and the whole way from one end of the town to the other for fivepence or sixpence. The hard-hit Europeans, forced to lay up their cars, took to the "*amcos*" like ducks to water, and the door to door transport problem, which the high charges of the old ordinary taxis made prohibitive, was solved. A still later innovation is the appearance of fleets of smart Austin Sevens; and as they run at the same low prices it looks as though the three wheelers, now showing signs of wear and tear after several years of faithful service, will soon be crowded out of European use, to be relegated, like the old *kossongs*, to a lower social strata of passengers. But they saved the situation, and deserve always to be remembered with gratitude.

The traveller soon realises their value through the lack of them in the West Java towns of Batavia and Bandoeng, where the full size taxis still have it all their own way. These towns being the seat of Government and the home of Government officials with fixed, though in most cases much reduced, salaries, the effects of the "slump" were less apparent, and no such hard time conveyances were introduced. It is true that taxi fares and all other charges—rent, hotel tariffs, food, wages, and so on—have fallen considerably in the last few years; but they all, and the cost of living generally, remain much higher at the western end of Java than at the other.

CHAPTER SEVENTEEN

Ancient Kingdoms

THE East India Company had been far too much occupied in making conquests and profits to waste any time over the historical or archæological possibilities of its colony. It was left for Raffles to sow the first seed of what was destined to develop into one of the best archæological organisations in existence; and he did so, with a thousand other forgotten things, in the intervals of entirely revolutionising the administration and native land law, pacifying an uneasy people hitherto in constant revolt against oppression, and writing a *History of Java* which is still the classic work of reference on the subject.

Raffles was the first white ruler of Java to make friendly contact with the natives. Those of his predecessors had been restricted to defeating and exploiting them. He made frequent and prolonged expeditions into the interior of the island and, gifted linguist that he was, talked much with the people and learned their customs and legends and beliefs at first hand. The existence of the Boroboedoer temple was well known to the population of the Sultanates, though, hidden as it then was in a tangle of tropical growth, it must have looked like nothing more than a small, symmetrical hill isolated in the midst of the surrounding ricefields. But the story of the temple buried in it had passed into legend, and it was Raffles who set a small army of men to work to uncover it. The tangle of vines and coarse grass and undergrowth, the accumulation probably of some four hundred years, was torn away to reveal the extraordinary structure that had lain so long hidden; and the work was continued after Raffles's departure, at least to the extent of preventing the lush tropical growth from blotting it out again. But it was not until the end of the century that the study of the wealth of archæological remains in Java was seriously undertaken. A research committee was formed in 1901 and all the then known relics of the vanished Hindu kingdoms were studied and described; and in 1907 the restoration of Boroboedoer was begun under

Colonel van Erp. The work took four years; and at the end this unique temple was revealed almost as its creators' hands left it, a thousand or perhaps twelve hundred years ago.

All travellers in Java nowadays visit Boroboedoer, and it would be strange indeed if they did not; for there is no other quite like it in the world, with its tiers of galleries illustrating the life of the Buddha elaborately carved in stone panels; its hundreds of cupolas and Buddha statues; its noble flights of steps; and its most lovely setting on the crown of a low hill surrounded by palms and ricefields. Yet wonderful as it unquestionably is, it seems strangely remote and empty of all human association. It may be because no record whatever of its origin or history has come down to us, and even legend, usually so rich, is strangely silent where it is concerned. Apart from its curious design, forming as it does a colossal cap to the hill itself, into the sides of which it is built and fitted, and its wealth of pictorial wall carvings, its principal interest is the proof it provides that in Java, as in Angkor, an amiable religious tolerance among the Indian conquerors and colonists permitted the Buddhist and Hindu faiths, the latter in its various forms of dedication, to Brahma, Shiva, and Vishnu, to be practised side by side. For within only a few miles of Boroboedoer and its attendant small temples of Mendoet and Pawon, both of them fine examples of restoration by the Dutch experts, which must have been the centre of a wealthy and important Buddhist community, there is an immense scattered group of Hindu temples on the site of Prambanan, the capital of the first Hindu kingdom founded in Java.

This group, known as Lorodjonggrang, covers many acres, and the Government Archæological Service, which in 1913 replaced the Research Committee, has (in 1939) been at work on its restoration for about twelve years. Here the wall carvings are much more varied and spirited than those at Boroboedoer, and suggest that the artists who carved them, perhaps students in the art schools of the day, may have been light hearted fellows who didn't care a brass farthing whether the temple they had been engaged to decorate was Brahman or Buddhist; and that, carrying the guess further, they found their style rather cramped at Boroboedoer by the necessity of confining themselves to the blameless career of the gentle Buddha, whereas at Lorodjonggrang they could let themselves go to their hearts' content on the bloodcurdling adventures of Rama and other heroes as told in the great Hindu epic *Ramayana*.

It is a pity indeed that so few of the overseas tourists who "do" Java are shown even a glimpse of Lorodjonggrang; for while Boroboedoer is impressive, these panels in the Hindu temples are not only remarkable but extremely entertaining. One series shows Hanuman, the Monkey King, leading the monkey army into Ceylon, to which they cross on a stone causeway, built ahead of them by monkey engineers who carry rocks on their heads and fling them down, hampered by giant fishes and crabs which try to drag the stones away. The army leads with it a dog on a chain, presumably as a mascot.

Then there is lovely Sita, Rama's fiancée, sending her ring to him by a bird as a token that she is in danger; and farther along the dove with an anxious air is delivering it. Rama, however, has other business on hand, slaying a giant with a blow that drives his face through his ribs! We see the good Monkey King captured by the wicked many-armed Ravenna, who orders slaves to bind oil soaked rags round his tail and set fire to it, all faithfully presented in stone in the minutest detail. Then Hanuman, with tail ablaze, leaps on to the roof of the king's palace, which is burnt to the ground and the city with it, giving the artist a fine opportunity to portray a scene of panic, even down to a terrified dog scrambling out of a lower window of the blazing palace.

This huge "temple-complex," as the Dutch call it, includes more than 150 shrines in three walled enclosures, one within the other. The central and largest one is dedicated to Shiva, and a pair of others, one on either side of it, to Brahma and Vishnu respectively. In them are elaborately carved statues of these gods.

All these temples are rich in decoration closely resembling in style that at Angkor, proving how close is the link between these two mysterious efflorescences of transplanted Indian art, and how feasible the theory held by many archæologists that the founders of Angkor came from Java.

Lorodjonggrang is not the only relic of vanished glory that

the Archæological Service have unearthed. Not far from Prambanan is another Hindu group called Tjandi Sewoe, guarded by two giant stone watchmen with clubs. In the same region are the ruins of a temple called Tjandi Kalasan, and of a Buddhist monastery. Farther away are the remains of a great palace or *kraton*, probably resembling in its day those still occupied by the sultans of Solo and Djokdja.

All this region belonged to the great Hindu kingdom of Mataram, not to be confused with another Hindu kingdom of Mataram on the island of Lombok, east of Bali, which at one time rivalled Madjapahit in importance. The name was retained when the kingdom was conquered by the Malay Mohammedans, under whose rulers it remained a rich and important state in whose many wars the Company several times took a hand. It was split in 1755, as the result of one of these, into the two present puppet Sultanates of Soerakarta and Djokdjakarta; but the old name is preserved in part of the Djokdjakarta territory. A traveller who visited Mataram in 1656 has left an interesting account of the road that ran from it to Samarang, and describes a bridge built of *djati*, "strong enough to carry a thousand elephants." It was 3000 paces long, and provided transport across the rushing torrent of the River Damak. So, after all, it seems that the poor ignorant natives of these islands do not owe quite all their engineering knowledge to the conquering white man!

There are many more shrines in much the same style as those at Prambanan and Sewoe, about forty miles away on the Dieng Plateau; and farther east, at Singosari, near the big modern town of Malang, are the traces of another large Hindu city. Here a picturesque native *kampong* is now snugly tucked in among the ruins of ancient temples; and as you walk along its neat bamboo fenced lanes, under the shade of palms and bananas, you will come here and there upon a space left respectfully open, dominated by a portly Shivistic statue in sandstone, looking out upon the tumbled remains of a temple courtyard. And at the entrance to the village, instead of the usual bamboo gateway, the way is guarded by two enormous squatting figures something like those at Tjandi Sewoe. A mile or so away are the remains of what must once have been a very beautiful bathing place ornamented with carved stone mouldings. There are records of a Hindu kingdom hereabouts in the ninth century, and of another at Soerabaya; and yet another, much earlier, where Batavia now stands, called Taruma, which vanished and gave place to Jacatra, as Jacatra gave place in its turn to Batavia. Taruma, however, though long forgotten, has at least left its name behind it in that of the River Tarum. A proclamation in Sanskrit, signed by a King Purnavarman, engraved on a stone found here, in characters similar to those used by the Pallavas of South India, is one of the meagre proofs still remaining of this perhaps great city's existence.

But most interesting of all these relics are those of Madjapahit, the greatest of the Hindu kingdoms that between them dominated Java for at least a thousand years, which is quite a chapter in a country's history when you reflect that it is as yet less than that since the Norman conquest of England! The actual remains of Madjapahit are sadly few and unimposing for the capital of a state which the records prove to have been of great wealth and importance. But the once great Hindu stronghold has left its mark in a curious fashion on the straggling *kampongs* that are now the only human habitations on the vast site it covered in its heyday. The builders of Madjapahit used brick rather than stone; and when the city had been sacked by its Mohammedan conquerors, and the temples and palaces abandoned or demolished, the peasants of the surrounding country, who crept back to their holdings when peace was restored, doubtless thought it a wicked waste that so many millions of bricks should be lying idle. That, at least, seems the most likely explanation of the fact that, instead of the split bamboo fences elsewhere universal in native villages throughout Java, here at Madjapahit all the compounds and gardens are enclosed by brick walls often further embellished with tall brick gateposts. These are set up without mortar, and are therefore very thick, so that the contrast between their solidity and the flimsy *bilik* houses behind them is oddly incongruous. Many of the irrigation ditches serving the surrounding ricefields are also lined with those same beautifully made bricks, all as sound and shapely as when they left their makers' hands anything from 500 to 1000 years ago.

Ancient Kingdoms

The remains of Madjapahit are not very easy to find; and the stranger who follows the vague native directions given in response to inquiries is likely to take several wrong turnings before he discovers the byroad that leads from Trowelan, an inconspicuous *dessa* a few miles from the big modern sugar town of Modjerkerto. This road soon degenerates into a rough track; and it is here that the brick walls, by the mere incongruity of their existence in so obviously poor a place, attract attention, and offer their silent, incontestible evidence that this *kampong* is not quite as others are.

As my car bumped slowly along the uneven track, the inhabitants of the houses inside the brick walls came drifting out, as is the native way, full of curiosity to see what a stranger might be wanting here so far from the main road; and in reply to my questions, and the offer of a cigarette, an unfailing key to Javanese good will, a dignified old man squatted himself on the running board and offered to show me the way. He took me first to a partly ruined red brick temple of much the same design as many of those in Bali, which latter in all probability were copied from those here, refugees from Madjapahit having fled to Bali when their country was overrun by conquerors. This temple, said my guide, was called Badjang Ratoe, and little was known about it; but he could show me better things if I would leave the car a little farther on and go afoot, for there was a stream ahead of us, and there the track ended. So to the end of the track we presently went, abandoned the car in the mud on the bank of the stream and, wading across, took to a slippery six inch path on the *bund* between two ricefields. Meanwhile I wondered as we slithered along whether in a few hundred years' time, perhaps, visitors from other lands might not be picking their precarious way along just such a path, guided by just such another *dessa* man, in search of the last traces of Batavia or Soerabaya! It is no more impossible, perhaps less so, than such an idea would have seemed to the inhabitants of Madjapahit in the fourteenth or fifteenth century, with a thousand years of power and glory behind them. Whereas the Dutch have been in Java less than 350 years, and their cities have been places of dignity and importance for little more than a century.

One of the earliest references to Hindu Java is contained

in the *Chronicle of the Buddhist Monk Fa-Hian*,[1] who relates that he went in A.D. 400 overland from China to India and in A.D. 414 returned by sea via Ceylon, whence he set sail "in a great ship with 200 persons on board, and a small ship in tow carrying provisions." On the way they visited Java, which he calls "Ya-vi-di," or "Jawa-dwipa," and relates of it that "all the people were of the Brahman religion, and he met only one or two Buddhists" on his travels through the country. Buddhism had therefore not yet gained the foothold it was destined to attain later; four centuries or so had yet to elapse after this Chinese monk's visit before the building of Boroboedoer.

It is to a Chinese source also, the records of the Yuan Dynasty, that we owe accounts of Kublai Khan's attacks on the coasts of Hindu Java in 1292 and 1293, at Soerabaya, Padjetan, and Toeban. The attempts at conquest were successful at first, but the enemy were beaten off eventually "by the skill of the men of Madjapahit," who had "great ships with Naga heads on the stem." The same records contain many references to the importance and elaborate administration of Madjapahit, mentioning, among other interesting details, that good maps of the country were obtainable, and that there was a complete "National Register" of the population! It is a little disconcerting to find that such a scheme was in full working order in a vanished Hindu state six or seven hundred years ago, which we have only now rather nervously organised in modern England!

However: *sic transit gloria mundi*. Madjapahit, once the centre and focal point of its Government Survey maps, is no longer even a name on ours. Lost among a maze of ricefields, located only through the good offices of a village native, the symmetrical sunken water temple towards which at last my guide waved a proud proprietary hand was indubitable proof of a splendid past, for it was worthy to be what legend claims for it, the bathing place of kings. Built on the plan beloved of Indian architects in their Golden Age, with intersecting squares and rectangles enclosing small square "islands" carrying groups of miniature shrines, the enclosing walls rose from the water in projecting tiers, decorated with carved heads and floral designs. Parts of this outer wall were still quite

[1] J. Legge (Oxford, 1886).

REMAINS OF A BRICK TEMPLE AT MADJAPAHIT, THE FORMER GREAT HINDU CAPITAL IN EAST JAVA.

ONE OF THE ISLAND SHRINES RICHLY CARVED—THE BATHING PLACE OF THE KINGS OF MADJAPAHIT, THE VANISHED HINDU CAPITAL, NOW IN THE MIDST OF RICE FIELDS.

A COUNTRY SCENE IN EAST JAVA.

A SPECIMEN OF THE CARVED STONE PANELS AT BOROBOEDOER.

A JAVA MOUNTAIN HOTEL AND PART OF ITS TERRACED GARDEN ABOUT 5,500 FEET ABOVE SEA-LEVEL.

Ancient Kingdoms

perfect; in others they seemed to melt imperceptibly into the high grass bank that in its turn merged into the pattern of the surrounding fields, giving to this strange isolated relic of vanished glory a dreamlike unreality.

A sense of hallucination persists. Turn your back and walk ten paces away and this last tangible trace of Madjapahit has vanished; you are in the midst of the familiar ricefields, and it seems impossible that you should have seen anything so utterly irrational; turn back and there it lies: an elaborate, costly, carven bath, with decorated walls reflected in the gleaming water that they imprison, set in the midst of fields whose silvery surfaces mirror only the slim green spikes of newly planted rice: no more numerous, perhaps, than the human life that crowded the sites of these very fields only a few hundred years ago. If a reminder is needed of the transience of temporal power, a visit to Madjapahit will certainly provide one. All over the wide region once covered by the vanished kingdom, scattered traces of it have been found. Not only the tumbled remnants of buildings, but carvings, pottery, and other relics of its arts, which are collected in a small *bilik* museum at Trowelan: so unassuming a place that the passing motorist on the high road is very likely to miss it. Here, watched over by a six foot stone figure from some old Shiva temple, is a motley assembly of small carved stone objects, many of them beautifully executed. Among the pottery found were water jars just the same as those used throughout Java to-day, for fashions in such things do not change though conquerors come and go. Another reminder of unchanging custom is the blue Chinese porcelain found buried among many of the ruins; suggesting that the old city was probably just as full of Chinese shops and tradesmen as are the towns of Java to-day.

The N.E.I. Archæological Service came into existence after the similar services in India and French Indo-China, but it very soon forged ahead. The methods employed by the Dutch experts were recognised as so admirable from both scientific and æsthetic points of view that they were paid the high compliment of being adopted by the archæologists responsible for the preservation of the Khmer ruins in Cambodia, at Angkor, and elsewhere.

The Archæological Service is included in the Government Education Department, and is rightly regarded as one of national importance in a country so rich in antiquities as Java. In the years that ended with the financial depression, exhaustive surveys were made of all the known antiquities in the island, a collection of many thousands of photographs and descriptive records have been made, hundreds of carved inscriptions excavated among the ruins have been deciphered and translated, and the restoration and reconstruction of many buildings has been carried out. Measures were taken to prevent demolition of antiquarian treasures, such as the removal of the Madjapahit bricks by too practical natives already referred to, and also their removal on the grand scale from their sites by well to do antiquarians, to Europe or the United States.

Since 1931 the activities of the service have had to be sadly curtailed, but even so, a great deal of invaluable work is being carried on. The immense undertaking at Lorodjonggrang is continuing, and the general care and upkeep of all the antiquities is maintained. The rule has been made that all discoveries made by natives must be reported to their regent, the discoverer, however, remaining as a rule the owner in the case of small objects, with the right to sell them, if he wishes, to the archæological authorities; but if he conceals what he has found the penalty is confiscation.

The relics of the Hindu period in Java have been visited by artists and antiquarians from all parts of the world; but the ordinary tourist still seems to be convinced that he has exhausted the historical monuments of the country when he has paid a hurried visit to Boroboedoer!

CHAPTER EIGHTEEN

Yesterday, To-day, & To-morrow

OLD BATAVIA, founded by Jan Pieterszoon Coen early in the seventeenth century on the site of the native town of Jacatra, which he had burned to the ground, was planned as far as possible on towns of the period in Holland. It lay on the sea front, divided into two by the River Tjiliwong, whose mouth only native craft could enter, larger ships anchoring outside. The town was enclosed within high walls and dominated by the Castle, in which the Governor and other officials had their quarters.

The roads and streets were named after places in Holland, and after animals supposed to be those native to Java. They included a Lion Street; but whether this was due to over-estimation of local fauna, or merely as an offset to Tiger Street, is not recorded. This Tiger Street, or rather, Tijgersgracht (Tiger Canal), was the Park Lane of Old Batavia, where stood the mansions of the wealthiest residents, and along which paraded the equipages of fashionable society in the cool of the evening.

On these vehicles the ostentation that was the hallmark of the time found one of its favourite outlets; and their elaboration was as fantastic as the dress of those who rode in them. To such a pitch did it come that in a report calling for restrictions upon them the East India Company stated that the "extravagant luxury, pomp, and costliness of these vehicles were helping to ruin the Company." Regulations were issued forbidding anyone except the highest Company officials to possess "a glass coach" or one that was "gilt or silvered," or was shaded with an awning of costly material; and taxes were imposed rising from 40 rex dollars up to 300.

Sedan chairs, here called *tandoes*, were much in use; and these too the Company censured severely as "far too luxurious and lavishly decorated." They were the chief hire transport, and there were stands at convenient points about the town, as well as halts where bearers could be exchanged, on payment of a fixed tariff rate from point to point. *Tandoes* were usually made to carry either one or two passengers; but there are records that they were even built for four! *Tandoes* are still used in the Java mountains: but they are built to carry one person only.

Along Jacatraweg, Antjolweg, and Molenvliet stood, and in some cases still stand, more fine houses. These were the quasi country residences of the wealthy burghers, just outside the business centre, and here the mansions all stood in spacious grounds. Fabulous sums were spent on these gardens, and immense was the competition between their owners to attain the most magnificent displays of colour: not, probably, so much for love of their beauty as for sheer vulgar ostentation and the desire to crow over their neighbours. But whatever the motive, all these plutocratic streets must have been a lovely sight indeed: especially the Molenvliet, where the great dignified houses with their lofty pillared porticoes stood back amid masses of croton, acalypha, coleus, alamanda, hibiscus, and other gorgeous shrubs that made blazing splashes of colour on the shaven turf, on both sides of the canal, separated from it by the avenues of noble *flamboyant* trees that are now all that remain of its former glories. And the people that moved about in this colourful scene were by all accounts as brilliant, though certainly not so beautiful, as their setting; for the sums squandered by the merchants upon their dress and that of their slaves were so outrageous that these also the Company made the subject of legislation, and restrictions were imposed under heavy penalties.

In the households, as in the gardens, competition and display were the characteristic note. The index to wealth, and thereby to social superiority, for there was no other standard in Company society, was the number of slaves that were kept, so that everyone tried to outdo his neighbour in the matter of staff. In some of those great old mansions, now converted into hotels or warehouses, it is on record that there were once more than two hundred slaves in a single household, all dressed in barbaric splendour worthy of some Oriental potentate in *The Arabian Nights*.

These slaves were brought from all over the archipelago in the Company's ships: the pitiful survivors of defeated island populations. As likely as not, many of the men and

Yesterday, To-day, & To-morrow

women who scurried hither and thither to do their masters' behests in those Batavia mansions, and serve him with *nasi besar* (now known as "rijsttafel": the Javanese rice feast that the Dutch adopted in the early days of their conquest, as the type of meal best suited to local conditions), were once people of high standing in their own islands; as strange to such work as the doctors, artists, writers, and others who, 300 years later, were to be driven out by the Nazis, and forced by circumstance to be house servants in the homes of England.

Few white women cheered the exile of the East India Company men in the early days, and we may suppose that the châtelaines of those handsome mansions were for the most part the brown skinned beauties with whom the Company founded the Eurasian families of to-day. But just what their status was we cannot know, for history is mute. Did they preside charmingly at their lord's table, and grace his board as well as his bed? Or did those lords, taking a leaf from the native book, keep their women in subjection like better class slaves, as creatures existing only for their pleasure and convenience? All things considered, the last seems most likely.

Strange to say it was not the Dutch language that predominated in Old Batavia. The Dutch might reign, but the population was extremely mixed. The language of the Portuguese traders had taken a firm hold, for there had been much intermarriage and there were many half castes. It may well be, too, that the similarity of Portuguese vowel sounds to those of Malay and Javanese had something to do with this language having been more easily assimilated; for to this day many Portuguese words are firmly embodied in Malay, and there is nothing foreign sounding about them. Then, as now, Malay was the *lingua franca* used by all nationalities, but Portuguese was a good second. It was in Portuguese that the services in the Portuguese Church were held, though the service was that of the Dutch Reformed Church.

Batavia and the other chief Java towns have seen many changes since those early days; but, although it was not to be expected that they could escape altogether the blight of modern "development," they still remain very pleasant places. According to old residents, and to photographs, Batavia and Soerabaya, as well as Samarang, which is still unspoiled, were, before the Great War, towns quite as beautiful in their way as the country around them. Even as lately as ten or twelve years ago, the rising tide of progress was only lapping at their unique charm, and their principal shopping streets were still unlike those of any other large towns in the world. For at that time those streets had only lately ceased to be wealthy residential quarters, from which the owners of the old houses had drifted gradually away to modern suburbs as the town spread and grew. Commerce had flowed quietly in to take their place; the stately old Colonial houses still stood back in dignified seclusion behind the trees and lawns of their spacious front gardens, but they had fallen from their high estate as rich men's homes, and had been turned into shops. So that when you drove round to do your morning's shopping you turned in between the flowering shrubs to a wide semicircular drive, and your car swept up with an air to the steps of a great *voorgalerij*, formerly pillared and open, but now glass fronted and converted by means of counters, shelves, and all the necessary paraphernalia for the display of groceries, hardware, drapery, jewellery, cameras, flowers, or whatever it might be.

There was a great charm about shopping in those days. You could match silks, buy cheese or coffee or carnations, or await the results of your latest Kodak film, knowing that you were sitting where a hundred or two hundred years ago the worthy burghers and their ladies too had sat, discussing the scandals of the day or the latest news from Europe; or even perhaps the machinations of that rascally fellow Stamford Raffles!

Then came the post war boom, with its fortunes made in sugar, quinine, coffee, rubber, and the rest, and the high inexorable tide of progress flowed over these two most charming cities, submerging much of their beauty. Soerabaya suffered most. The great boom in sugar caused a sensational rise in land values, and the shady, quiet, front gardens that hid the old houses along its central avenue found themselves described as "valuable business frontages" at fabulous prices per metre. That was the end of them. So rapid was the transformation as to savour of magic, and black at that. Gone now are the gardens and the trees, the flowering shrubs with their masses of brilliant blossom, and their setting of velvet lawns.

The long, once gracious avenue that ran through the heart of the town is now almost as conventional as Piccadilly, except that you may catch a glimpse here and there of one of the old dignified porticoed mansions, peeping shyly through an occasional gap between the big modern stores, like old-fashioned country cousins elbowed out of the way by a more assertive younger generation. These few survivors are built in behind the new shops and shut out for ever from the once shady avenue upon which they used to look out so proudly; spending their last years in the condemned cell from which they will soon go the way of their vanished contemporaries.

There are reminders of earlier periods in Soerabaya's history as you go farther back through the old town. Here the houses were built close on the street and touching one another, like the relics of the same period in Banda and Amboyna. Many of them still stand, pillars and all, still immaculately whitewashed, for such is the admirable Dutch law, and still roofed with the crinkly reddish tiles that contrast so pleasantly with their white walls. But their glory, such modest glory as they had, is long departed. Some are warehouses; posters deface their walls and doors and stout outcurving pillars; and here and there, taking advantage of their narrow *stoep* raised two or three steps above street level, a *toekang djahitan* (sewing man) will squat before his sewing machine, busily stitching at the garments he makes up so neatly and swiftly for a few cents apiece. Others of the old houses have been turned into Chinese shops and restaurants; but they all seem to have a rather self conscious air, as though they can never forget that they have seen better days.

In Batavia, though there are many changes, the layout of the town with its intersecting canals and double avenues did not lend itself so easily to such complete transformation as in Soerabaya, and though here, too, many of the old houses have vanished, many others happily remain, and means have been found to build plenty of modern shops without sacrificing the avenues of trees.

The suburbs of both Soerabaya and Batavia are charming; and here it is Soerabaya that has the advantage. Its wide boulevards with their *tjimaras* (casuarinas) and *flamboyants*, and their charming bungalows, each standing in a garden that is a little paradise of shade and brilliant flowers, must surely be the pleasantest suburban dwelling places in the world: a far cry indeed from what in England is conveyed by the term. Nor are they any the less pleasant because a trickle of commercial progress is penetrating them, quite inoffensively, in such a way as to save suburban housewives many a journey to town. It is a little startling nevertheless to see quite modern houses, large and small, already converted into shops just as ruthlessly as their *démodé* ancestors. A snug little bungalow tucked away behind a mass of bougainvillea, in a secluded cross road off one of the boulevards, may prove to be a spick and span Chinese grocery store with shelves full of shining tins adorning the walls of what was but recently the best front bedroom. And in one very select neighbourhood a large modern house announces itself as "Dames Kapper en Permanent Huis"—or in other words a ladies' hairdresser's. More staggering still, an imposing, not long built mansion on a commanding corner of the aristocratic Darmo boulevard is labelled in huge letters: DARMO VLEESERIJ EN WURSTFABRIEK (butchery and sausage factory)! Imagination quails at the thought of what our British snobbery would say to such a metamorphosis of some impressive Gentleman's Residence in, say, Branksome Park, Bournemouth! The residents would probably petition the council for the tainted thing's removal, or else evacuate the neighbourhood themselves in a body. But in such matters Dutch common sense prevails; they merely welcome the opportunity provided by the intruders to shop at easy distance, thus saving them the tram fare or a bicycle ride to town.

Native as well as European taste in architecture has changed of late years in the towns. Old-fashioned Javanese houses have no windows, and inside their *bilik* walls the light is very dim; but nowadays many of them are being modelled on European style in miniature, with windows and verandahs, not unlike Australian wooden bungalows in design; so small that the heads of their owners, who are by no means tall, touch the verandah roof. The effect of these rather attractive little homes with their tiled gables and tiny verandahs facing each other across the ten foot "gangs" that serve them as streets is somewhat that of rows of dolls' houses. And if you turn up one of the lanes between blocks of shops in some of the suburban streets you will find yourself at once in a sort of Lilliput in the very heart of your ordinary full size workaday world.

All visitors comment on the fearful and wonderful arrangement of the Soerabaya tram stop islands which appear to have been designed for the express purpose of decimating the population. They are not placed in the middle of the road in the usual way, but are in pairs, with the two tramlines running between them, and motor traffic in both directions as well. So that the pedestrian who reaches one island alive has to dodge cars coming both ways before he gets across to the next: a much more hazardous adventure than it sounds when there is no speed limit, and no means of knowing whether a fast approaching car intends driving on one side of the island or the other. It says much for the intelligence of the population that there are not more accidents, when it is remembered how many safeguards in the way of "Look Right," "Look Left," and so on, are considered needful to safeguard the people of London.

The larger towns in Java have now followed the lead of the rest of the world in adorning their principal crossings with traffic lights. They are engagingly simple affairs like large square dark-lanterns, and hang in the middle of the road from cables strung across from trees at the roadside. The square face is divided into three horizontal sections, covered with red, yellow, and green glass, bearing the words "*Stop!*" "*Awas!*" "*Djalan!*" (Stop! Look Out! Go!) Native drivers like them immensely because of the fun they get out of pulling their unfortunate ponies up on their haunches when the light changes! At all events the lights are as meticulously obeyed here as in any European country.

The Dutch in Java were in the vanguard of radio progress and for many years the station at Malabar, near Bandoeng, was said to be the most powerful in the world. Radio-telephone communication with Europe was brought to the highest perfection long before it was possible in British Malaya to telephone from Singapore to Penang.

Family chats between parents in Holland and their married sons or daughters in Java are a regular institution. The ordinary charge for three minutes' conversation between any private house in Holland and another in Java is fifteen guilders—25*s*. at par. But at New Year 1938 the service was further popularised by the announcement that six-minute talks would cost five guilders only during the holiday period. The result was that there were more than 6000 happy exchanges of "voices across the sea."

The country post offices of Java are delightful: dazzlingly whitewashed outside and spotlessly clean within. And the courtesy and efficiency of the native assistants, smart and slim in their starched white jackets and *batik* headdress and *sarong*, are just as pleasant as their cool airy offices. The system under which they work is admirably thought out in every particular, and foreigners need have no fear of difficulties even if they should wish to cable home from some remote country *dessa*. In such small offices telegrams are telephoned to the nearest telegraph office. On the wall by the operator's telephone there hangs a chart displaying the letters of the alphabet in large print side by side with the numbers 1 to 26. Each letter corresponds to a number: $A=1$; $B=2$; and so on. All native post clerks have learnt Roman type and script, so when the message is spelled out letter by letter it does not matter in the least whether it is in Dutch, French, English, Malay, or any other language known or unknown to them, provided it shares the same alphabet. They simply telephone the numbers corresponding to each letter, and mistakes are rare.

The fingerprint system is much used in Java. You cannot get a driving licence without leaving the mark of your thumb on the police records. And in every post office there is a book of black ink paper on the counter wherein every native employee sent to cash a postal order or collect a registered packet must press his finger tip, and "sign" a form with it.

The post offices in Batavia and Soerabaya, though pleasing to the eye, are trying to the temper, for they share to some degree the disproportion of pretentiousness to efficiency characteristic of Australian G.P.O.s. In Soerabaya, as in Sydney, you gaze with admiration at the architecture and seek in vain for the proper place to buy a stamp.

The ground plan of the big Java offices might serve as models for those in cities the world over. But the customer who enters the cool, light, airy hall anticipating that his business will be as easily expedited as the setting suggests will certainly be disappointed. All round the lofty skylighted building, spacious as a church and spotless as a hospital ward, with its tiled floor and polished brasses, are dozens of "*lokets*," all numbered and labelled with their particular mission in the postal scheme, each of course designed to be presided over by one of the pleasant, helpful *djeroe toelis* (clerks) we all like so well. But alas for the optimist! The available funds must all have been spent on the buildings, so that there were none left to staff it. You try one after another of the "*lokets*," only to find them tenantless and marked "*gesloten*"; and from those that are open, long queues like those waiting to enter theatre pits or galleries stretch from side to side of the great hall, crossing one another in the middle; moving very, very slowly as each client holds great argument with the clerk about his or her business.

An elderly uniformed official who wanders hither and thither superintending all this with a fatherly, benignant eye is always ready to give courteous information as to which of the queues you should join. But sad to say, if you take your place at the tail of the one indicated, arriving at the "*loket*" some ten minutes later, you are just as likely as not to be told that you should have gone to some other. And then, having patiently repeated the process and arrived in due course at the number indicated, you may be directed back to the very one you have just come from!

But there are ways and means of getting round these small drawbacks in the service of the otherwise so admirable *Post Kantoors*. If it is merely a matter of stamps, then one glance at the long queue from outside is enough for the customer who has discovered that certain Chinese storekeepers in the town have provided for this oft recurrent contingency, shrewdly anticipating that those who come to buy stamps will often buy their attractively displayed goods as well! Or, if a visit to the post office itself is necessary, a very small tip, or even none, will send your native *djongos* (house-boy) rejoicing to stand in queues for hours if need be; for to him it is a pleasant opportunity of chatting to acquaintances all bound on the same errand.

Official parsimony in the matter of personnel crops up in some curious ways. The inhabitants of one big and busy *dessa* deeply resented the closing down of their post office in favour of a new one in a recently popularised mountain resort some miles away; and to add insult to injury, they have even been deprived of their native postman, whose munificent wage was ten guilders (16s. 8d.) a month, on the score of economy necessitated by the depression! Their post bag is now brought by an erratic Chinese motor bus, and deposited at the tiny office of the local *wedono*, where it is sorted, more or less, in the intervals of dealing with water supply complaints, disputes over boundaries, and handcuffed criminals just arrested for some petty misdemeanour or other, who squat outside the door and on the steps chatting with the policeman in charge of them, and look on with interest as you enter and help the clerk to hunt for your mail amid a heterogeneous muddle of papers relating to all the affairs of the local authorities which clutter two small tables and overflow on to the floor.

Java has much to offer to lovers of the cinema. Excellent French, German, Dutch, and Austrian films are shown, as well as an occasional English or American one; and the general quality is far above the average of those seen in English speaking countries. Best of them all, up to 1938, were the Vienna productions; it remains to be seen whether their standard will be maintained under the Nazi régime.

All foreign sound films are shown with captions added in Dutch; and the news reels are the same as those elsewhere, only described, of course, by a Dutch commentator. It was in a Java cinema that I met with the exception to what I had hitherto believed to be an invariable rule: an entire absence of humour in both Dutch and German mentality; to one or the other, I never discovered which, belongs the credit of showing H.R.H. The Duke of Windsor's visit to Berlin to the strains of *The Vicar of Bray*!

In addition to the films shown in the regular cinemas, some of which are air conditioned, especially fine ones are imported and shown by the "Kunstkrings" or "art circles." These latter are among the many admirable Dutch institutions that might well be emulated elsewhere. The "circles" are groups of subscribers to a fund which makes it possible to engage musicians, dancers, and other artists, with the certainty that their fees and expenses will be adequately met. In every white community of any size in Java there is a "Kunstkring" with a hall or theatre of its own; and by this means the "exiles" in the Far East are able to see and hear many of the world's great artists who would otherwise not be able to take the financial risk of visiting the colony. Any artist who thinks of including Java in a professional tour has only to write to the secretary in Batavia and, always provided dates are available and the eclectic standards of the selection committee are satisfied, the appearances are fitted in and the success of the show is assured.

A kindred institution to the "Kunstkring" is the "Lezengezelschap," which also would be a welcome addition to the amenities of life in British colonies and dominions. There is one of these reading clubs also in almost every district. They send out "boektrommels" weekly, containing collections of the leading Dutch, French, German, English, and American periodicals, and a novel or two, for circulation among their subscribers. By this means, at the cost of only a few shillings per month, it is actually easier to keep in touch with contemporary affairs and opinion when living in this far away foreign colony than it is in England, at hundreds per cent. greater expense. The English papers in these collections usually include *Punch, Illustrated London News, Bystander, Sphere, Strand,* &c.

The English visitor to Java is constantly reminded of his national insularity by the popularity among the Dutch of English books on railway bookstalls and in shops and libraries; shaming him with the thought of what surprise the sight of Dutch, French, or German novels would cause in similar places in a British country. Several reasons probably contribute to the popularity of our light literature in the Dutch East. One is the excellent teaching of languages in Dutch schools; another is the abundance of English cheap editions, which it does not pay to publish in Holland for so small a population; and yet another is the average Hollander's desire to improve his knowledge of English. Hence, when you travel by train you may be pretty sure that some of your male fellow passengers (the women are less ambitious in this regard) will be reading one or other of the excellent "sixpennies" that are such a boon nowadays to Dutch and English alike, and which are even cheaper to the former on account of the high exchange value of the guilder.

Nowhere are the genuine blessings of civilisation that the Dutch have brought to their colony more marked than in their admirable hotels, and many years' experience has convinced me that it is the Dutch and not the Swiss who deserve the title of the world's best hoteliers. The first hotel of which there is any record was a "Stadsheerenlogement," a "Municipal Boarding House for Gentlemen," established in Batavia in 1754 in response to complaints from the residents that no "genteel accommodation" was available for gentlemen visiting or staying in the town. It was a licensed house under the control of the East India Company, and the licencee was entitled to keep six carriages for hire. The number was later increased to twelve, so it may be inferred that in those days too the Dutch hotel keeper knew his job, and the house did good business. In 1798 it was still flourishing, and "two gilded coaches" were added to the hire vehicles available to the public. In 1811 the records state that "owing to altered circumstances" the establishment ceased to exist. The English took over in that year; and the horrid inference suggests itself that there may have been a lack of persons sufficiently "genteel" to keep it going.

There is, however, no lack of support by the English in Java nowadays for the abundant "genteel accommodation" provided by the Dutch; nor of regretful appreciation that it is so much better and cheaper than in their own colony just across the straits. Probably nowhere else in the world is such civilised comfort and cleanliness and such excellent service to be had for so reasonable a cost as in Java, where in the most modestly priced *pension* you will find spick and span tile floored bedrooms equipped with the very latest of shining chromium, plateglass, and porcelain fittings, and bed linen so white that it almost dazzles you, lightly starched and smooth from the huge roller ironing presses installed in all Java laundries.

Hotels in Java, with the exception of a few tourist hotels *de luxe*, are almost all built on only one floor, often planned so as to enclose inner courtyards on to which open the "*voorgalerijs*" or verandahs that go with every bedroom. It is delightful to sit here in the very early morning and drink your coffee, looking out on the great rain trees that shade the courtyard; listening to the wakening birds and to the murmur of native life in the distance as it streams along the road outside; with perhaps a *tokek* lizard in some hidden corner adding his queer contribution to the drowsy chorus now and then.

In the warm coastal regions, hotel dining rooms are often open to the air on two or even three sides; and in these a small, rather charming diversion is sometimes provided by that humblest of birds the house sparrow, which thrives in Java as in most other parts of the world. He finds these big, lofty, virtually open air rooms very much to his taste, and makes himself perfectly at home, hopping about the tiled floors in search of crumbs, perching cheekily on brightly polished brass finger bowls to steal a drink, and roosting cosily at night in long closely packed rows on high ledges near the ceiling, chirping sleepily now and then as the blaze of electric light disturbs his dreams.

Another of the diversions of the Java hotels, with the rather embarrassing publicity of their open verandah sitting rooms, is the stream of pedlars who appear one after the other, offering a variety of goods that it would be hard to beat in a whole day's shop gazing. Approaching noiselessly on their bare feet, the first warning of their presence is a softly spoken "*Tabek, N'ya besar*"—and you look up from whatever you may chance to be doing to see a figure standing patiently awaiting your attention. These vendors never try to force their goods upon you in the infuriating manner of their English prototypes, but depart at once without argument, as silently as they came, if you should respond to the opening greeting with an emphatic

"No!" Given the slightest encouragement, however, the whole stock in trade will be laid out on the floor for your consideration.

The goods vary in different parts of Java. In Batavia, your first visitor may offer you sets of thin silver teaspoons with handles formed of tiny *wayang* figures, always wrapped in pink tissue paper. The next time you look up you will perhaps see a stocky little fellow squatting between two huge concrete flower pots containing shrubs in full bloom: a load that must weigh a couple of hundredweight at least. Regretfully waving him away, you will be disturbed by a woman *batik* seller, more persistent than any of her male rivals. Sooner or later the *toekang sepatoe* (the shoe man) is sure to appear, complete with block and tools, ready to do any repairs that may be required, and very neatly too, for a few cents. Then perhaps a vendor of wall hangings adorned with elaborate paintings of familiar *wayang* characters, an adaptation of native art to European material that is most decorative. Next, two heavy upholstered armchairs, for which a motor van would seem a more reasonable mode of transport than one small coolie; a table, a set of bookshelves, or a big gong, may be presented to your notice, followed by a man so hung about with white curving snakeskin belts as to suggest a Medusa's head. You will certainly have a visit from the peripatetic Woolworth's with his stock of haberdashery, perfumery, bath sandals, coat hangers, mosquito *obat*, soap, face cream, pins and needles, shoe laces, tooth paste, studs, suspenders, nailbrushes, and a hundred and one other oddments: a collection so ingeniously put together that it is seldom it does not remind you of something you really need.

In West Java this enterprising tradesman appears with two big round baskets hung from the end of his *pikoelan*; but in East Java he wheels in front of him a little shop with glass sides mounted on four wheels like an old-fashioned perambulator, tinkling a bell and calling "*barang*" (a much used word meaning all kinds of goods and chattels) as he goes.

Every kind of fruit in season is also carried round for sale; bunches of roses and other flowers fresh from the mountains; strong well grown seedlings ready to plant out in your garden if you have one; cakes and pastries; the daily paper and a

Yesterday, To-day, & To-morrow

variety of light reading, including fashion books and patterns for industrious dressmakers. There will be little flowering trees just coming into bloom, their roots tucked into earth filled sections of bamboo: a picturesque and practical method of portage enabling so many to be packed on one tray that they look like a miniature Japanese garden.

In the Preanger local specialities are spoons and salad servers, paper knives, pendants, and *wayang* figures all made of polished buffalo horn, and weird birds with outspread wings, the tip of the horn serving as beak; model *krises* six or eight inches long of horn and bone, tiny ones mounted as brooches, and wooden *wayang golek* puppets.

Tasikmalaya specialises in fine grass weaving, and bags and purses not made elsewhere in Java are offered to visitors here. At Djokja there are bags of another kind with queer little figures, birds, and animals interwoven in coloured grass. In East Java *krises* copied from old and beautiful designs are brought for sale from Madoera across the narrow strait that separates the islands: a strait only 2000 yards wide at one point, and served by a steam ferry. The wood-carvings for which Bali is famous, particularly half life-size heads of native types, are another favourite stock in trade of the house to house vendors. This Balinese carving is being exploited for the tourist trade into something almost approaching mass production; but so far, happily, it does not seem to have caused any appreciable deterioration in the work of these gifted people, many of whom appear to carve as instinctively as they breathe.

A native craftsman in Soerabaya makes crocodile-skin handbags equal to any to be found in London shops. He finishes a half dozen or so, the work of weeks, then packs them up and sets off on his bicycle to offer them from door to door: thus earning enough to support his family in a tiny quasi-European dolls' house hidden away in a *kampong* behind a big block of shops. A visitor who happens to receive a call from this clever little person will have a chance to buy a first class piece of work at about a quarter the ordinary price.

The Chinese *klontong* (pedlar) with his odd little rattle like a tiny drum mounted on a six-inch handle, which he twirls as he goes with a sound so characteristic that once heard it is never forgotten, and his big pack of embroidered goods so neatly wrapped in white sheeting, is a familiar and ever popular figure in Java as in Malaya.

An interesting combination of native and European commercialism is to be found at the annual fairs held in the large towns: the *Pasar Gambar* at Batavia, the *Pasar Malem* at Soerabaya, and others. Here every sort of commercial enterprise makes an advertising display, and the European salesman of modern electrical or hygienic apparatus courts your custom every bit as assiduously as do the native vendors of wood-carvings and *wayang* figures. The entertainment offered, however, is entirely Oriental. There are Chinese plays galore; and Malay "opera," so called, presenting Shakespeare with Antonio in a black dress coat, near-white trousers, and co-respondent's shoes, and Shylock as a Chinese clown.

Of all the queer little experiences that befall the English visitor to a Java town, none perhaps is quite so odd as a sound that will sometimes burst upon his astonished ears as he sits peacefully on his verandah, enjoying a "short one" and a cigarette, before dinner in the soft breeze that tempers the warmth of the tropic evening. Suddenly, out of the darkness near at hand, the quietness is shattered by the strident florid jangling of a barrel organ in full blast, grinding out the tunes familiar thirty or forty years ago. They transport you in a moment back to childhood; back to gaslit rooms and dark foggy winter days, before phones or planes or radio or motor cars had reduced a pleasant world to distraction, and nothing worse than barrel organs disturbed our peace. Why and when they came to Java no one seems to know; but there they are, some of the oddest of anomalies in these model modern tropic cities.

These and a thousand and one other innovations have been grafted by degrees on to the ancient simple ways of Java: things great and small that have become part of the fabric of ordinary everyday modern colonial life, and seem to us as permanent and inevitable as the sunshine and the ricefields.

But what the future may have in store no one can tell. These are dangerous days for Java as for the rest of the world;

and it may be that this happy colony, created by the Dutch on foundations laid long ago in blood and tears by their ancestors, is fated to be overwhelmed as completely by modern forces of barbarism as it was three centuries ago by the Dutch East India Company, and before them by Indian and Malay conquerors. But one thing is certain. Whatever else may happen, the beauty and the essential spirit of this lovely land and of its people are indestructible. Its mountain ranges will still stand serene and mysterious in their delicate veil of hazy blue against the primrose skies of dawn; robed in royal purple at sunset or before approaching storm: or rich and green and smiling in the midday sunshine, as they have stood through all the human cataclysms, so shortlived and petty in comparison with their age-long repose, that have raged around their feet.

Bombs may destroy Batavia and Soerabaya as they have destroyed Warsaw; and as Coen destroyed Jacatra. But though they score a million wounds in the forests that clothe the mountain heights, and in the richly cultivated terraces brought into being by generations of toiling workers, they can never destroy them. Nature, generous in these regions as perhaps nowhere else in the world, will heal the wounds and cover the scars in the forests and hillsides; and the Javanese cultivators, patient and untiring as Nature herself, will repair and replant the terraces.

There may be a "new order in Asia," in which all our laboriously built up civilisation will have no more place than that of the earlier conquerors who came, and played their part, and vanished from the scene, leaving behind them only a few ruins for archæologists to ponder over. But beneath the surface changes, great as some of them have been, brought about by each of these phases, that strange, secret, immortal thing that is the soul of a people has lived on: untouchable and remote as the lives of the birds and butterflies, the ants and the rest of the humble creatures that go about their affairs oblivious to all human interference.

And when these present days of storm and stress have drifted into the past, when they are of no more account than to add one more to the pages of history, the Java mountains will still look down unmoved upon generations, as yet unborn, of cheerfully toiling people in their fertile ricefields and their *kampongs* tucked so snugly among the green bamboo groves. And other strangers from overseas will look and marvel as we do at these same scenes, changeless yet ever changing in their eternal beauty as the heavens themselves.

INDEX

Advertising, 76
Agave, 179
Ancient kingdoms, 234–242
  Madjapahit, 238, 240
Animals, 158
Ants, 208
Arachis, 172
Aret, 33

Badjang Ratoe, 239
Bananas, 72
Barbers, 78
Basket making, 144
Batavia, Old, 243, 246, 247
Batik, 138
Betel nut, 181
Bilik, woven bamboo, 68, 144
Bird life, 210
Birth, 54
Boroboedoer temple, 234
Bosch, van den, 142
Brass, 146
Bridegrooms, 43, 53
Brides, 46, 49, 52
Buffalo hide, 147
Buffalo horn, 147
Burial places, 56–58

Calves, 166
Charcoal, 206, 207
Children, 122–123
Christian missions, 94
Cinemas, 252

Cleanliness, 30, 96
Coffee, 204, 206
Coffee disease, 205
Cotton goods, 143
Crafts, 144–150
Crops, 172 *et seq.*
Cruelty, 159, 161, 165

Daendel, Governor, 214
Dancers, 133–134
Death, 55
Deer, 165
Dessa bank, 75
  government, 59
  officials, 60
Dieng Plateau, 237
Dogs, 163
Domestic animals, 158
Doves, 165
Dress, 87–90
Dutch East India Co., 94, 243
Dyes, 140

East Monsoon, 120
Education, 24, 25
Erp, Col. van, 235
Eurasians, 151–157

Factory district of Soerabaya, 92
Fingerprint system, 250
Five-day week, 119
Flower growing, 194
Forestry service, 192

Index

Fruit, 202
Fruit-tree grafting, 204

Gambir, 181
Gardens, 171
Gogok bangan, 33
Goldsmiths, 146
Grass weaving, 144
Groundnuts, 172

HEADDRESSES, 79
Hotels, 254–255

INDIGO, 130, 142
Insect pests, 207
Irrigation, 31

JACATRA, 243
Javanese, artists, 149
    characteristics of, 17–24
    children, 123
    cleanliness, 30, 96
    dress, 19–20
    women, 122–137

Kampongs, 82–85
Kapok, 174–176, 184
Katella, 174

LEATHERWORK, 147
Leper colonies, 94
Libraries, 26
Loewak, 206
Lorodjonggrang temples, 235

MADJAPAHIT, 238, 240
"Magic," 100 *et seq.*
Malabar radio station, 249

Markets, 64, 70–75
Motor bus services, 229
Music, 85

NATIVE cleanliness, 30
    fashion, 36–37
    financial standard, 34
    food, 34–36
    houses, 84
    ingenuity, 32, 33
    newspapers, 25
    ways, 30
N.E.I. Archæological Service, 241
Nurseries, 194

OPIUM, 80
Oranges, 202
Orchids, 209
Oxen, draught, 160

PAINTING, 149
Paper making, 193
Parang, 144
Pasar, 64, 70–75
Pea-nuts, 172
Pedlars, 255
Pets, 163
Pieterszoon Coen, Jan, 243
Ponies, 158–159, 161, 162–163
Post offices, 250
Pottery, 145

RAFFLES, 234
Railways, 222
Railway travel, 223–229
Religions, 86 *et seq.*
Religious ceremonies and conventions, 86

Index

Rice planting, 125
Roads, 214, 220
   Great Post Road, 214–216
Rubber estates, 130
Ryoks, 42, 44

SAMARANG, 246
Sarong, 19
Schools, 80
Selendang, 65
Servants, 135, 207
Sirih box, 180, 182
Sisal hemp, 179
Soerabaya, 246, 249
Soya beans, 176
Storekeepers, 80
Sugarcane, 177–179
Sultanates, 218
Superstitions, 100 *et seq.*

TEA, 77
Tea estates, 126, 127, 128, 129
Teachers, 80
Temples, Badjang Ratoe, 239
   Boroboedoer, 234
   Lorodjonggrang, 235
   Mendoet, 235
   Pawon, 235

Temples, Tjandi Kalasan, 237
   Tjandi Sewoe, 237
Tile-making, 145
Tjandi Kalasan, 237
Tjandi Sewoe, 237
Trams, 231
Trees, 185

UMBRELLAS, oiled paper, 148

VANILLA, 179
Vegetable growing, 201
Vehicles, 218
Veterinary clinics, 166

WATER, running, 107–108, 209
Wayang beber, 27
Wayang plays, 26–27, 28
Weaving, 143
Wedding festivities, 47 *et seq.*
Weddings, 39 *et seq.*
Whip-making, 147
Wild cat, 206
Women, 122, 125, 128, 130–137
Women's dress, 66, 67
Woodcarving, 148
Wooden sandals, 148

Some other Oxford Paperbacks for readers interested in Central Asia, China and South-East Asia, past and present

CAMBODIA

GEORGE COEDES
Angkor

MALCOLM MacDONALD
Angkor and the Khmers*

CENTRAL ASIA

PETER FLEMING
Bayonets to Lhasa

ANDRE GUIBAUT
Tibetan Venture

LADY MACARTNEY
An English Lady in Chinese Turkestan

DIANA SHIPTON
The Antique Land

C.P. SKRINE AND PAMELA NIGHTINGALE
Macartney at Kashgar*

ERIC TEICHMAN
Journey to Turkistan

ALBERT VON LE COQ
Buried Treasures of Chinese Turkestan

AITCHEN K. WU
Turkistan Tumult

CHINA

All About Shanghai: A Standard Guide

HAROLD ACTON
Peonies and Ponies

VICKI BAUM
Shanghai '37

ERNEST BRAMAH
Kai Lung's Golden Hours*

ERNEST BRAMAH
The Wallet of Kai Lung*

ANN BRIDGE
The Ginger Griffin

CHANG HSIN-HAI
The Fabulous Concubine*

CARL CROW
Handbook for China

PETER FLEMING
The Siege at Peking

MARY HOOKER
Behind the Scenes in Peking

NEALE HUNTER
Shanghai Journal*

REGINALD F. JOHNSTON
Twilight in the Forbidden City

GEORGE N. KATES
The Years that Were Fat

CORRINNE LAMB
The Chinese Festive Board

W. SOMERSET MAUGHAM
On a Chinese Screen*

G.E. MORRISON
An Australian in China

DESMOND NEILL
Elegant Flower

PETER QUENNELL
Superficial Journey through Tokyo and Peking

OSBERT SITWELL
Escape with Me! An Oriental Sketch-book

J.A. TURNER
Kwang Tung or Five Years in South China

HONG KONG AND MACAU

AUSTIN COATES
City of Broken Promises

AUSTIN COATES
A Macao Narrative

AUSTIN COATES
Macao and the British, 1637–1842

AUSTIN COATES
Myself a Mandarin

AUSTIN COATES
The Road

The Hong Kong Guide 1893

INDONESIA

DAVID ATTENBOROUGH
Zoo Quest for a Dragon*

VICKI BAUM
A Tale from Bali*

'BENGAL CIVILIAN'
Rambles in Java and the Straits in 1852

MIGUEL COVARRUBIAS
Island of Bali*

AUGUSTA DE WIT
Java: Facts and Fancies

JACQUES DUMARÇAY
Borobudur

JACQUES DUMARÇAY
The Temples of Java

ANNA FORBES
Unbeaten Tracks in Islands of the Far East

GEOFFREY GORER
Bali and Angkor

JENNIFER LINDSAY
Javanese Gamelan

EDWIN M. LOEB
Sumatra: Its History and People

MOCHTAR LUBIS
The Outlaw and Other Stories

MOCHTAR LUBIS
Twilight in Djakarta

MADELON H. LULOFS
Coolie*

MADELON H. LULOFS
Rubber

COLIN McPHEE
A House in Bali*

ERIC MJÖBERG
Forest Life and Adventures in the Malay Archipelago

H.W. PONDER
Java Pageant

HICKMAN POWELL
The Last Paradise

F.M. SCHNITGER
Forgotten Kingdoms in Sumatra

E.R. SCIDMORE
Java, The Garden of the East

MICHAEL SMITHIES
Yogyakarta: Cultural Heart of Indonesia

LADISLAO SZÉKELY
Tropic Fever: The Adventures of a Planter in Sumatra

EDWARD C. VAN NESS AND SHITA PRAWIROHARDJO
Javanese Wayang Kulit

HARRY WILCOX
Six Moons in Sulawesi

MALAYSIA

ODOARDO BECCARI
Wanderings in the Great Forests of Borneo

ISABELLA L. BIRD
The Golden Chersonese: Travels in Malaya in 1879

MARGARET BROOKE THE RANEE OF SARAWAK
My Life in Sarawak

SIR HUGH CLIFFORD
Saleh: A Prince of Malaya

HENRI FAUCONNIER
The Soul of Malaya

W.R. GEDDES
Nine Dayak Nights

C.W. HARRISON
Illustrated Guide to the Federated Malay States (1923)

BARBARA HARRISSON
Orang-Utan

TOM HARRISSON
Borneo Jungle

TOM HARRISSON
World Within: A Borneo Story

CHARLES HOSE
The Field-Book of a Jungle-Wallah

CHARLES HOSE
Natural Man

W. SOMERSET MAUGHAM
Ah King and Other Stories*

W. SOMERSET MAUGHAM
The Casuarina Tree*

MARY McMINNIES
The Flying Fox*

ROBERT PAYNE
The White Rajahs of Sarawak

CARVETH WELLS
Six Years in the Malay Jungle

SINGAPORE

RUSSELL GRENFELL
Main Fleet to Singapore

R.W.E. HARPER AND HARRY MILLER
Singapore Mutiny

MASANOBU TSUJI
Singapore 1941–1942

G.M. REITH
Handbook to Singapore (1907)

C.E. WURTZBURG
Raffles of the Eastern Isles

THAILAND

CARL BOCK
Temples and Elephants

REGINALD CAMPBELL
Teak-Wallah

ANNA LEONOWENS
The English Governess at the Siamese Court

MALCOLM SMITH
A Physician at the Court of Siam

ERNEST YOUNG
The Kingdom of the Yellow Robe

Titles marked with an asterisk have restricted rights.